The Man, Confidence

A Greek POW in World War II

The Man of Confidence
A Greek POW in World War II

by
Anastasios Aslanis

Sunflower University Press®
1531 Yuma (Box 1009), Manhattan, Kansas 66502-4228 USA

© 1995 by Anastasios Aslanis
Printed in the United States of America on acid-free paper.

ISBN 0-89745-183-X

Cover illustration: Pen and ink, by Floyd W. Gibson, Salina, Kansas.

Edited by Amie J. Goins

Layout by Lori L. Daniel

To My Children

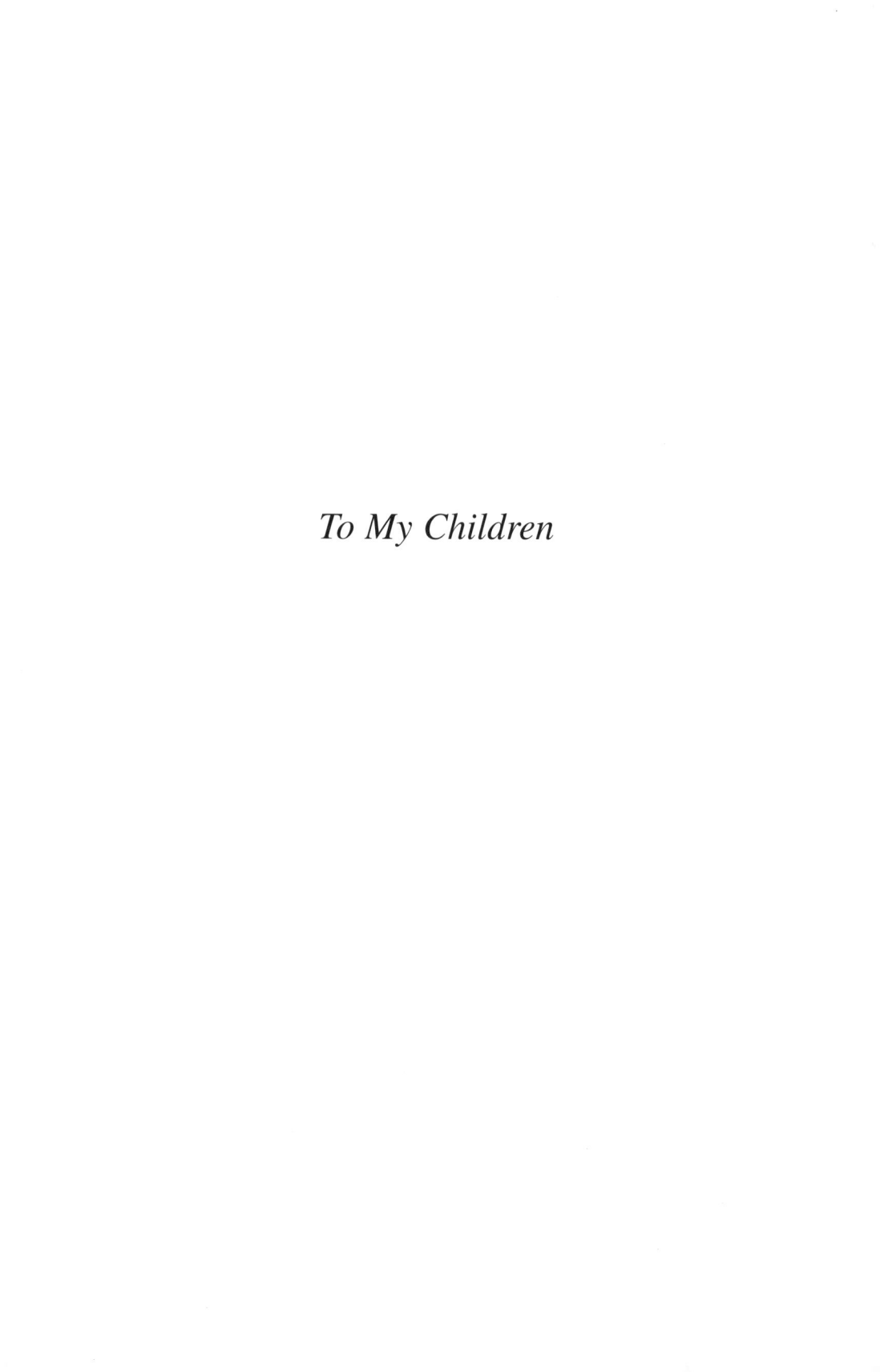

Anastasios Aslanis, 1945.

In 1929, the Geneva Convention established rules governing the humane treatment of war prisoners. Among other things, the Convention required that prisoners be allowed to elect a leader from among themselves. This was "The Man of Confidence."

This book is neither an accusation nor a condemnation. It is an account of men in the deepest hollows of hell, fighting to get through the darkness a glimpse of the sun.

Contents

Preface	xiii
Introduction	xvi
One	1
Two	8
Three	15
Four	23
Five	32
Six	42
Seven	53
Eight	60
Nine	69
Ten	77

Eleven	84
Twelve	93
Thirteen	103
Fourteen	108
Fifteen	113
Sixteen	126
Seventeen	136
Eighteen	143
Nineteen	154
Twenty	163
Twenty-One	173
Twenty-Two	189
Twenty-Three	200
Twenty-Four	211
Twenty-Five	220
Epilogue	229
Appendix	234
Index	254

Preface

IN the fall of 1950, at the University of Michigan, I received a telephone call from my aunt in Wilmington, Delaware. She read to me the contents of a letter from the U.S. Immigration and Naturalization Service, regarding my deportation hearing the summer before. Among the derogatory statements: "... The respondent is not a person of good moral character and cannot be reasonably found to be such a person."

"They didn't believe your story," my aunt said.

The judgment tore through me like a bullet. I could never have imagined that the honor I had earned in battle would be destroyed by such a brutal assassination of my character.

The deportation hearing itself had been the consequence of an act committed without cause by a Greek army officer in

Heracleion, Crete, five years before. With a stroke of his pen, he had wiped out my four years of military service with the statement that at the time of my capture by the enemy I did not have an official military capacity. In truth, I had been on my way to Rhodesia to be trained as an RAF pilot.

It was after this deportation judgment that I decided to write about events that had taken place in a German POW camp in 1944, leading up to the trial of Nazi camp commandant Rinke. I soon finished a book that I titled *No Price for Freedom*. I was, however, reluctant to give the story to the press. A great number of memoirs had been published since the end of the war, with unique details of courage and heroism with which I felt mine could hardly compare. It was, after all, a story of justice in a prisoner of war camp, not a battlefield account.

My university friends convinced me to let the chairman of the English department see the book, if for no other reason than perhaps its literary merit. I gave him the original manuscript, sent a carbon copy to Wilmington, and went to work for General Electric in Detroit. When, a year and a half later, I asked for its return, the chairman replied that the manuscript had been lost. "The janitor," he said, "must have disposed of it with the other stuff on the desk."

In 1955, in East Lansing, a package arrived from my aunt in Wilmington. Among some other papers of mine was the carbon copy. I made a duplicate, and asked the editor of Michigan State University Press, Edwin Wintermute, for an opinion. "It's a dandy!" Wintermute said of the manuscript. "A document of human courage! A book which must be published." At his suggestion, the title was changed to *The Man of Confidence*. The names of the persons involved were also changed.

The circumstances surrounding me at the time, however, were so adverse that it was unthinkable to have a university press put its seal of approval on my work; I was, by that time, a man condemned to the firing squad in his own country. During the Greek civil war that had followed World War II, the Greek government, misled by the army officer's statement in Heracleion, revoked my permit to study in the U.S., and issued a death sentence.

My book was thus rejected, and, in a fight loud enough to be heard outside the building, Edwin Wintermute resigned.

In 1963, I self-published the work, but without the corrections contained in the original manuscript.

In this, the second edition, some of those corrections have been included; others are no longer significant. The Introduction and Epilogue have been added, and all the names are real.

Anastasios Aslanis
Upper Montclair, New Jersey

Introduction

THE village of Haghia Semni slept under the blanket of the night's mist as if it had no cares in the world. Nothing beyond it was real, like an abyss at the end of a cliff, hidden until one takes that fateful leap into it. I was leaving the world I knew, quite certain that the feeling of belonging would go along with me, that the rest of the world was like everything around me, and that I would come back a better man if only for daring to know it.

My future until that time had been a matter of course — I would spend so many years in school, and then a career away from the mountains of Crete. This was Mother's vision of it. Father, on the other hand, insisted that I become a farmer, like him. My professors in the Gymnasium, the Intermediate school at Heracleion, spoke of greater things, politics among them. My heart pounded whenever I could be alone in the valley dreaming of places like Asia Minor, where my parents belonged before the tragedy of 1922, when the Greek army was defeated by the Turks, causing the land to fall into Turkish hands.

I had begun my eleventh year in school when suddenly the war stopped me from going any farther. Coming back to Haghia Semni bored me. Father lectured endlessly about the *ancients*. In six months, since the schools had closed, I was at the point of rebellion, yet I could find no excuse that would permit me to go away.

We celebrated the birth of Christ in December 1940 with song and dance, made louder this time by Greek victories on the Italian Front. The Greek army was advancing deep inside Albania; the town of Argyrocastro had been taken only weeks before. The whole world had turned its eyes to Greece, the land where freedom had been born, and saw that it could survive.

And yet, a dark shadow hung over this unexpected success, dampening the joy of victory with a cold, chilling thought. Hitler would come to Mussolini's rescue when the snow on the mountains began to melt. The words of the classics professor at the Heracleion Gymnasium, George Philippakis, spoken at the school's closing, echoed with growing significance, as if they had been meant for all of us in the room: "The time is now to set books aside and take up the sword."

Father had no idea of what I thought. I did not have the proof that would convince him, either. In fact, I could not tell anyone what my thoughts were — that the war would be brought to my doorstep and I would be called upon to fight — as I was not yet 16. The eventual fall of Greece seemed inevitable to me. It was sad on one hand, yet promising on the other — I would find the reason I needed to leave home.

I felt alone. I spent my time laboring on the farm. Of my three brothers, only Constantine, two years behind me, was old enough to understand. During those beautiful moments he and I shared, the pain of being home was absent, as we worked and played in the fields.

As the weeks went by, we pruned and fertilized the grape vines, and broke up the soil for the sun to pierce through. With no laborers to hire any more, Constantine and I did all the work. But there were no markets, as Germany, the main buyer of raisins, was by then cut off. The futility of it all further convinced me.

I told my mother of my decision to leave, but gave no indication how far I had planned to go — only that I was going "into Heracleion." The disintegration of the Greek army, the end of life as we knew it, the expected fall of Crete — all were contrary to the hope Mother held that the schools would soon open again and I would return to the classroom as before.

The day was April 6, 1941. My three brothers were asleep. Father, as always, had left for the vineyards. I would have to travel the 32 kilometers to Heracleion on foot. Our horse had been conscripted by the Greek army — Father always blamed this on a General Alexakis, who lived not far from us. He kept his fingers in everybody's affairs, Father maintained, except his own. I didn't know where I would stay, how I would live, only that events yet to unfold would help me find a way. I had no idea I would never come home again. Being alone, I felt free in a way I had not experienced before. My heart pounded with anticipation.

I said nothing to my brothers before they went to sleep. They would ask when they woke up what had become of me. Mother would explain to them that I had gone to Heracleion. After all, that is where I was most of the time — in school. Only God and I knew the extent of my plans.

I wondered if Greece, and then Crete, would fall to the Germans as I had feared. I hoped that it was only a dream, a product of adolescent fantasy. But it all became real when I reached Heracleion and saw people crowding the radio inside a cafe, listening with grim faces to the news. Basil Peirasmakis, a classmate from the Gymnasium, was among them. "The Germans," he said, "have attacked Greece."

Basil worked at the British base beside the airfield at Heracleion, an advance RAF squadron of mainly ground crew, sent to prepare the airfield for planes expected later. The base commander, Squadron Leader Mason, was the man to speak to, Basil said, if I wanted work. Basil had invited two of the airmen, Fred Addison and Jack Bassett, to his home. I could learn from them how to approach Commander Mason.

Jack Bassett put in a good word for me. This was the first time I had used my newly acquired skill, the English language, as I spoke with Jack. Basil spouted words he had learned at the base, which fell somewhere between Greek and English. Suddenly, the air raid alarm went off. The town, and Basil's house, sank into darkness. The roar of planes overhead was drowned in the blasts of anti-aircraft fire, aimed with the help of searchlights. Moments later, bombs exploded nearby; the earth beneath our feet groaned as the bombs burst. Then the planes went away, and the party atmosphere at the Peirasmakis home quickly returned.

The German attack gave substance to my fears. Their numbers indicated defeat of the handful of Greek foot soldiers trying to stop a juggernaut. Two of the Greek forts in the Metaxas Line — the fortified defense against Bulgaria named for the late General Metaxas, the Greek Prime Minister — had blown themselves up in a valiant effort to take as many of the Germans with them as possible.

I went to my aunt's house in Heracleion, vacant since the outbreak of the war. She had moved with her children to the village farmhouse when her husband, a cavalry man, left for the Albanian Front. I felt lonely, the way one feels when he is suddenly abandoned in the world, while everything around is unfamiliar.

By the following day, April 8th, the Germans had entered Greece through Yugoslavia. The front collapsed by the 9th, and while the Germans were racing south after capturing Thessaloniki, I had obtained a job with the RAF squadron in the kitchen, in the hopes of easing my enlistment with the British forces.

Easter had no joy that year. British planes shuttled between mainland Greece and Crete, ferrying what they could salvage of the battered British force. The Greek royal family and government officials came through Heracleion, on their escape from the Germans, as the Greek army on the mainland had surrendered. In Albania, the Greek army was outflanked and dissolved. On April 16, Greece fell to the Germans. On May 1, German warplanes bombed the British positions at the airfield near Heracleion. All fighting forces on the island, British and Greek, came under the command of a New Zealander, Major General Bernard Freyberg. The battle for Crete had begun.

By the second week of May, the bombing was uninterrupted, but the British anti-aircraft guns, a battery of Bofors 40mm guns around the airfield and one in Heracleion, remained silent to preserve ammunition. Resupply became difficult, if not impossible. Sea battles with the Germans and Italians raged close enough to be heard. They kindled the morale somewhat, like drops of fuel to a fire almost extinguished. But the situation was grimmer at sea, a ship lost each time, as the British navy fought to prevent the Germans from landing. Ships were precious. They were needed to help Great Britain in the Battle of the Atlantic. The British had leased bases on many islands to the United States in exchange for 50 destroyers only a year before. Thus, Crete, whatever its strategic importance, would have to be abandoned. I was certain then that the British would leave, but when?

The RAF camp at the airfield — except for the kitchen and the officers' mess — was an assortment of small, white tents spread under the olive trees, in an attempt to hide them from the view of German planes. In front of the officers' mess, five Lewis machine-guns were fortified inside a wall of sandbags. A deep, narrow trench zig-zagged between them, exposed to the planes overhead. From there, the camp sloped downhill to the berth of a dry river. A barren hill rose above the other side, hiding the sandy flat beach from the fire of the Lewis guns in front of the officers' mess. An asphalt road separated the airfield from the British camp, winding downhill and turning by the sea around the hill to the beach. Anzac (Australian-New Zealand) units manned the stretch between the camp and the city.

I mustered all the courage I had and confronted the British squadron leader in the officers' mess. It was now or never, I thought. I stood at attention in a soldier-like manner to impress him. "Basil and I wish to enlist in the British air force," I said. Squadron Leader Mason, middle-aged, tall, and clean-shaven, was surprised. He promised to consult with the Air Ministry and let me know. I felt relieved that he did not reject my request. Events, I was certain, would convince him.

The bombing of the British positions grew more intense from one day to the next, and with the anti-aircraft guns silent, the German Stukas and Messerschmitts bombed and strafed the ground at will. They flew quite low. The pilots, bare to the waist, were visible, watching the movement in the British camp through their field glasses from the cockpit. Four British Hurricanes that had flown in were set afire by German planes as soon as the pilots had stepped out.

On the side of the hill, near the kitchen, civilian workers had dug a shelter. But it really didn't matter where one hid; the Germans could see everything on the ground. The corporal in charge of the kitchen came and dragged me into the shelter. I heard the Stuka's siren, then the whistle of bombs falling and, immediately, a hollow grunt directly above the shelter, but no explosion. Upon inspection afterward, we found two bombs wedged into the earth, two feet above the cave's ceiling.

All civilians in the RAF camp were ordered to leave. Basil and I were granted our wish to join the RAF, and given quarters with the Squadron.

My father came to see me in an attempt to talk me into returning home. I met him in the makeshift cafe by the regimental barracks occupied by the famous Scottish infantry regiment of the British army, the Black Watch, which had taken up quarters in the vacated buildings.

"The Military Academy is now in Heracleion," he said. "They are accepting youths of your education. You could apply." (The cadets were later executed by the Germans.)

The idea did not impress me at all. I wanted to fly, not read. He said nothing further and left. He, too, could see what I had seen all along. The call to arms had reached out to me.

In the lull of dusk, British airmen gathered under the trees and talked of home. The corporal in charge of the kitchen set the mood with his harmonica. For a few moments, the noise of warplanes was forgotten and the sound of music brought back the hope that the men would soon be going home. The music blended with the quiet of the evening into a sort of farewell for me, envy and sadness mixed. I had no home anymore. Home was any part of the earth where I could be free.

Without knowing it, Basil and I were the beginning of a new Greece. The old had passed into history. It showed in the eyes of the airmen watching.

In the succeeding days, I was given an Enfield rifle, and one of the airmen drilled me in its use. It was heavy, and the wood was cracked, but it was exciting to have it. I had also been given an RAF uniform. The squadron leader and the other officers had come into the camp from headquarters. At last, it appeared that we might leave. One of the officers gave me a concerned look.

"He is coming with us," Squadron Leader Mason explained.

Nothing, I thought, could prevent me from becoming a pilot in the British air force.

Father never began anything on a Tuesday. "Bad omen," he always said. Tuesday was the day in history when Constantinople had fallen to the Turks, and Greece had ceased to be. Tuesday, the 20th of May, 1941, would turn out to be no exception. The air was filled with German warplanes. They cruised overhead not more than 250 feet above, keeping everyone pinned to the ground. The sun had turned toward evening in a clear, blue sky.

From both sides of the uninhabited island of Dia, north of the airfield on Crete, swarms of low-flying Junkers 52s suddenly appeared. At once, the anti-aircraft batteries opened fire. The Ju-52s flew over the hill, leaving a streak of mushroom-like umbrellas, as they circled over the beach and turned back to sea. Everything on the ground aimed at the falling parachutists. One contingent, approximately battalion strength, was dropped on the two hilltops overlooking the barracks within 200 yards of the camp. The Messerschmitts and Stukas cruising overhead opened fire on us. In the shadow of the nearby Ida mountain, the tracer bullets and shells flying through the air toward the falling Germans created a panorama of tragic beauty, with death, like a messenger from hell, spreading the darkness of eternity. Within minutes, the Ju-52s disappeared, leaving their human cargo to the shelter of the oncoming night.

The landing of the German parachutists broke the last link that I had with the past, sealing my commitment to this war. I was free to be myself, to do and feel as I wanted, without concern whether or not anyone agreed with me. I was in the center of the fighting, which had moved from the continent of Europe to an airfield in Crete. The only exit was the sea, and it, too, was in German hands.

All night long, machine-gun fire stuttered in the darkness, aimed at the battalion of Germans who had fallen on the hilltops. They were wiped out by morning. Civilians killed stray parachutists who had landed in the city. News spread that Max Schmeling, the heavyweight boxing champion, was among the parachutists, and that he had been wounded. We spent the night outside the officers' mess, finger on the trigger.

Three British tanks went toward the sandy beach where the bulk of the Germans had landed. They didn't come back. In the morning, a fourth tank rambled down the winding road, never to return. It moved slowly, as if to stretch the time between life and death, knowing what had happened to the three before.

Jack Bassett and seven others were ordered to Rethymnon to reinforce the garrison there. On Thursday, May 22nd, the Germans retaliated against the civilian resistance by bombing Heracleion. On Friday, artillery shells began to hit the British camp. A truck came by, laden with dead British soldiers.

A Ju-52 crash-landed on the hill opposite the officers' mess, bringing heavy equipment to the Germans on the beach. Clearly, the Germans were getting stronger. We were ordered to save ammunition and to fire only when confronted directly.

On Saturday, May 24th, under the cover of darkness, we prepared to move to Pateles, an underground command center in Heracleion. British Ford trucks drove to the camp as quietly as possible to avoid German detection. But, suddenly, the Germans opened fire with everything they had. This lasted for some time though no one was hit. Following this outburst, we got onto the trucks and quietly rolled away. The next day, as we waited to leave for the British training base in Rhodesia, Basil and I discussed our future.

On May 27th, Fred Addison asked me to go with him to the base's food supply depot. The quartermaster, a chubby, jovial major, wanted to know how I came to be with the British.

"Do you think we will hold?" he asked me, as if I were more familiar with the fighting than he.

"You will evacuate," I answered. The major looked at me as if I were a military prodigy.

The following day, the 28th, was unusually quiet. The order came to stand by. Basil went to say goodbye to his family in Spylia, where they had found refuge from the bombing. I went with Addison into Heracleion. We had expected to return in an hour at the most, and would have if the German planes had not returned.

In the Square Venizelos, with the lion fountain, browsing among the rubble, I found three jackknives hooked to a steel ring at the end of a chain. I tried to separate one but couldn't. The German planes were overhead, and Addison kept prodding me to hurry, so I put all three knives in my pocket, and we left.

A British truck came by, and the driver yelled for us to climb on. Craters gaping wide in the middle of the street and delayed-action bombs made driving difficult. I looked at the Greek army center in the row of municipal buildings along the street. It was deserted. Every young man's record was kept there to mark his courage — or his cowardice. The center itself had become the target of enemy planes; its occupants were gone and the records burned.

We managed to reach the Venetian walls at the end of the Tris Camares park as a Stuka circled overhead, aiming for our truck. At the turn of the road, downhill along the walls, the aircraft dived. I jumped off the truck and rolled down the slope to the road beneath, then waited for the vehicle to come by. There was no sign of the truck or Addison, so I began walking toward the underground command post.

At the first street barricade, an Anzac sergeant stopped me. I gave him the password for that day, which was "macaroni," but he was not satisfied. He led me instead into the basement of a schoolhouse. There, an Australian army officer spoke to me in Greek. The grin on his face puzzled me, as did his knowledge of the language.

"What news from the city?" he asked.

"Not good," I replied. I pleaded with him to let me rejoin the RAF squadron. He refused. He ordered the sergeant who had brought me in to make certain that I didn't leave the building. The order for evacuation had been received; I could not return to my unit.

"Do as the others are doing," the officer told me.

The others — Anzac soldiers — were busy destroying heavy weapons, to keep the Germans from getting them. A column of British troops from the airfield appeared, heading for the schoolhouse. The Germans on the beach seemed unaware of the British withdrawal taking place, and I convinced myself that it would all be well in the morning; I would find and rejoin the squadron in Alexandria. I waited for the evening to come.

One

WHEN darkness fell, we moved down to the port. Six British destroyers and three cruisers moved along the pier as we quietly walked in, trying to avoid attention from the Germans nearby.

I kept the few things I could carry with me — my rifle and a round of ammunition, together with the three jackknives, which I hooked by the chain through the buttonhole of my shirt pocket.

Our group embarked on the HMS **Hereward**. Going aboard the ship, I took a last look at Heracleion, the town where I had been raised, trying through the darkness to say goodbye to a land I had cherished above everything else.

"Hurry it up!" a ship's officer shouted, standing with one foot on board and the other on land.

We were all aboard by midnight. I had followed the crowd of troops on board and climbed down through the open hatch to the decks below. We were directed to the bottom deck of the destroyer and found a place for ourselves to rest while the convoy moved away. I took off my helmet and laid it on the table. Standing in the middle of the room packed with two-story bunks was the only table on this deck. I braced my rifle and lay with my back against one of the bunks, trying to get my thoughts together and guess what pleasant or unpleasant surprises this movement might mean to all of us.

I was exhausted and very hungry. One of the crewmen appeared at the open hatch above and told us that we were not going to have any food until we reached Alexandria because of the shortage of rations left on board. A meal would have tasted very good at that time. We had been fighting against the Germans for over a week without much sleep or food, and we would have gladly welcomed something hot and edible. But since we suspected the trip to Alexandria would take not more than a few hours, we were just as glad to stay hungry for one more night.

Someone inquired of the crewman's rank. "I'm Norman, the padre on this ship," the red-haired sailor replied before disappearing from the open hatch.

As I was sitting there leaning against the bunk, I tried to make a comparison between the British evacuation of Dunkirk and our evacuation of Heracleion. The only chance of pulling through safely depended on how long the darkness lasted. The Germans had occupied the bases in Greece and around Crete, and in order to get through safely, we had to sneak past them, unobserved in the dark, thus avoiding any aerial attacks. I felt the ship rock, and I was sure we had moved out of the port. With this conviction, I settled myself comfortably and very soon went to sleep.

I don't know how long I slept, but when I awoke I heard gunfire on the top deck. I was surprised to hear this, as I was expecting at that time — four in the morning — to have been clear of the Stuka range. I couldn't possibly imagine we were still outside of Heracleion, caught by German dive bombers and making a desperate effort to escape. I asked one of the others, who seemed to have stayed awake all night, what had happened. He didn't know for sure, but he told me that we had finally pulled out and that we were being attacked by German planes.

Having been under constant aerial bombings for the last 30 days without much protection, the ship's decks overhead seemed to offer safety. I paid little attention to the fact that we were being bombed, considering myself invulnerable in the ship's depth, and I went back to sleep. But not for long, however, as a sudden jolt awoke me. As I opened my eyes, I saw the ship's lights dim and then go out at the same time as the hum of the engines stopped.

"They got us!" an officer yelled.

I did not want to believe the young Australian officer, but from what I was seeing and hearing, there was no doubt we were hit. The next thing I worried about was how severely. I didn't see any water gushing in and if it had, it would have entered our deck first. In the dark, I saw the others climbing up through the same hatch we had come in the night before. I followed in line. As I reached the top deck, I looked up. The sky seemed to be full of German planes. Perhaps a hundred — or more. They circled like vultures, taking aim at the wounded ship.

The ship fired in a frantic effort to bring them down before they let their bombs loose. I heard that all-too-familiar whistle, so I took cover under the bridge. The bombs fell into the sea, lifting water high into the air. The sun, barely up, pierced the splintering mass with a rainbow.

I climbed to the top of the ship to see where the rest of the convoy was. I saw nothing but blue sea. We were alone, without power, and had only the *Hereward's* guns and ammunition for protection. I looked around me. The smokestacks were burned completely, and the fire had also destroyed the boats cradled around them. The bombs had fallen through the smokestacks into the engine room.

Machine-gun fire was getting heavy so I went down to the deck below the bridge and stepped into a cabin at the end facing the lower half, trying to decide what to do. Upon entering the cabin, I saw two sailors tying life belts around their waists, shoulders, and every other part of their bodies where a life belt could be tied. Next to them was a heap of deflated life belts. I picked up a couple, and one of the sailors showed me how to blow air into them.

"These can't hold me in the water," I said.

"It's all that's left," the sailor replied.

Two of the crewmen dragged in a third sailor, half-naked, his body covered with blood.

I went outside. Some had already abandoned the ship. I looked for a boat, but there was none, except those about the funnels that had been burned. I took off my shoes and laid down my rifle; then, saying a short prayer, I jumped into the water. I swam back to a life raft still secured to the ship — the only thing left — and rode onto one side. Others swarmed from the deck above to the same side, and the raft capsized. More kept coming down onto the raft like ants. Then again came the sound of Stukas diving, with that frenzied whistle before the bombs were released.

"We've got to get away from the ship!" someone screamed.

"We can't," another shouted. "The ropes are trapped under. We can't untie them."

When the life raft capsized, the ropes that tied it to the ship had twisted and the knots remained underneath. Soaked with water, they had become stiff.

I reached in my shirt pocket. The three knives were still there. In my haste, I threw one to the sailor at the rope carelessly, and it fell in the water. I was better with the second knife, which the sailor caught, surprised.

"Look out!" someone screamed.

I covered my head with my hands. Bullets flew all around us. Again came more bombs, and more still. One would think the Nazis had gone crazy seeing the helpless ship bounce on the blue Mediterranean Sea.

"They will not stop until they see it sink," I thought.

"The ropes are loose now," the sailor said. "Paddle with anything you can find. We've got to get away from the ship."

We must have been some 500 feet away when the ship's ammunition locker was hit. Then the fireworks started. Huge black clouds engulfed the valiant destroyer. Wild flames pierced the massive inferno like a hungry beast devouring its prey. I don't know why, but in spite of the panic and confusion I felt sorry for the ship rather than myself. In its hour of death, the lifeless structure seemed to have possessed feelings. When the hungry waves swallowed their helpless victim, I felt that a dear friend had died in the most savage way.

The crowd on our raft increased as we picked up all those we could along the way. I heard a cry. Somebody was calling for help nearby. I looked around, but could not see anyone. The waves obscured my view. We paddled with our hands and feet in the direction of the scream. On the crest of a wave we saw a body, thoroughly burned. He could still utter a few words. We guessed the rest. He was the only survivor from the engine crew; the bursting steam had scalded all of them to death. We placed him in the middle of the raft, even though it made it sink a little more. He fell unconscious.

The sea had begun to get rough and long high-rising waves prevented me from seeing what happened to the rest of the men around us. The Germans were still over us and once they finished off the ship, they turned their fire against the survivors.

"Hey, look!" someone shouted, pointing overhead.

"He is dropping something," another yelled.

"It's one of ours — a Hurricane," a third man screamed.

We thought he was dropping a life raft, but soon discovered it was his long-range fuel tank, in order to go into action against the German planes around us. Bullets began to zip around the raft. Machine-gun fire from the German planes continued, but as the sea became wilder, the waves obscured their view, and we were indeed fortunate to find in nature the only means of protection against an enemy that held all the cards.

We all rode on the raft, neck high in the water. There must have been 50 or more.

"It's sinking!" somebody screamed.

"Don't worry," another voice assured. "It won't sink."

I wondered if it was actually sinking, as a sudden fear gripped me.

The sea had become quite rough. The raft rode up and slid downhill, as each wave moved under us without warning.

"Sit down and hold on tight!" someone commanded those sitting on the high side of the raft. But they wouldn't listen. Panicked, they tried to swim away. As the crest of the wave hit the lighter side, the raft turned end-over-end, tossing all of us off. I found myself underneath. The raft was pushing me down. Then I felt myself being pulled slowly away from the rest of the crowd, but I was able to emerge to the surface. The raft was only a few feet from me. I swam toward it as fast as I could. I grabbed somebody's leg, pulled myself near, and tried to climb on. But it was impossible; my clothes, soaked in the water, were dragging me down.

I held onto the leg. It was all I had to keep me from drowning.

"The oars are on top now," the same man who had cut the ropes before yelled. "We've got to get them loose." Instinctively, he looked for me.

I remembered that I still had one knife left. I tossed it toward the middle of the raft. He picked it up and cut the oars loose.

The sky was clear by then; the German planes had disappeared, and, except for the rough sea, everything was quiet. Suddenly, I saw something pierce the horizon. At first I thought it was a British ship coming to our rescue, but it seemed unlikely that the Germans had let anything sneak past their bases without giving it the same treatment that they gave to the *Hereward*. As the spot on the horizon grew bigger and came nearer, I saw the Italian flag.

Up to this moment I had never suspected that I was going to find myself in the hands of the Italians. I thought I would drown eventually when fatigue and cold water had drained the last bit of my strength; or that if I managed to stay afloat until dark a British ship would come to our rescue. But I never thought Italians would pick the survivors from the sea.

I had been in the water nearly eight and a half hours. The cold had stiffened my limbs. I could not move without feeling pain. As the torpedo boat drew near, a sailor aboard threw a rope, which I grabbed. I pulled myself and the raft toward the boat. I felt two strong arms lifting me up. As they laid me on the deck, I must have reached the limit of exhaustion, for I fell unconscious.

When I came to my senses, the sun was hitting hard on all my body. The rest of the crowd from my raft was also on the deck. I heard them cheer as the Italians picked the last man from the water. It was the captain of the sunken destroyer. Three more torpedo boats were near; they had picked up other survivors, and because they could not see any more bodies in the water nor hear any more screams, they concluded that all those alive, at least, had been rescued. So they started on their journey back.

From that moment on I could not be sure about the future, and I could not expect anything but surprise. I had been saved from drowning, and so had 200 others, but I was no longer free. Still, I was glad to be alive. I had little strength as yet to stand up, and my limbs were stiff, so I lay there in the sun and let the torpedo boats take me away from freedom.

We stopped at the island of Kaso, east of Crete, and let ashore the most seriously wounded, including the burned sailor from our raft who had died. From there the torpedo boats went on until they reached Scarpanto (Kárpathos), northeast of Crete. About five o'clock the same afternoon, they docked at the pier. A company of guards was already waiting to take us to a small bungalow, where we received some food —

macaroni and a small loaf of bread. The floor was bare earth covered with hay; it seemed comfortable after so much struggle. An Italian doctor came later and examined those in need of medical help. The rest of us, who suffered only from exhaustion, were taken the same night on an Italian destroyer to the island of Rhodes, in the Dodecanese Islands between Asia Minor and Crete.

The heat inside the ship was unbearable, and, with only hot water to drink, I passed out. When I came to, I felt myself being thrown into a truck. We drove for almost a half hour before we were told to get out and march into a barracks. We were left there for the night, to rest on the cement floor, all without clothes, except for a few like me who had not thrown them away. I would have gone to sleep but for the army of bedbugs that inhabited the barracks. These insects climbed on the wall and, centering themselves on the ceiling directly above the prisoners, they dropped like paratroopers. No one else was able to sleep that night, either. When morning came, at last, a couple of Italian officers took our names and ranks. Later in the day, we were given some clothes, and in the afternoon were given food. The same night we were moved to a camp inland.

Two

I spent three weeks on the island of Rhodes, in a camp by a small village called Psitos, a few miles south of the city of Rhodes. For the first time, I realized that I was no longer free and that my life no longer belonged to me. Although the Italians were bland and unable to cause hardship, in the first few weeks I began to see that everything I had known and everything I had cherished was no longer mine.

I found it hard to believe that I was going to be there for long. Common sense suggested that it would be a while before I could get out, and yet I felt that I was only going to be a prisoner for a few days. I thought somehow things would change. I thought this because I could not believe it was possible to lose everything in so short a time. As the days went on, however, I began to realize that all I had left was just myself. I didn't know anyone around me. There was no place to look for help. The only way to freedom was escape.

To reach Egypt from the island of Rhodes meant crossing several hundred miles of sea, all within range of the German air patrols. The thought never occurred to me that I didn't have a chance of getting away unobserved. I felt that all I had to do was get to the beach during the early part of the night, steal a boat or even use just a board, and set out to sea. I made all kinds of plans, but the only reasonable one for escape seemed that of overpowering the camp guards or one or more vehicles in the event we were moved, then make our way to Turkey, where we might be able to get through to Egypt.

I had to realize very soon, however, that the enemy was making its own plans. Before mine could be organized, we were taken on a transport ship to the mainland of Italy. Although we were in the heart of the German and Italian armies, the British navy dominated the seas; thus the ship stayed in port during the day, traveling only during the night when it could not be seen.

A few days later, we reached Pireus, and after a two-day delay, moved up through the Corinth Canal and docked outside Corinth in the bay. I was locked in the cabin downstairs, but I could look out through the porthole, which was left open. I kept watching a little house that showed distinctly among the rest. In that little house I had started my first days of grammar school. My grandmother took me into her home until I was old enough to walk the one mile to the school in Crete, where my parents lived. I used to sit next to her by the window and watch the sea. The beautiful view, high above the beach, stirred my imagination to all sorts of distant lands.

I used to swim in that same water many days in the summer when I could sneak away without Grandmother knowing. I used to spend all day at the beach sometimes. There were people there — I could see them. There were people walking on the streets where I had walked before. The window at the house was still open, but I was a prisoner, and the shadow of Nazi occupation hung over the beach where once there was sunshine.

Two days later, the ship was joined by three more passenger vessels carrying the Italian prisoners liberated by the Germans on Crete. Traveling only at night, as usual, under the escort of two destroyers, we reached Bari a week later.

We were taken ashore by a regiment of Italian guards and led through the streets of Bari to the railroad station, where, to our surprise, we were put on third-class coaches instead of the customary boxcars. Some Italian officers and soldiers came through the train and gave us rations for the trip — two cans of meat and four loaves of bread, each the size of a big tomato.

I couldn't sleep that night on the train. I kept looking outside through the window. The land seemed almost the same as the land of my own country. Olive trees were everywhere, just as in Crete. Life in the cities and villages we went through seemed to follow a normal peacetime course. Nothing was different, but I was a prisoner now.

I can't remember exactly how many other things went through my mind as I sat looking out the window. But I remember that as the train rolled northward, my hopes for freedom faded away. I knew very little about wars and how long they lasted, but for some reason I thought it would probably be two years before I could be free again. So, as we kept moving, I said goodbye to Greece — to freedom, to everything, locking in my heart all those things I had loved when I was free, thinking that I could let them out in two years when the war would be at an end.

By morning we arrived at Capua, the first organized prisoner-of-war camp that I saw. A guard detachment was at the station to take over. We marched to the camp, and as we approached, we saw others gathered near the fence inside, staring at us and yelling out names. These prisoners had been captured a few weeks before in Libya, when the German army pushed ahead toward Tobruk. The names they were calling were of their comrades whom they thought might be in our group. To me they were all strangers.

We had a shower while our clothes went through the fumigation machine. When that was done, we were taken inside the camp to spend the next three weeks. Ten prisoners were placed in each tent. There were ladders and straw to make up a bed, and a couple of blankets for cover. We had some food the same afternoon, which, to our surprise, was not bad. I met the others in my tent the same night. The one next to me, a Maltese, was on the *Hereward* when we were sunk. His nickname was Toby — a short, jovial character with a thin, childish voice. Others in the tent were from London, and one from Australia.

In the morning, we lined up at the square inside the camp, and learned of the restrictions we were subject to and the regulations by which we had to abide. This was the first time that I learned there was such a thing as the Geneva Convention. The same day I learned that according to this Convention, prisoners of war were subject to labor of any kind, except when it had immediate connection with war, and that the detaining power had no right to execute a man without supplying the Red Cross official proof of his guilt.

I learned further that the Geneva Convention required the prisoners to elect one of their number — the "Man of Confidence" — to represent them before the International Red Cross and the detaining power. I learned a number of other things in this same camp, which had no importance to me until a few years later. But the main thing I learned over and over was that I was a prisoner.

The second night, as I returned to the tent from a stroll in the camp, I heard lively talk in the dark.

"I'll be glad when Saturday is here," said one. Several other men agreed.

"What's all this about Saturday?" Toby inquired.

"We're getting another Red Cross parcel," the first man said.

The Italians had given the prisoners a parcel a couple of weeks earlier, and we learned they had had several consignments since. According to our tentmates, they were going to issue one parcel per man each week from then on.

I was puzzled, as I was unfamiliar with the whole routine, but Toby seemed to know. Satisfied with what I had heard, I went to sleep. I didn't learn until Saturday, when I received my first Red Cross parcel, that it was a food package prepared by Britain and other countries and placed at the disposal of the International Red Cross, which was authorized to distribute them to prisoners of war in enemy hands. It contained ten pounds of food, including butter and biscuits, and it was encouraging to see for the first time that we were not entirely forgotten.

We stayed in Capua for three weeks before we were moved again to northern Italy, to a camp near Bolzano on the Mediterranean side of the Alps. We spent two months there and were moved again to another location near Udine farther east — a concentration camp at Grupignano, later identified simply as Camp No. 57.

The billets we were placed in were in no way protected against drafts — the boards were too far apart to prevent the wind from whistling into the rooms. There was a brick stove in the center of the billet, but no fuel.

We had enough beds, but the blankets were too short.

The camp was divided into five compounds, each separated from the next by a barbed-wire fence, but going from one compound to another during the day was not forbidden. The camp commandant, Calcaterra, gave the appearance of a mild colonel, not the strict, hard-boiled man he was at heart, but he obeyed the stipulations made by the Geneva Convention.

There were times in the camp when Red Cross parcels arrived regularly, making life tolerable. There were also times when Red Cross parcels did not reach the camp for months, during which we had to rely on Italian rations alone — 40 grams of rice or macaroni and 250 grams of bread per day per man. At times like these, death made its way into the camp; cold and hunger froze our hope for survival.

Christmas 1941 was getting near, and, to our disappointment, we learned that Japan had entered the war by attacking Pearl Harbor. Up to this time we had been predicting that the war would end by Christmas, though we had no evidence to support this. The addition of this new enemy, the Japanese, brought to our side a new ally, the United States, but it was obvious that the war would be prolonged. As if this were not enough, the Germans took Tobruk and pushed toward the Nile. Celebrations were held by the Italians everywhere. Desperation and mourning reigned over the camp.

So that we should learn of the Axis's successes, the Italian colonel installed loudspeakers in each compound, and a regular summary of the news from the Italian sources was broadcast throughout the day. We learned of the fall of Corregidor, the surrender of the Allied fleet at Singapore, the landing in Borneo, and the Allied preparations for the last defense in Australia. "Lord Haw Haw," who we later learned was the British traitor William Joyce, occasionally made his comments on the situation, which was, at that time, favorable to the Axis powers. But we never stopped believing that the end would be in our favor.

It was as a result of the first attempt for mass escape that things became even worse. In the course of eight months, a group of prisoners succeeded in completing a tunnel. Although originally all who took part in the digging were to escape, the narrow exit, a few feet outside the barbed-wire fence, completed last, provided time for only 30 men to leave before daybreak.

It was a big surprise for the camp commandant when their escape was discovered. We were made to empty all the billets and undergo a thorough search until finally the entrance to the tunnel was found under the barracks in a new compound. I was standing by my belongings outside when a prisoner remarked, "What are they looking for?"

"They've lost Libya," another prisoner by the name of "Shots" sarcastically replied.

From that day on, every privilege that the Geneva Convention had granted us was withdrawn. Each week we had to move everything out of the billets and every inch of ground beneath the floor was checked. Communication between compounds was forbidden, and a little canteen, where we bought cigarettes and toilet articles, was closed. Red Cross parcels were withheld. The Italian part of our rations was cut to practically nothing. The most disappointing fact, however, was that all 30 of the escaped prisoners were caught one after the other within a month.

A new prisoner, George Vardakos, was brought into the camp in the summer of 1942. He had been captured weeks before as an accomplice in acts of sabotage and was brought to Italy for internment. He was quite relieved to learn that he could finally talk to someone who spoke his tongue.

As the months rolled by with no Red Cross parcels, hunger began to take over once again. The winter this time was not as cold, but the lack of food made us feel it more than we had the year before.

We spent the whole winter of 1942 without Red Cross parcels. During the Easter week of 1943 I was in prison, which Calcaterra had built within the camp, for not saluting an Italian officer. In this prison for the first time — the day was Tuesday — I received a letter from home and learned that my family had not been hurt by the Nazis.

When spring was over, the prisoners' situation began to improve. Red Cross parcels began to arrive again and starvation once more was alleviated. Meanwhile, another tunnel was under way. The Italians were aware of such a possibility and watched every inch of the camp for traces of freshly dug earth, making digging almost impossible. By the water closet, the Italians had built a six-by-nine-foot carpentry shop. They were digging a new sewage pond for the water, and the dirt was being deposited by the carpentry shop. Although Italians supervised the work, the digging was done by the prisoners, and this offered the opportunity for the second tunnel. Under the noses of the Italians the tunnel was begun, with its entrance inside the carpentry shop. The Italians were in a hurry to remove the loose dirt from the pond as soon as possible, but actually this pile of dirt was never completely eliminated, because what the Italians took away during the day was replaced by the earth dug from the tunnel at night.

The summer of 1943 was well along when something changed the mood of the prisoners throughout the camp. One of the men in our billet, Shots, whose last name was Simmons, had managed to get liquor from one of the Italians and got drunk. Shots was well liked because his sense of humor and jokes gave us some entertainment once in a while. Unfortunately, a guard smelled the liquor on his breath and reported to the commandant that Simmons was intoxicated. When the guard was sent to take the prisoner to jail, Shots began to amuse himself with the guard, and in his usual joking manner had hoisted the empty bottle in his hand. The guard took this as a threat. He aimed his rifle at Simmons and fired. Shots bounced around with laughter still on his face and dropped. He was rushed to the infirmary, but did not live.

Although Commandant Calcaterra permitted the greatest funeral ever carried out for a prisoner of war in the camp, Simmons's death had aggravated us. He was harmless, a friend to everyone, always amusing and entertaining. His death seemed unjustified. But like every other hardship, this faded with future events.

Three

WE were still at Camp 57 in August 1943, when the war began a different trend. The Allies had taken North Africa and had landed in Sicily; the Japanese were stopped in the Pacific, and the American forces were taking on the offensive everywhere. We no longer had to hear the views of Lord Haw Haw. We had our own source of information, secret transmissions from the British Intelligence Service, from which we learned the truth. We were familiar with what was happening at the front.

Once again I began to feel that freedom was getting near. This time it seemed that the whole war was coming to an end. From my knowledge of history, it seemed that Italy would not stay on the Nazi side much longer. I was very confident that the Italians would surrender as they had done in the First

World War and abandon the Germans.

For the first time in all these years my thoughts turned back to my education, which had been interrupted when the war broke out. Feeling that I had already lost my chance for any more fighting in this war, I began to make plans for continuing that education when the war would end. My original aim was to become an engineer, and it was back to this that I turned my aspirations. Using books on mathematics, which had been supplied by the Red Cross, I learned algebra, trigonometry, and calculus during August and the first days of September 1943.

On September 13 the good news arrived — Italy had surrendered. More than pandemonium reigned that night. I took a big pair of scissors and started to cut down the barbed wire. I hated that wire; it had deprived me of everything a free life can mean. I wanted it down — wanted to do it with my own hands. The idea of using the second tunnel was abandoned since we no longer were prisoners, and we turned to celebrate the memorable event.

But in spite of all the joy, I couldn't very well tie a number of things together in my mind. With the rate at which the Allied forces were advancing in Italy, it would require weeks, or maybe months, for them to reach our camp. On the other hand, the Germans had already seized control of the important centers in Italy. In Udine, the town nearest to the camp, Genoa, Rome, Naples, and other Italian cities, the Germans were already in control. Furthermore, the camp's commandant had declared himself loyal to the deposed dictator Benito Mussolini. It appeared impossible that he would set the prisoners of war free. And he didn't.

I spent the night trying to plan my escape. By morning, it was already too late. In the sentry boxes were no longer Italian guards, but two Germans in each, and a garrison outside the camp had taken over. Once again my hopes for freedom were frustrated. The sight of the Germans around the camp convinced me that I would be inside the barbed wire for quite some time yet.

My predictions came true about noon the same day, when the Germans walked into the camp and gathered all the prisoners into the front compound. The German major commanding the Panzer battalion called the Man of Confidence and gave him a brief order.

"*Sagt euren Leuten, sich innerhalb der nächsten Halben Stunde fertigzumachen* (Tell your people to get ready within a half hour)," the major said through a German interpreter, "or else all of you will die."

Then he warned, "If one man gets out of line, if only one does, my troops have orders to mow down all of you. Understood?"

Between two rows of guards standing with their fingers on the triggers of their machine-guns while the remainder of the battalion stood at some distance from the roadside, we were marched to a train of cattle cars waiting a few miles outside the railroad station of Udine and were thrown in. Behind us, machine-gun fire combed the barracks in the abandoned camp. The Germans were making sure that no one had remained hidden inside.

It was very hot that day, but we were not allowed to ask for water. We were locked inside those cattle cars — as many as 60 or 70 men, where ordinarily there could only be 40 — and the train took off. When the doors were unlocked again, we were at the Salzburg railroad station in Austria. We were put in groups of five and made to march to a camp two miles away.

From my experience, I thought nothing worse could take place in Germany than what had already occurred in Camp 57, but it did not take long before I knew better. In a valley below, surrounded by high mountains, was an extermination camp for Russian POWs.

As the gates closed behind the last man in the column, another long sentence in a concentration camp was sealed. We were put through a registration routine; each received a prisoner-of-war number — the only thing anyone would know about us if we did not manage to survive. My number was 32202. We were told to wear it around the neck at all times; anyone caught without his number would be shot.

When registration was finally finished at the end of the day, a certain number were assigned to each barracks. These barracks, with four walls and a roof hanging on, were packed with three-story bunks, the top bed only two feet below the roof. A scant mattress of straw was thrown on each ladder-type bed. We were given neither blankets nor food.

From the first night I began to learn what it was going to be like in a Nazi prisoner-of-war camp. Five men were fired on that same night because they had walked to the water closet within the camp. Another guard began to shoot at one of the billets because the prisoners were trying to warm water for tea made out of tree leaves, to quench their thirst.

In the morning, at 5:30, we were forced out of the billets for roll call. Fortunately, I learned that day that the Nazis had heard of the Geneva Convention. The stipulation they liked, however, was the one calling for a man amongst the prisoners to represent them officially before the Red Cross — because it served their purposes more than those intended by the authors of the Convention. Having one man to represent the whole body, they could easily force others, through him, to comply with their wishes. This was the reason they asked for a Man of Confidence.

We elected the same man that had held the post while in Camp 57 in Italy — a regimental sergeant major from Australia, whom we all liked and esteemed as a conscientious person and an honest soldier. The unfortunate thing, however, was that he could not speak German, and he did not trust a German to act as his interpreter. He called on any one of us who knew any German words at all to do the interpreting for him. No one moved. As he called a second time, pointing at me, I stepped in front of the column. The German officer, meanwhile, was losing patience with him.

"Don't you see that he doesn't understand?" I told the officer in German.

"Oh, so you understand!" the German spouted. "Explain to him, then, what I have said."

From that day on, I was the one to do all the interpreting. Unfortunately, the things I had to interpret were not those that would make life bearable, or even tolerable, in a Nazi prisoner-of-war camp. They were instead the restrictions, threats, and punishments that the Nazis were going to impose.

We were told during this gathering that our stay in this camp was only temporary, that we were soon to be moved into another, and that it would be useless to make any attempts to notify the Red Cross of our whereabouts. The commandant of the camp would undertake to send our identities to the Red Cross headquarters in Geneva when it was possible to do so. The same day I found out what the food situation was like in a Nazi POW camp. We were allowed 100 grams of bread per day and 50 grams of potatoes; nothing more. Many times we received much less.

Later in the day, I learned that the Germans had allowed one billet next to us in the same camp to be used as an infirmary. Immediately, through our Man of Confidence, I managed to get the commandant of the camp to attend to those in need of medical care. At this opportunity, I walked over to the infirmary and met some men I had seen walking about. They were Russians who had been there since 1941 and whose lives had been spared by a miracle rather than Nazi kindness. One of the

Russians approached and asked me who I was. He didn't seem to be well educated, but he was friendly and, in his broken English, told me the shocking story of his 2,000 compatriots.

"You see over there, *Kamerat*?"

I turned my head and looked through the barbed wire at the narrow bed of wheat fields where the Russian had pointed. It was covered with hay, which was rotting now into fertilizer.

"What about it?"

"Two thousand men, women, and children are in there," the Russian said. "We were seized by the Nazis during the occupation of Kiev; we were forced to march into Germany with no food, getting beatings on the way until finally about two thousand of us reached the camp. Then they threw us into a compound — the one you are in now, and locked us there without food. I was lucky. Me and my two comrades were taken to this infirmary. The others all died. They carried them out, dug a big hole in that field, and covered them. Some were still alive," he said with a coldness that could only grip a human being when the unthinkable has become an everyday experience.

I stood there looking at the place, completely bewildered. I could hardly imagine that these things were true. I don't know whether in my heart I really believed him, or if I believed only part of his story. This was something beyond my comprehension, and, in my mind, impossible to have been done by human beings. Still, he seemed emphatic that he was telling me the truth. Although at the time I doubted his statements, later on I fully believed every word he had told me, because of things I was to see myself.

In the meantime, the Man of Confidence, accompanied by a guard, was heading toward me.

"Will you please come with me?" asked the sergeant major.

The guard took us to the *Lager Offizier's* office. As we walked in, a big, well-built man stood at attention behind his chair and greeted us. We did not return his salute, and he became furious.

"*Können Sie nicht mal grüssen, Mensch?*"

"What is he saying?" the sergeant major asked.

"He complains that we did not salute him when we entered," I said.

He ordered the guard to take us both out, and then we were marched in again, in order that this time we salute, but we went out of the office and came back in the same manner. For some strange reason, he gave up.

Taking this as an opportunity, he told us that as prisoners of war we were forced to salute German officers just as we had to salute the officers in our own armies, and explained that it was a matter of common courtesy to greet anyone, regardless of whether he was an enemy officer or one of our own. He recommended that we mention this to everyone else in the camp.

In his office that morning, I learned a few more things about the Geneva Convention, namely that when prisoners of war were to be moved from one camp to another, their destination should be made known to them beforehand as well as the reason for the move. I also learned that the Man of Confidence, who in German is called the *Vertrauensmann*, received certain rights by the Convention to enable him to work more efficiently for the welfare of his fellow prisoners, and that he was allowed to contact the Red Cross officials in Geneva at any time by mail and report any violation of the Geneva Convention.

What I realized most, however, was that whether his services to his fellow prisoners were to be valuable or useless was determined completely by the Nazi camp authorities. To them the Man of Confidence was just another prisoner, and unless he did as they wanted, he was treated worse than the rest. I looked at the sergeant major in the office, thinking over these things. He must have been a man of courage and must have liked his countrymen very much to accept the job that bore the price of his life.

We were given a list of instructions and warnings covering our behavior in Nazi POW camps, which we were to announce to the other prisoners that same day at roll call. The only fortunate thing we found out at this meeting was that we were going to have a bath, and this seemed to be the best news of the day.

We left the office without saluting, again to the amazement of the Nazi officer. The *Unteroffizier* escorted us back to our compound. As we passed alongside the field where the Russians were buried, I couldn't help but ask if it were true that 2,000 human beings were covered there. The German nodded in the affirmative.

"How did this thing happen?" I asked him.

He told me that they were too expensive for the German government to feed, and that their extermination relieved the government of this unnecessary expense.

"How dare you treat human beings like that?" I asked.

"*Die sind doch keine Menschen! Die sind Russen!* (They are not human beings, they're Russians!)"

His cold affirmation and merciless thinking froze the blood in my veins. Wanting to convince me, he took us into a small compound at the entrance of the camp where some Russians still were kept, after being brought there a few months before. We entered the compound and came to a billet that seemed empty. As we walked in, however, frightened and half-naked Russians disappeared between the three-story bunks and lay down quietly.

"*Steht mal auf!* (Get up!)" the guard yelled harshly.

Debased, frightened young Russians began to gather near the fireplace that had never been used. One could see in their faces the expression of fear and the expectation of the worst.

The Nazi took crumbs of bread out of his pocket and threw them before his feet. At once, those starved Russians hurried up to the bread crumbs, each trying to get there first, pushing the other fellow away, yelling and swearing at one another.

I was not amused with the scene, as the Nazi expected me to be. Neither was the sergeant major. To make things more spectacular, however, the *Unteroffizier* drew out his pistol and ordered the Russians to disperse before they could get all the crumbs. I asked him if we could go back to our compound. He stepped on the remainder of the crumbs and buried them with his boots in the black earth of the damp floor before leaving the billet.

This stout, cold-blooded Nazi believed that he had convinced us of the *Führer's* claim that the Russians are not human beings and that they deserved the treatment they were getting. The incident began to tie in with a few things I knew about Hitler's Germany — about the master race that the Nazi maniac was going to build, and it all seemed to add up. In the meantime, the guards who were to take us for a bath were ready, and as we got inside the billet we told everyone to go.

We were taken out of the camp, higher up into a separate section on the road to the railroad station. The only building there was a billet, which I thought would be the shower room. Instead I found that there was no shower at all. A few beer barrels cut in half were thrown here and there on the ground, and a small tap on a boiler inside the building was letting water drip into cans, which Russian prisoners were to empty into each one of the barrels outside. This warm water, mixed with cold, was what we were all to use for a bath. After the first man was through, the next was in the barrel and finally the whole crowd — more than 2,000 — had had their first bath in weeks, using the same water. By the time half the group was through, a mixture of mud and dirt, rather than clean water, was left in the barrel. Still, it was water, and we felt a little bit grateful.

    We returned to our compound just in time for the second roll call of the day. No one seemed concerned about feeding us. The Nazis were anxious only to have these roll calls over and make sure that we knew all the restrictions. *When* we were to eat was a matter very unimportant — *what* we were to eat was already standardized, no different from what we had been given at the Italian camp. We lined up in rows of five in the little side space adjacent to the barbed wire, 300 per group, and after the roll call, the *Lager Offizier* called the sergeant major and me, and gave me a notice to translate. It concerned relations between prisoners of war and women in Germany:

Vom Oberkommando der Wehrmacht

Den Kriegsgefangenen ist jedes Verhältnis mit deutschen Frauen streng verboten. Kriegsgefangene die mit deutschen Frauen erwischt werden, sind sofort und ohne Vorwahrnung erschiessen. Der Grund ihrer Bestrafung wird noch am selben Tag den anderen Kriegsgefangenen bekanntgegeben.

From the Army High Command

Any relationship between prisoners of war and German women is strictly forbidden. Prisoners caught with German women are to be shot immediately without warning, and the reason for their punishment will be made known to the other prisoners within the same day.

Four

WE spent nearly a week at the end of September 1943 in this camp, outside Salzburg. The climate was damp, and the valley was never free of fog. Although it was early fall, the weather was as cold as if winter was at its worst. During this week I was the busiest man in the camp. Each time the Germans wanted to communicate something to the men through the Man of Confidence, I was dragged out of the billet to do the interpreting. It seemed as if they expected me to condone their plans and contribute to their success, regardless of the effect they would have on the welfare of the prisoners. In their minds, I was their prisoner and, therefore, the only choice I could have in the matter was to agree with them.

But not so. In the two and a half years that had preceded, I had come to know each of those prisoners, if not by name, at least by sight; many had become good friends and dear to me. The fact that no one was Greek — they were all from Australia and New Zealand, with the exception of one — did not alter our friendship. I objected, consequently, to every Nazi attempt to worsen conditions, which the Geneva Convention had established as a minimum. The Nazis were nothing less than an enemy who had to be defeated and had to be fought at every step, at every opportunity, in every place. The idea of being used as an interpreter seemed hateful to me, but I was urged, by those friends I had made among the prisoners, to undertake this responsibility. The others felt that they would have the opportunity to impress upon the Nazis their need for food, clothes, and medical care. Nevertheless, as the week drew to a close and we were notified to move, my relief from such an assignment came with it.

We were told that our destination was Goerlitz, a city some hundred miles south of Berlin. We were again thrown into cattle cars. I was glad that this time the Germans did not mention to any of the guards who took over that I could speak their language. I felt very much at ease when I was back in the same lot with the other prisoners. Locked inside the cattle cars, where the only light came through a narrow opening near the ceiling, screened with barbed wire, we made our way to Goerlitz in two and a half days. We passed through Munich, Dresden, and other large German cities, but it was hard to see anything through the little openings above; they were too high to reach. Besides, the traveling was done during the night.

A guard company from the camp in Goerlitz was at the station to take us over. We had to march a little way — about eight kilometers to the camp itself, so the march began early in the morning. Throughout the city I kept seeing prisoners dressed in uniforms different from ours, escorted by German guards, or sometimes alone, working at various jobs; later I learned they were French. It seemed as though the city was inhabited by war prisoners rather than civilians.

The air of the town reminded me of my own home where I used to walk free and at liberty to do as I wanted, but it was altogether different going through Goerlitz. We had to march in fives; we couldn't break off lines, as the guards were ready to shoot anyone attempting to do so. But worse, we didn't know whether Goerlitz was the last town we had to go through, or whether this moving from one place to another was going to continue indefinitely — always from camp to camp, town to town, and always as complete strangers. Some civilians stood on the sidewalks and watched our column march by. I don't know if they felt pity or contempt. There was no spitting, but from the expressions on their faces I could also see that there was no sympathy.

In Goerlitz, for the first time, I realized that we were not fighting just one maniac; we were also fighting a great many others, for the spirit of aggression that Hitler had indoctrinated and the arrogant and inhuman attitude that he displayed was manifested right there by those civilians — ordinary Germans standing on the sidewalks. Knowing that my chance to share in the fighting was lost, I was sorry that I had to march through Goerlitz as a captive, swallowing the bitter pill of my misfortune. But I tried to salvage in myself the feeling that although I was a prisoner, I was far from being defeated.

This was Goerlitz in 1943. The camp was four kilometers out of town, almost as far as the railroad station. We had to carry with us all of our belongings, and the march was long and tiring.

As we arrived at the camp we were ordered to stand on the side of the road and wait. The German camp officials had already arranged for a thorough search before we were allowed in. Each group of 300 lined up in fives and were marched to a field that the French prisoners in the camp used for soccer games. While a number of guards stayed at the perimeter of the field, others went through all our possessions, taking away those things they thought we shouldn't have, leaving only a pair of shorts and underwear, our uniform, and a greatcoat. Rings and other valuables were confiscated, and the prisoners received a receipt to claim them at the end of the war.

When the search was finally over, we were placed in billets of the same type as those we had occupied in Austria. I was not asked to act as an interpreter. No one but the prisoners knew I could speak German. This was a relief, and I hoped it would continue.

The process of distributing prisoners to the billets was over late in the afternoon of the same day, when French prisoners told us they had prepared some soup for us. This was a friendly gesture, and a remarkable one; they had pooled their own rations together and had foregone their daily meal for our sake. We realized that inside the barbed-wire fence we were all the same people — we were all Allies, each fighting the same war. Within the camp we felt that we were one group with one objective, one destination, and almost invariably the same ideals. After two days of traveling and a whole day of search out in cold weather, a small bowl of potato soup given to us by the French was gratifying, indeed.

Later that day, I decided to take a walk inside the camp. It was divided in two rows of compounds separated by an elevated road through the middle. One end of the road led to the German commandant, the other to the rear exit of the camp. There were no villages or forests within sight. The entire camp was located in a vast, quiet plain, and the monotony of nature, combined with the wilderness of the surroundings, complemented the misery inside. Once in a while an army vehicle drove through the highway nearby, breaking up the quiet.

The only center of activity was headquarters — the *Kommandantur*. It was there that our destinies and our futures were being decided. We had no access to the gate. We could not know what was going on inside the brains of the Nazis in charge of our camp. As far as we were concerned, the elevated sentry boxes, with the machine-guns and searchlights, were the limit of our stepping ground. Those sentry boxes were always the same: one or two guards on duty, not much movement, not much excitement; but we knew that they were the end of our territory and hopes. As long as we remained inside the barbed wire, those sentry boxes would continue to be quiet. The minute we stepped closer to the wire than the five-foot mark, the sentries had orders to open fire. I wondered at times how I managed to convince myself that within such a small territory I was going to spend so many years — so long and dull.

As I walked along the road I came to the French compound. Prisoners were moving around in the barracks, others were just returning to the camp from outside, coming back from work. The entrance to the French compound was near the main gate, which was alive with movement. I walked in the compound without making an effort to talk to anyone, although many of the French greeted me and seemed eager to open a conversation. I noticed that they were all smoking cigarettes — we had been without them for weeks — and though I was not a smoker at the time, I knew how hard it had been for some friends of mine, especially George Vardakos.

The sight of tobacco gave me the idea that I might be able to get some for George, at least. I had nothing to trade except a watch, which I had thus far managed to salvage from the searches conducted by the Germans. I approached a Frenchman and made my proposition: 50 cigarettes for a wristwatch.

My approach apparently was not proper, because the man declined politely to accept the watch and at the same time assured me that he was out of cigarettes himself, though he believed the Belgians in the next compound might have some.

"*Viens avec moi!* (Come with me!)" he said.

I followed him to the next compound, and we both entered the only billet there, inhabited solely by Belgians. He began to inquire if any of them had cigarettes, but the same disappointing answer was repeated as we went on asking. They all declined politely to admit that they had any, mainly because they did not feel it was decent on their part to take my watch. On the other hand, it may have been the common instinctive attitude of each prisoner to keep everything he had for himself, knowing that there was no source to replace his own supply once it was gone. A watch was practically of no use — time was unimportant in a prison camp; but cigarettes and food were extremely valuable.

Having failed to make a bargain by the time we had reached the other entrance to the billet, the Frenchman led me back to his own barracks. He called a friend of his by the name of Robert, and mentioned to him that one of the newly arrived prisoners was looking for cigarettes.

As I heard him ask what the prisoner wanted, I walked over and introduced myself. Robert was very polite; he shook my hand cordially and asked if we three could sit at a table and get acquainted.

A third Frenchman interrupted us, asking what Robert had done with his "dixie" — the type of eating utensil we all used. A large bag was hanging on his shoulder and his face looked fatigued. As he saw me there, he became embarrassed for having broken into our conversation so abruptly.

"*Pardonnez moi!*" he exclaimed, looking surprised.

He shook my hand, telling me his name — Raymond, from Lyon, France. Just as he finished introducing himself, the fourth member of this friendly group came in, swearing at the Germans. His name was Jacques.

"What is it that you do?" I asked Robert in French.

"We have a small library here in this barracks. I am the librarian," Robert answered.

Jacques was the Man of Confidence, and Raymond explained that he worked in the kitchen.

The conversation began to warm up as each one learned about the other. The first Frenchman, whose nickname was Dédé, had returned ill from a working camp and was still recuperating, which was why he was allowed to stay in the main camp. The other three had assignments within the camp as they were above the rank of corporal, and according to the Geneva Convention they were not subject to labor by the detaining power.

We became better acquainted and more interested in one another's experiences as time went on that evening. I thought that Jacques did not take the Germans as seriously as a prisoner in their hands should. He seemed to have an air of superiority and was amused on every occasion by their mentality and behavior.

"They are like cows," he said. "They tread heavy, but they have no sense of direction. They go wherever Hitler tells them."

In spite of his carefree attitude, Jacques was a very intelligent man, as were the other three. Jacques was from Paris; one could see it in his conversation and accent. Before the war, Robert had been a bank official in Le Havre, France. He was married and had three children — the last one born two months after his capture. When the conversation came around to this point, Robert was uneasy. He had never seen his youngest child and, like every father, he was anxious to survive and be reunited with his family. Because memories of his background seemed painful, we changed the subject.

Dédé was a university student living in Oran, Algiers. The only one in his family still living was his aunt; he had no brothers or sisters.

Raymond was also married, with two children, but he had heard nothing from or about them since 1942. He felt that something had happened, but he could not inquire. The only word of communication prisoners of war were allowed with relatives at home was one letter each week on a little card mailed through the International Red Cross. We were fortunate that we were allowed at least to do that.

It was getting late and I was ready to leave the company that I had enjoyed that evening, when Dédé pulled me down by the arm, insisting that I should stay. I knew my presence there prevented them from preparing anything to eat. They had already missed their daily soup, but they didn't seem to care. I took this as extreme politeness, but Dédé explained to me that they were receiving Red Cross packages from home and at that time they did not find it necessary to resort to the German allotment of potato soup. In fact, he asked me if I wanted to stay and have dinner with them. This seemed out of place for me — they were prisoners the same as I. What is more, there was no indication that a few weeks from then they would not be in the same situation as I was — without Red Cross packages, having to depend on the German rations alone. But that didn't seem to worry them at all. Their disposition, as well as their spirit, after more than three years of oppression in that same camp, amazed me. I tried to leave, but Dédé would listen to nothing except my acceptance to stay. I finally consented and stayed for a few more hours.

A professional cook, Jacques went outside to prepare some spaghetti. Dédé, Robert, Raymond, and I continued our conversation. What they were interested to know was how I felt toward the war and its outcome in general. They wanted to know my background — I was very young at the time, only 19 — and they were curious to learn why I had enlisted at such a young age. As soon as I answered most of their questions, the subject of our conversation changed to religion. Dédé took a little picture from his wallet and handed it to me.

"I would like you to keep this," he said. "It may be important."

I looked at the picture. It had a mother and beside her a child on bent knees, praying to the Almighty that their loved ones be returned from captivity.

> *Seigneur, ramenez no captifs come un*
> *torrent du midi. . .Ceux qui sément dans*
> *les larmes moissonneront dans la joie.*

> Dear Lord, return our captives like
> a torrent of the south; those who sow
> in tears will harvest in joy.

Although I was not a Roman Catholic, a deep esteem grew in my heart for their religious convictions. I always kept the little picture. Somehow it seemed that this prayer had a meaning for me, just as it did for them. For the first time I began to realize that somewhere back home someone was kneeling, praying for my return.

The conversation was getting serious, however, and the time seemed appropriate to learn of their experiences during the early years of their captivity. Robert, who had been in the camp all the time, told me of an incident early in 1942. Guards had rushed into the camp one morning and had locked all other nationalities in their billets, prohibiting anyone from stepping outside. Then five trucks drove in, onto which they loaded dying Russians and covered them with a large canvas sheet. Robert, at the time, was in the library adjacent to the Russian compound and could see what went on through the window. Some of those Russians were still alive, and they tried to lift the heavy canvas tied to the truck. The Germans brought some back into the camp later the same day.

"They thought they could still get some work out of them," Dédé remarked.

"What did they do with the rest?"

"They buried them."

I was shocked at the commonplace of this brutality, recalling the 2,000 buried Russians in the camp outside Salzburg. But just then, Jacques showed up with a big kettle of spaghetti. His smiling expression washed away our sad thoughts, and a pleasant mood returned as we enjoyed his cooking.

Although originally I had only gone to the French quarters to trade my watch for cigarettes, I had already spent a good part of the night doing everything but that. During those hours, however, I had begun to see that one could do a great deal to improve his own conditions within the barbed-wire fence if he made the required effort and showed the necessary courage and endurance the situation demanded. I had enjoyed their company to the greatest extent I ever enjoyed anything — if possible in a prisoner-of-war camp — and when I finally left to return to my billet, I no longer had to make a bargain for cigarettes. Each one gave me a pack free. I did not want to tell them that they were not for me, but even if they had known I intended them for someone else, they would still have gladly given them.

I returned to my billet with four packs of cigarettes, which meant relief for George, and carried with me a wonderful impression of the four Frenchmen. As I lay exhausted on my ladder, I went immediately to sleep.

At six o'clock the next morning, we were awoken by shouts and yells from the guards firing into the billet to make certain that we heard.

"*Aufstehen! Na los!* (Get up! Get going!)"

We were taken down to the soccer field for a roll call. At this gathering, we were informed through a German interpreter that each of us was to fill out a card with his particulars and hand it over to the *Lager Offizier*. The card was a request from the Red Cross for a statement of whereabouts. We were told that the name of the camp was *Stammlager* (Stalag) VIII-A but that we were not allowed to mention the location. We were told further that we would be there for an indefinite time.

One day passed after the other, and I learned a little more about the way the Nazis handled war prisoners. Their first move was to detect any Jews, who were usually sent off to, we found out later, extermination camps. The next move was to make us realize that we were defeated, and *they* were the only power within our realm of existence that could dispose or spare our lives as they pleased. In this the Nazis made sure that there was no misunderstanding.

What surprised me was that from the last guard to the highest ranking officer in the camp, all were alike. Whenever an officer — many times without reason — felt like beating a prisoner, the guards were more eager than he to carry out the job.

One day, I was standing near the barbed-wire fence that separated the Russian compound from ours, when I saw one of the guards pushing with his bayonet two Russians attempting to move a bag of potatoes into the kitchen. One of them had only one leg and was struggling to stay afoot; the other was legless completely, walking on crutches. Since the day of their capture, they had worn the same uniform, which had been through the fumigation machine quite a few times. This was all they had. They slept, lived, and walked in them.

A prisoner's appearance had quite an effect on the Nazis. Often depending on how clean or well dressed he looked, the Nazi would decide whether the prisoner's life should be spared or eliminated. A great part of our "salvation" was, I think, due to this Nazi way of thinking. Since the Red Cross provided us with uniforms, and because we kept our appearances up, the Nazis decided that we were worthy of living, while others who did not have this privilege or did not keep themselves in good form were gradually eliminated.

Five

I think it was at the end of another two weeks that the first working party from Stalag VIII-A was detailed. The Man of Confidence, whom I knew very well from Camp 57 in Italy, told me that I was assigned to the working party, but that I had my choice to stay at the camp if I so desired.

"What do you mean, Sir?" I asked, curious to know what the sergeant major meant by "choice" in the matter. I knew that sooner or later we were all going to be forced into labor camps, under the threat of death.

"You are to be their Man of Confidence," he said.

My anxiety increased as I realized the risk involved in such a responsibility. During the two weeks I had spent in Goerlitz, my association with those four Frenchmen, the spectacle of the Russian prisoners, and the knowledge that quite a few prisoners with a similar responsibility had lost their lives, made me hesitate to respond one way or the other.

"I am afraid I will have to think it over, Sir," I replied.

The sergeant major stood silently for a moment while I tried to get my thoughts together. The comparatively great difference between the French prisoners and the Russians, and the background of their current treatment convinced me that although we, as prisoners, no longer possessed anything, not even our clothes, there was an opportunity to make the Nazis treat us humanely. I felt that we could eventually force them to realize that in spite of our status we were still human beings, and make them accept the Geneva Convention as a right to which we were still entitled.

"George Vardakos is in the list with the working party," the sergeant major added, and left.

I spent the entire day trying to come to a decision. I had very little background — if any at all — to depend on. What the sergeant major needed was a man of experience, a courageous leader who not only would bring the prisoners' welfare to a human level, but who also, even at the risk of his own life, would fight the Nazis until they realized that the treatment they gave to Continental prisoners could not be enforced upon British soldiers. My only qualification for such a position was that I could speak German.

However, George had been ordered with the party, and I could not very well leave him alone in a camp where he could understand neither German nor English and where he would have no one to associate with for the remainder of his imprisonment. George had often expressed the fear that if he were ever left by himself, he would be forced to give up every hope of survival and walk through the barbed wire with the intention of getting killed. I kept thinking of his fear, and I began to believe that if there was any reason at all for me to accept this task, George was that reason.

I also began to feel that there was perhaps some other motivation in the sergeant major's choice, that maybe he had seen something in me which he could not find in anyone else, which made me fit to undertake a job as difficult and dangerous as he knew it to be.

"Cheer up, Tasos!" someone said, using my nickname, as he saw me sitting on the bed worrying.

I responded with a contrived grin. Just then, George returned from a stroll in the compound.

"How about a game of cards?" he asked.

"I'd rather take a walk, George," I said. "Will you come along?"

I had hardly walked halfway along the main camp road, listening to George's impressions of his first weeks in Goerlitz, when I became convinced that I should go with the labor detachment. I kept talking to George and consciously heading for the office where the sergeant major stayed.

"Glad to see you here so early!" the sergeant major grinned. "I take it you've decided to go."

"Yes, I have. But I have a feeling I will need someone else's help, too," I said without pleasure, and with a little regret.

Looking back, I don't know whether by saying this I was referring to God or some other power, but I knew I wasn't strong enough to carry the task alone.

"Sergeant Day also will be going with you," the sergeant major said. "This way you shouldn't have difficulty maintaining discipline among the prisoners. Sergeant Day is from New Zealand and is a member of the British army. He ought to give you considerable help as a senior non-com. You are leaving tomorrow," he continued. "You will have your medical examination in the morning and you are expected to leave by noon. Your destination is a sugar factory in Klettendorf, a suburb of Breslau. This is all I can tell you. The rest is up to you."

George did not seem to understand anything about what we were saying, so he kept pacing around the office waiting for our conversation to end.

"Before you go for the medical examination in the morning, report to me," the sergeant major said. He shook my hand cordially, indicating he was pleased with my decision.

"I wish you all the luck," he said, as I turned around and walked to the door. "God bless you!"

I did not say a word. I just didn't know what to say.

"What were you talking about?" George asked when we left the office.

"You are leaving Goerlitz for a working camp," I said.

"Work? What do you mean?" he asked with concern.

I explained to him that he was detailed with a British labor detachment, and he was scheduled to go the next day.

"Aren't you coming with me?" George asked anxiously.

"That is what we have just been talking about," I said.

George heaved a sigh of relief. "Don't leave me alone," he said.

When we reached our billet, it was time for chow.

"Grab up!" a prisoner shouted from the doorway as I was ready to sit down on my bed. We held our mess kits and lined up for the thin potato soup — our only meal for the day.

George wanted to know more about this working camp as we sat down drinking what the Nazis called a meal. I wished I could answer all of his questions, but I didn't know any more than he what the future was going to bring.

"We'll see tomorrow," I replied. "Meanwhile, we can get some rest."

That night, I tried to pull myself together and plan what to do the next day. I had already made the decision that I was going.

It now remained to do the job. I could not tolerate any effort on the part of war prisoners to help German production. That, I was told before my capture, was one thing I should always try to avoid. Of course, going to a working camp as a Man of Confidence, I myself would not have to work; the remainder of the prisoners, however, would. I knew that prisoners of war were excluded from labor that had direct connection with warfare, that we had the right to refuse this type of labor — if one could believe that prisoners had any rights at all. The Nazis certainly didn't seem to believe so. From the Frenchmen I had learned more about the Geneva Convention, but to the Nazis it was only a piece of paper, worthless as far as they were concerned; they always laughed when one dared mention it.

It was getting late, so I decided to go to sleep and wait for the next day. I looked at George before I turned on my side. He was sound asleep.

The medical examination in the morning did not take long; the German doctor seemed to know beforehand which prisoners were healthy and which were ill. Those found able to stand on their feet were lined up behind the main gate for a thorough search.

"I am Sergeant Day," a big, stout, mild-looking man said as he approached me in front of the group. "My friends call me Bill. But my name is really Cyril."

We were ready to leave by noon. Each of us was given one day's rations — the equivalent of one meal — for the entire trip. After a two-hour march back through Goerlitz, we were locked up inside the same cattle cars that had brought us there two weeks before. Bill and I were together. We were 200 in all, 50 men in each cattle car.

We left Goerlitz at four o'clock the same day. Everyone else in the cattle wagon seemed content to be at least moving to another place, as if conditions might be different. I wanted to share their contentment but could not very well do so. Sitting in the middle part of the boxcar with my back against the locked door, I was trying to devise some plan for the following day's activities.

I had no idea what the living quarters of the labor detachment would be like, but I made a list in my mind of those things I believed would benefit the welfare of the prisoners. First, the thing that worried me the most was food. Was it going to be the same as in Goerlitz — better, or worse? Then the medical care, Red Cross supplies, a million other things.

All of the 200 men with me had smoked their last cigarette before we left. Now, their craving to smoke had aggravated to the point where they were using tree leaves or any other kind of leaves they could find to roll up, regardless of the effect this would have on their health. Since our departure, they had been asking consistently if I knew whether the Germans were going to give us cigarettes at Klettendorf or whether we would soon get Red Cross supplies.

Although I was not a smoker, I shared their agony to the same degree, and the fact that I did not know the answers to their questions made me nervous and agitated — perhaps because I understood how they must have felt.

Late at night I tried to sleep; I couldn't, however, until the last couple of hours before morning. When I awoke, we were already approaching Klettendorf.

I stood up for a while, gazing through the small openings near the ceiling at the empty fields outside of the forests we were passing through every now and then. It was a cold morning. I could feel the draft through the walls and openings above.

We arrived at Klettendorf about ten o'clock. A small locomotive pulled the four cars to the outside entrance of the factory grounds. A herd of German guards were spread around the tracks. Once again I heard the locks close behind me and we were back inside the barbed wire just as we were the day before.

"*Wer ist der Vertrauensmann*? (Who is the Man of Confidence?)" one of the Germans yelled.

"I am!" I answered, and stood in front of the mob. He took me inside and showed me what was to be our living quarters.

It was one of the shipping rooms in the same building as the plant. The only difference from our living quarters in Salzburg and Goerlitz was that a number of lockers had been provided for our use, something we hadn't had before.

"Well, this is it!" I said to Bill, who stood in the middle of the warehouse, trying to find in our new quarters some improvement from the old. The German wanted to know who Bill was. He accepted my explanation, apparently in a hurry to have things settled as quickly as possible.

"Let the men in!" he ordered. "You two come with me!"

We followed him to his office, where he introduced himself.

"*Ich bin der Kommando Führer* (I am the camp commandant)," he said in a growling voice. I noticed that he was a sergeant.

He was a fairly old man with red eyes and false teeth. A bayonet hung on his side, swinging back and forth as he walked. He wore a pistol on his left thigh. His office was adjacent to the first half of the warehouse, with an entrance through the partitioning wall into our quarters.

This was an opportunity I had longed for all night. Now that we were in his office and he had identified himself as the commandant of the camp, the time was right to find the answers to all those questions that had bothered me along the way. First of all the food situation. We could not work with one meal a day like the one we received in Goerlitz, and we were not going to.

He seemed to be in an awkward position suddenly. He said that he was willing to give us four meals a day if he could, but his orders were that we only get one, with a slight increase in the amount per person.

"Do you expect these men to work while they starve?" I asked.

He moved his hands in a gesture of desperation, as if he were trying to indicate that his personal feelings were the same as mine and that he would not hesitate to grant my request if it were up to him. But it was up to the higher authorities to change the orders. When I asked him what medical care the camp provided, he led me back into our quarters and showed me, on one side of the warehouse, a fairly large section separated from ours with a wooden half-partition. A few cots were scattered inside, and a few aspirin with a bottle of iodine and some cotton were lying on a desk.

"*Das ist euer Revier* (That is your infirmary)," he said. Again, he repeated that he would like a better-equipped facility if it were within his power to have it.

By this time I was beginning to be convinced how far the Nazis would go in giving us humane treatment, even when they knew that we were intended for work. They were trying to get all they could out of a man's strength while granting him the least comfort in return.

I did not feel desperate, but I was angry.

"I suppose if I asked you for Red Cross supplies, you would repeat your own feelings," I said.

He did not seem willing to answer for or against this time, as he stood hesitating. Meanwhile, the remainder of the prisoners were settled in the quarters — each allotted one bed with a mattress, one blanket, and one locker split among three. Some had already started complaining that the number of lockers was not enough. Others began to repeat the same question: cigarettes and food?

"When do we eat?" one man shouted in German.

On hearing this, the *Kommando Führer* led me out into the courtyard where he showed me the little kitchen. Two old ladies were boiling potatoes, barley, and carrots in a big cylindrical container, preparing some kind of soup. It was to be our evening meal — the only meal. I gave word to the others, who had been anxiously waiting, that the soup would not be served until five o'clock, and this seemed to relieve the tension — at least they knew we were going to have a meal.

I asked the *Kommando Führer* if we could return to his office. I slammed the door behind me as we went in. He looked at me with a little bit of surprise.

"You told me your side of the story," I shouted. "Now listen to mine. I am the Man of Confidence here, and I intend to get these things at any cost. First, I want two meals for the men. Second, I want medical supplies for the infirmary. Third, I want cigarettes and Red Cross supplies. These men aren't pigs. They are human beings just like you. Unless we get these things starting today, we are not going to work for a single hour."

"I am not responsible for that," the *Kommando Führer* said with surprise. "You can talk to the captain of my company or the factory manager. Either one has more authority than myself."

"Show me, then, to the captain," I said.

He went to the telephone and called the company office. I heard him tell the captain that I desired to speak to him in person.

"I will be right there," the captain answered at the other end of the line. As we stood waiting in the office, a young man from New Zealand, who struck me more as the scholarly type than as a fighting man, was brought in by another guard. He seemed upset.

"All I can find is some cotton, some aspirin, and iodine," he said. "Could you ask the *Kommando Führer* for some more medical supplies?"

"I'll see if I can get them for you," I said, trying to calm him.

"How soon?"

"Later tonight, perhaps."

The captain was late, so I decided to see the factory manager.

"I'll take you there," the *Kommando Führer* prompted, readily. Bill remained behind to tend to other problems the prisoners had. We went straight to the manager's office. He was not there, but the inspector was somewhere around the plant. We found him in the research lab on the second floor. He seemed glad that he finally had obtained help for his plant. The *Kommando Führer* broke up his remarks by telling him the purpose of my visit there. He told me that there was nothing he could do to get cigarettes for the camp, because cigarettes were rationed and he could not get permission from the ration officer. Furthermore, he said that he was only responsible for production in the plant. He indicated that I could talk to the superintendent and maybe he could do something more.

I realized that what the Germans were trying to do was discourage me, since each one I had seen so far had done nothing more than recommend someone else. Very much disgusted, I asked the *Kommando Führer* to take me back to the camp.

When we returned, the captain was already there waiting for us in the office. He had called on Bill, but because he did not speak English and Bill did not know German, they had decided to wait for me.

"*Was ist los?*" he asked as we went in.

As I had done with the *Kommando Führer*, I made my demands to the captain. He became very uncomfortable and began to walk around, complaining that he was not authorized to do anything except provide the guards for the camp.

He did not seem to be an objective, capable individual. In his manner

I perceived a sort of weakness, and of this I took the greatest advantage.

"All right!" I said. "You claim that you can't do anything. Then let me go to Goerlitz."

"Goerlitz?" the captain asked, wondering. "You no longer belong to Goerlitz," he said, realizing my mistake. "You are under Sagan."

"To Sagan, then," I said.

He thought for a while, then he asked me what I thought we needed and why I believed my trip to Sagan was necessary.

"Some time ago, I heard of a thing called the Geneva Convention. Now I know that you Nazis don't believe in any agreements. I want a copy of that Convention. Unless I have that copy in my hands, as soon as I can get it, I can't do a thing before consulting the man above me, and that is the Man of Confidence in Sagan."

The captain turned to the *Kommando Führer*. "Don't they," he said to him, pointing at me, "don't they have a copy of the Geneva Convention?"

"*Ich weiss nicht* (I don't know)," he answered. "They don't get that from us," he said.

I was getting nervous. I walked to the window overlooking the courtyard, while the captain and the *Kommando Führer* talked to each other. I noticed that the men were already lined up receiving their first meal.

"You'd better go and eat," I told Bill. "I'll handle these two myself."

As soon as Bill left, the captain started to say that those things I was asking could not be settled the first night and that perhaps we could discuss the situation better in the morning. From my short experience thus far, I could see this as one more excuse, and as soon as the captain finished what he had to say, I made my demand precise and clear: "Either we get what we are entitled to, or no one goes to work in the morning!"

I felt safe in making this threat, as I suspected that any labor disorder in our camp would be reported by the factory superintendent to the German division command as an inability of the captain to properly supervise and handle the labor detachment. This would become quite an embarrassment for the captain, especially if my threat was carried out. Even if he had used a firing squad to make an example of a few men, that in itself would remain as an unpleasant episode for the Nazis to conceal, and the captain would be the one to answer for such a situation to his superiors.

"When do you want to go?" he asked.

"Tomorrow morning," I answered.

The captain turned to the *Kommando Führer* and asked when he could get a guard ready.

"*Morgen früh, glaub' ich* (Early tomorrow morning, I believe)," the *Kommando Führer* answered, standing at attention every time he was addressed or spoke to the captain, clicking his boots in the German military fashion.

"*Dann sehen Sie zu, daß alles in Ordnung geht!* (Then you see to it that everything works out all right!)" the captain answered.

"*Jawohl, Herr Hauptmann!*" the *Kommando Führer* hurried to obey. Then rubbing his hands, now that he had left the task of carrying out my request to someone else, the captain smiled as he headed for the doorway, and added, "*Ich hoffe, daß alles klappt!* (I hope everything goes well with you!)"

Six

WHEN the captain left, the **Kommando Führer** and I went through the details of my trip to Sagan. As I was curious to know why Sagan was the central camp instead of Goerlitz, he explained to me that because we had been moved away from Goerlitz and were within the domain of Stalag VIII-C, we were automatically placed under its jurisdiction, and that anything we wished to obtain or report should be addressed to Stalag VIII-C, Sagan, Germany. He also told me that this was a newly established camp, a fact that meant considerable time must pass before any Red Cross supplies could arrive.

I learned from this **Kommando Führer** how the German labor detachment system for prisoners of war functioned. Each was supplied with working manpower from a main camp and when the work in a labor detachment was completed, the prisoners employed there were returned to the central camp for use as labor elsewhere. I also learned that those who were reported sick during the week, from natural causes or accident, were to visit an army physician and receive adequate care. Tuesday was to be such a day.

Now that I had won one of my demands — perhaps the most important one — I considered it a proper time to let the *Kommando Führer* know a number of other things I had in mind. I made it clear to him that I wanted the *Sanitäter* (nurse) of our detachment and Sergeant Day to be unobstructed in carrying out their duties toward their fellow prisoners. I told him further that if there was ever any violence because of the hostility of the guards, which might endanger the prisoners' lives or welfare, I was the one who should be told of the situation, and that the guards should not proceed to settle on their own their differences with the prisoner involved. I told him that if these things weren't done, I was going to report any arbitrary punishment imposed by the guards on prisoners to the Red Cross, and that I could find a way for the information to get there.

He did not raise any objections, and in the days that followed, he seemed to abide by this. I was still talking with the *Kommando Führer* when Bill dropped in.

"I saved some soup for you," he said. "Aren't you going to eat anything?"

Then, pointing at Bill, I stressed the point again that he was one of the two men whose duties I expected the guards to avoid interference with at all times.

I left the *Kommando Führer's* office with Bill and went back to my quarters, a separate office within the warehouse made by stacking the lockers side-by-side to create privacy. I told Bill the news about the trip to Sagan.

"Did you finally manage to get it?" he asked with surprise.

"Yeah," I answered, "but I don't intend to go myself. I think it is best that you go. I will give you a list of all the things that I want done. I want you to be sure that the Man of Confidence understands our determination here to maintain a humane level of welfare in spite of Nazi attempts to the contrary."

"I'll do my best," Bill said.

"The captain here has authorized me to buy German cigarettes from the camp's canteen, in case Red Cross shipments are not yet in, and charge them to the factory here. He has promised to have the guard, who is going with you, verify this, so if you can't bring anything else back with you, you've got to bring the cigarettes."

Bill himself was acquainted with the necessities of our labor camp as well as I was. I felt, however, that my instructions were necessary to give him an exact idea of what he had to do.

The enthusiasm in our camp was beyond description when the news spread that they were finally going to get cigarettes. Almost everyone came to ask if it were true.

"You will all be smoking cigarettes two days from now," I said. And with this feeling prevailing in our quarters, the day ended.

When everything had quieted down, I went over in my mind the situation that had developed during the day. I could not help but see a great deal of weakness on the part of both the *Kommando Führer* and his captain, and I began to hope that as soon as I obtained a written copy of the Geneva Convention, it might become possible to make the Nazis recognize that they had to abide by it. I was encouraged to think this, as I knew that the German *Kommando Führer* was not willing to undergo any embarrassment that might lead to his replacement. This almost inevitably would mean "the front," where he hated to go, while here he could use his post to promote his own prestige as a noncom. His captain was not the rigorous Nazi soldier who would rather kill than find himself embarrassed because of prisoners' claims or desires. I felt that those Germans I had met thus far in this camp were not impossible to control. I also realized that in order to succeed in my objectives I had to continue to stubbornly support my claims in the same manner as I had done this morning — and maybe even with greater determination — as I suspected that, although that day had been easy, it could be very different in the future.

I knew from conversations with other prisoners in Goerlitz, especially the French, that others who had adopted the same attitude as I had at some time or another disappeared because, in one instance, they happened to display weakness, which induced the Germans to believe their courage was not real. As I thought of all this, I began to question myself, whether I was following those same steps or whether, in fact, I was not afraid of the Nazis. I could not reach a conclusion, but I could see beyond doubt that my only hope, if I were to keep fighting them, would be to avoid showing any weakness as those others had done. This seemed to reassure me that I had everything to lose if I weakened, and possibly something to gain if I didn't. With this conviction in mind, I went to sleep.

I was glad to see Bill leave for the central camp in the morning. I bade him goodbye at the station, while in my heart I hoped that he would succeed in his mission and that he would realize the importance of my points. A little fact about Nazi mentality I had picked up previously induced me to feel that any success depended mostly — if not entirely — on how far ahead I could anticipate danger or the ultimate end of their plans and actions.

When I returned to my quarters, the inspector of the sugar factory was there waiting. He told me that everyone had to go into the plant and be assigned a job. The guards were already in line waiting for the *Kommando Führer* to give the signal for the takeoff. Our *Sanitäter* approached me almost instantly with a number of complaints that he had been trying to voice for quite some time that morning, with very little success.

"Quite a few of the men reported sick," he said, "but the Germans forced them to line up for work just the same."

I took the list from his hand and called all those men out of the line. Then, turning to the *Kommando Führer*, who wondered what I was doing, I said that those men were to stay there until the doctor decided whether they were fit to work.

"*Verflucht nochmal*! (Damnit!)" he groaned. "Come on, let's go! Out!" he ordered the remainder of the prisoners.

Curious to find out what the prisoners would be asked to do, I followed them. The inspector walked along with me.

Within two hours, the Germans had placed everyone on the job by just taking the number of men each foreman needed and assigning them to their duties.

I walked with the inspector to his office. There were a number of things I wanted to know, which only he could tell me with authority: the extent of working hours, the pay, and the working uniforms. He seemed willing to do anything I asked him, and although he promised me everything, only after some struggle did I finally manage to get the uniforms.

The inspector informed me that the prisoners were to work on the same basis as the civilian workers, with the same amount of food allotted them, and the same pay. He said that a shift consisted of 12 continuous hours of work — that we were to have both day and night shifts, and that we were to have no Saturdays or Sundays off. As the inspector said that, I asked him whether he knew that prisoners are entitled to a 48-hour rest period each week, according to the Geneva Convention. He assured me that they were going to get their 48 hours of rest, except that instead of getting this rest at the end of each week, we were to get it at the end of the sugar campaign, which was to last approximately three months. Then we would receive the equivalent of 48 hours per week as a rest period but, in the meantime, it could not be otherwise.

"*Ich kann nichts mehr tun,*" he said, indicating that that was all he could do in this respect.

I took some time to think of a solution to this new situation. All of these prisoners had been in the same camp with me in Italy and so far in Germany. I knew very well how many times they had starved, and the loss of health that had resulted from their repeated periods of suffering. I could easily see that a 12-hour shift was going to be too hard for men who had already spent three and a half years inside prisoner-of-war camps, especially with only one meal a day and a hard bed to lie on during the hours of rest. The thought came to me that perhaps if three shifts worked instead of two, the number of working hours could be reduced.

The inspector thought my request was reasonable, but he said that there were not enough men to make up three shifts. For the time being, it would have to be two shifts of 12 hours each. He indicated that if I wanted to reduce the number of hours, the man to see would be the German commandant of the central camp, as only he had the authority to supply or withdraw war prisoners from our labor detachment. This meant that once again I had to see the Man of Confidence at the central camp.

With Bill already at Sagan, I wished I had thought of that the evening before. I told the inspector that I was going to insist on reducing the number of hours, as well as getting the 48-hour rest period at the end of each week. This done, I left with the remainder of the men who were to be used on the night shift. I walked back to my quarters to find that the *Sanitäter* was in trouble with the guards. I told him that if he was ever again provoked for any reason, to let me know and that I had already taken steps for disciplinary action against the guards interfering with his work. The guard protested that he didn't know that the man was the *Sanitäter*, but abstained from further arguments.

In this busy morning I had not had time to see what had happened to George, so I went back to the plant and found that he had been put to work at the conveyor belt in an underground tunnel that brought the unrefined sugar to a temporary storage area. I asked whether he felt the work would be too hard for him, but he thought it was all right, for the time being. As I came out of the tunnel, I was stopped by the inspector, who decided to show me around the factory.

Although at first I did not understand his gesture, during the tour I discovered that his main objective was to impress me with the German engineering skill and perfection. I refrained from any comment, but I was glad that through the tour I could get an overall impression of the sugar plant. Most of the equipment in use was old and had undergone repair quite a few times. Its life was almost at an end. The inspector excused this by saying that it was difficult to replace the equipment.

One of the most interesting parts in the factory was the research department. A young lady, who introduced herself as the chemical engineer, was the only expert there. Filled with tubes and chemicals, the research department looked like a perfect laboratory. Many times later I visited this same laboratory, trying to escape from reality into the dream world of the engineer.

As we toured, I asked every prisoner I came across how he felt at work after two and a half years of captivity. Some gave me the impression that work seemed to relieve part of the tension that persisted during the years they spent in Italy. Others told me that the Geneva Convention was wrong in allowing the detaining power to use prisoners of war for labor, regardless of its nature.

I left the factory to return to my quarters. I was tired and tried to get some rest. I lay on my bed wondering how Bill was doing. How would the men feel if he returned without cigarettes? What would I do if the whole trip was in vain? In my heart I kept wishing him success, as if this wish could help him through the distance. It wasn't all bad, however. There was one good thing to expect the following morning, as, for the first time, the men who reported sick were going to see a doctor.

I did not go with the group, because there was no one else to leave behind in the camp. The *Sanitäter* knew a few words of German — all that was necessary in a medical case.

Instead, I asked the *Kommando Führer* if I could go with him to the hospital in Breslau and get some more medical supplies for use in our camp. He agreed to this without hesitation, and that same evening our infirmary had something to offer those who needed medical care.

Complaints regarding food continued to increase, but my main hope rested not with the Germans — as every attempt in that direction had failed — but with the Red Cross. I managed, however, to discover that the food allotted each prisoner depended on the type of work he was doing, and while some men were allowed one pound of bread per day, others were allowed two. Upon my request, the bread rations were distributed to each prisoner individually in the exact amount allotted him, but the soup rations were all put in the same big kettle, thus increasing somewhat the amount for all.

The *Sanitäter* returned from the doctor with the sick the same evening and assured me that the doctor was a conscientious man, and that the sick had received proper care. He showed me a list of prescriptions the doctor had recommended. The *Kommando Führer* informed me that I could also obtain those drugs from the main hospital in Breslau at the expense of the plant.

The acquisition of these small comforts seemed to give some encouragement in the otherwise depressed atmosphere. The last man I saw that night was the *Kommando Führer*, who came to tell me that the night shift was to replace those working in the day. Thus, a second day ended in our new prisoner-of-war camp. The following day, the one I — and everyone else — anxiously awaited, Bill was due back.

The weather was beginning to get cold at that time, and our clothing was inadequate against the severity. I had read some time before that in the war against the Russians, the Finns managed to overcome the weather by taking cold showers in the open, and this induced me to try the same thing. The shower room was in the same plant, and because I had nothing else to do, I went and took a cold shower, intending to keep it up regularly.

This done, I took a walk around the plant. I was anxious to see how the prisoners were being treated at work. I found George sitting in a little cave on the side of the tunnel. His work was not hard — he only had to shovel back the few lumps of sugar that had fallen off the rubber belt during their underground travel. The inspector, who was making his usual tour of the day, found me there. In an effort to open a conversation, he asked what I thought of the installation. He then told me to follow him out of the tunnel, where he showed me the heap of brown sugar that had begun to pile up in this immense warehouse. With an expression of pride on his face, he told me that in peacetime the warehouse was filled completely with sugar, and that their objective at present was to produce only what Hitler had ordered. I asked him whether he did not think that every man should be employed in the job of his own capacity. I had seen many of the physically weak employed in the stacking department, where they lifted 300-pound bags of sugar. He promised that he would see to it that each prisoner would be put on the job he could do without much strain and labor. This he did in the same afternoon.

Before I left the plant he asked me to come with him to his office. This was more of a personal invitation. He was curious to know what my background was and my views about the future. I told him that when the war was over — and this, of course, would be with victory on our side — I was planning to study engineering and live the rest of my life as a professional engineer. He wanted to know what had induced me to plan for an engineering career, but I assured him that I had this intention long before I had left Greece. At that point, his secretary returned to the office and went to the desk on the opposite side of the room. She was extremely attractive and, as usual, the inspector took advantage of the fact.

At that time in Germany, under Hitler's regime, marriage had very little meaning. Promiscuity was practiced throughout the country, encouraged by every government agency and individual — an idea that some women welcomed wholeheartedly, while others resented it severely. This lady seemed to fall in the second group. I learned this a few minutes later, when the *Kommando Führer* stepped in and began a campaign to convince her to follow him to his room. Her answer was somewhat interesting.

"I am married," she said. And when the *Kommando Führer* used up every form of persuasion he could invent, she told him firmly but politely, "A good wife remains always true to her husband."

It was getting about noon and Bill was due back any time, so I returned with the *Kommando Führer* to my quarters. I made an inspection of the room to see if everything was properly cleaned. I was satisfied that it was, and the *Sanitäter* began to gain my regard for having maintained this cleanliness in our quarters at his own initiative and labor. The infirmary also was in much better shape than when we first came in. With the drug supply complete, blankets and linen added, it looked more like a place to receive the sick. It was much cleaner than our quarters, on the other side.

Because there was no change in the 12-hour work shifts until the end of the week, those in the day shift lived continuously under artificial lighting without seeing a trace of daylight for seven consecutive days. This, I feared, might prove detrimental to their health, and I believed that a change in environment and a little fresh air might help. I sat at the table in my office, trying to think of a solution. If the prisoners could take a walk, I thought, some time during the day, after they had their necessary sleep, it would help a great deal. I made this suggestion to the *Kommando Führer*, who accepted the idea readily. The men did not seem to care in the beginning, but later on they seemed to agree it was a good idea.

I spent the rest of that afternoon with the *Sanitäter*, trying to get him acquainted with the possibilities of improvement in the infirmary and the difficulties that might obstruct such improvements in the future. I expressed to him the hope that very soon he would not have to rely on German medical supplies, which were still inadequate in quality and quantity, as I was doing my best to get Red Cross supplies flowing into the camp as soon as it was possible under the circumstances.

About two hours before the night shift went to work, Bill finally arrived from Sagan. I was waiting for him in front of the guard room. He was carrying two huge packages, and the guard who was with him was carrying two more — the cigarettes were there. I helped him carry them into our office, and we distributed them to those who were still in the room, keeping the other half for those who had not yet returned from work. I was anxious, however, to find out how Bill had made out on the other matters. He said that the central Man of Confidence had welcomed my suggestions, and he was going to try every single point I had brought forward, and make it work.

From Bill's description of the central Man of Confidence, it seemed that my initiative and determination to go all the way in establishing a human level of welfare was greatly admired by him and it offered a practical line for him to follow in his own efforts. He said that Red Cross supplies had not arrived in Sagan yet, that the British prisoners had only been there for two weeks, and that these shipments were expected to arrive at any time. They were to include medical supplies, food parcels, and clothing. He assured Bill that we were to be the first to receive part of these supplies when they arrived. Bill's description of the Sagan camp left the impression that it was the same as Stalag VIII-A in Goerlitz, part of the camp inhabited by British with the remainder by Russian and French prisoners.

When the day shift returned and received their share of cigarettes, an enthusiasm for life once again began to be felt, but there was still the question: "When do we get some food?" The answer came a week later when the first Red Cross parcels arrived. I asked the *Kommando Führer* to let us have these parcels immediately after their arrival, something he did without much argument. Along with the food came medical supplies and parcels designed for the sick.

The atmosphere that prevailed in our camp when these packages were issued was not new, as we had experienced the same feeling before. Everyone seemed happy, at least temporarily — having something to eat and something to smoke. Not a week had passed after this when the first clothing supplies began to arrive, together with more food parcels and medical supplies. It seemed that finally the Red Cross's efforts were coming through and that conditions were improving in our camp to a satisfactory degree.

During this time I continued to oppose any suggestion made by the *Kommando Führer* until my views and the welfare of the prisoners were first recognized and maintained. This began to give me an advantage over him, and he eventually came to realize that the usual Nazi method of intimidation and force could not succeed with us and that the best way for matters to be settled was to *ask* me rather than *tell* me what to do.

The prisoners became slowly acquainted with this attitude of the *Kommando Führer*. They began to respect my efforts and acquired a great deal of confidence in their success. The extent of their faith surprised me; they seemed to believe that as long as I was there with them, everything was going to be all right. The man who felt this way most was Sergeant Day himself. He was well acquainted with my attempts and efforts on the prisoners' behalf, as well as the dangers involved. What gave me the greatest pleasure, however, was the fact that the Germans had realized that there was no other way to treat us than the humane way, and although at times they could have killed me to avoid disagreements, they spared my life. My attitude seemed to have impressed them so much that they considered it unmanly to dispose of me.

As the days rolled by, my position, as well as that of my comrades, grew more and more secure. I spent most of this time trying to find out other things that would improve the prisoners' welfare. The *Sanitäter* continued his usual duties, taking the sick to the doctor every Tuesday, and attending to those in the infirmary during the week. The gravely ill were sent to Sagan for hospital care.

Each one of the prisoners had acquired a new uniform as soon as fresh clothing supplies arrived, and in spite of the long working hours, our appearance in the camp was clean and neat — something that had its effect upon the Nazi way of thinking. With constant pressure on the mill superintendent, I managed to get overalls for those who needed them at the plant, and once again everything seemed to be in order — this time in much better order than anyone could ever have expected or believed.

Seven

AT the end of the second week at Klettendorf, the first payments were made to those who had worked at the plant. The unfortunate part, however, was that there was nothing we could buy with this money without the necessary ration cards. But at the prisoners' request, I managed to get the **Kommando Führer** to let us buy beer twice each week — something which proved to be a satisfying experience.

In the course of the third week, the first movie was shown in our quarters. Such things were not ordinarily permitted for war prisoners, but the **Kommando Führer** in this case overlooked the restrictions, and this comfort was added to our living. The film was a Nazi production, but we sat and spent two hours just as we would have done outside the barbed wire.

As the first month in this working camp passed, it seemed

that things were becoming more or less routine for everyone except myself, who had to maintain the situation that thus far had prevailed.

I was seated at the table talking with Bill one evening when suddenly one of our workers rushed in and told me that I should go to the plant in a hurry.

"George has had an accident," he said.

I took the *Sanitäter* with me and while Bill followed us, I rushed to the plant. As I came down into the tunnel, I found George lying in the cave with his hand pressed on his waist, his face curled from pain. I asked the *Sanitäter* what he thought, and he seemed to believe it was a case of appendicitis. I ran upstairs to the night inspector's office and asked him to call the local hospital. He did this without any other questions, but unfortunately there was no ambulance available at the time, as the only one in their service was not expected in until the next morning. Wasting no more time with the inspector, I ran downstairs and, with a stretcher that I found in the first-aid room, Bill, the *Sanitäter*, myself, and one of the prisoners carried George back to our quarters and laid him in the infirmary. Meanwhile, the *Kommando Führer* had returned to the guard room. I told him that the local hospital had no ambulance available and asked him to call the hospital in Breslau. He did not hesitate, and we walked together to the telephone station, a few hundred yards away from our quarters at the exit of the steel fence that closed in the factory grounds.

I was nervous and confused as I feared that the hospital might not consent to send their ambulance for a prisoner. They had refused to do so for others before. But I could not bear to think of George lying helpless in the camp, his body twisting with pain. My heart was beating hard as the *Kommando Führer* finally started to talk to somebody on the other end of the line. I could not hear what the answer was, but from instinct rather than any calculated reason I stood at the doorway as if I were trying to make it clear that the only way the *Kommando Führer* could leave the room was by finding an ambulance.

When the telephone conversation was completed, the *Kommando Führer* told me that he was only talking to the night clerk and that the superintendent of the hospital was expected at the telephone any minute. As the phone rang again, I held my breath, hoping the superintendent would not refuse the treatment that George needed. When the *Kommando Führer* turned around and told me the ambulance was on its way, I felt relieved, thinking that perhaps there was a good chance to save George's life. We walked back to the camp and waited ten minutes before the ambulance arrived.

Four German *Sanitäters* brought a stretcher inside the infirmary and, after giving George a morphine injection to ease the pain, they carried him to the ambulance outside. George could still speak while I walked along beside the stretcher to the ambulance.

"Don't let them take me away," he begged.

He looked at me as if he felt that my going along with him would help his operation. As soon as he was place inside the ambulance, however, the *Sanitäter*, who was in charge, told me that George was quite safe, and assured me that he was going to receive every treatment and care a person under such circumstances needed (something which George did not understand). Although up to this time I was intending to go along to the hospital, I realized now that the *Sanitäter* meant what he said and I stepped outside to return to my quarters. George begged me to stay — he felt that he was safer with me than with the doctors who were going to help him. I tried to explain that he was in good hands and told him that I would be down at the hospital to see him the following morning. As the doors closed, George's pleading faded away while the ambulance moved on.

I didn't sleep that night, in spite of the assurance that the German *Sanitäter* gave me that George was going to be all right. Finally, in the morning, the *Kommando Führer* walked into my office and told me that I was free to visit George at the hospital and that he had a guard ready to take me there.

This was the first time I was going into the city of Breslau. The largest city in upper Silesia, Breslau formed the center of communications and industrial arteries in eastern Germany. When we arrived at the hospital, the clerk at the desk told the guard that visiting was forbidden. I was already in, however, and without waiting for permission I went upstairs and asked a nurse passing by if I could see the prisoner who underwent an operation the night before. She gave me his room number and accompanied me there herself. I opened the door and walked in.

George was lying on the bed half conscious, with a faded look in his eyes.

"Hi, George!" I said.

He tried to talk, but he could hardly be heard. He spit blood in a container, which the hospital kept by him on a wooden stand with a drawer. There was a glass of water that he was allowed to use for a few swallows. I pulled the chair to the bedside, but the nurse informed me that it would be best if I did not try to induce him to talk.

He had undergone the operation a few hours before, and according to the doctor's orders, he was to remain undisturbed for a day or two until the wound began to heal. I laid by his side a few bars of chocolate, which I had brought with me from my Red Cross parcel, and gifts from Bill and others in the camp. I tried to assure him that he was all right, and that there was absolutely nothing for him to worry about. I did not know if he heard me — he was hazy and didn't seem to react in any way. I patted him on the forehead and followed the nurse outside.

To relieve my tension, the nurse informed me that she was going to take particular care of George, and that so far he had received the same treatment any other human being would have received without discrimination. She also told me that she, herself, was going to see to it that the same treatment continued until George recovered completely — something that was expected to take about two weeks. I asked her if she could get the doctor to see him at least once a day, and she agreed without hesitation.

When I went downstairs, the guard was still arguing with the clerk about whether visiting was permitted or not.

From the hospital in Breslau, the guard and I went to visit a prisoners' hospital where some of the men from our labor detachment were being treated. I wanted to give them the Red Cross parcels they had not received since their absence from the camp and also to learn of their living conditions and extent of care. In contrast to the hospital where George was kept, the prisoners' hospital was nothing better than the same kind of billet that housed prisoners in central camps, with a little more heating. Prisoner *Sanitäters* were taking care of the sick.

They seemed glad to see me there, especially when I told them that I had brought with me their Red Cross packages — something that always relieved the prisoners' tension and worry. I tried to learn from them how they were being treated, and they seemed to have no complaints. When the purpose of my visit was accomplished, the guard escorted me back to the camp.

I had hardly walked into my office when the *Kommando Führer* dropped in and handed me a small book with the censor's stamp on the outside cover.

"This is for you," he said.

I looked at the title. It was the Geneva Convention. Along with the book he handed me a package of letters, the first mail to arrive in the camp. I looked through the letters, but there was nothing for me.

I spent the rest of the afternoon reading over and over the Geneva Convention until I had learned every detail. Up to this time all I knew about the Convention was what I managed to find out by asking other prisoners, who at some time or another had read it. Now I had the whole thing in my hands, and it seemed to me as if I had the greatest weapon man could invent. Now that I knew for sure what rights the Geneva Convention bestowed upon prisoners, I had something definite to depend on besides the purely human instinct of common decency and welfare.

The days continued to pass. Bill and I spent most of the time together — that is, the time we did not have to spend fighting or arguing with the *Kommando Führer*. I learned from the inspector that my wish for an eight-hour shift was going to become a reality. More prisoners were expected to arrive, who would relieve the ones in our camp from 12 hours of strenuous work. It would be a matter of weeks only, he said, before the eight-hour shift could go into effect.

A few days later, however, a detachment of slave labor, consisting of young girls between the ages of 16 and 25, arrived at the plant for work. They were poorly dressed and fed, but they had to work the same number of hours as we did, and in the same jobs.

The sight of women in the mill caused a great deal of excitement to the prisoners of our camp who, for the last two and a half years, had not seen a woman at all. But their wretched appearance and the treatment those women received from the Nazis caused pity and anger in our hearts.

In the course of the same week, another detachment of slave labor arrived, this time consisting of French political prisoners in much worse condition than the women, and in much poorer health. These prisoners were wrapped in blue uniforms with the pants permanently sewn on a pair of wooden boots. Large white bands were sewn around their arms and legs, to indicate that they were political rather than war prisoners. They looked pale and weak. I watched a group of these individuals trying to push a wheelbarrow without much success. Their guard, a Gestapo member, infuriated because of their inefficiency, pulled a pistol out of his belt and started to beat them in an effort to give them more strength. I stood there helpless, knowing that if I attempted to give them a hand, I would only be inviting a harsher punishment on them — perhaps death.

We were not allowed to approach either type of these prisoners. If any one of us attempted to talk or give anything to them, they would be punished instead of us. Although the Nazis would not shoot any one of us at will, they could shoot any one of the political prisoners without excuse if they felt like it, and the slightest attempt on our part to have any contact with them was sufficient grounds for their punishment.

This day gave me the worst and most pitiful feeling I had ever experienced. As I watched the helpless prisoners struggle to push the wheelbarrow without success, being beaten and whipped by the Gestapo guards, I could not help but see what a Nazi victory in this war was destined to bring.

During my trips to the sugar plant I managed occasionally to approach these prisoners and give them cigarettes and bars of chocolate without being seen by the Gestapo guards. I could speak French, so I asked one of them about his background. He told me he was a doctor, captured while operating a radio station for the Allied command in France. Such an act of resistance was considered by the Nazis to be an act of treason, and he was sentenced by a German court to 40 years' internment in a fortress. To escape from hardships and certain death in that fortress, he and his mates had volunteered for work. He seemed to think that their present condition was far better than that which existed in jail.

More pitiful by far was the spectacle of these prisoners trying to lift the 300-pound bags of sugar, which even we could not move. They looked like lifeless statues, immune to pain and suffering, the only way they could look, I suppose, as any protest was met by punishment — the only punishment the Gestapo knew: beating a man to death. Quite often, whenever I had the opportunity to talk with them, I tried to convince them that victory was going to be ours, that the war against Germany would soon be over, and that their suffering was only temporary. I realized, however, that I didn't have to do that because in their hearts, in spite of everything, their conviction of victory was as strong as mine.

In the days that followed, the conditions in our labor detachment improved. New British prisoners arrived, and the working hours were reduced to eight. Everyone seemed to be content, feeling safe in some way, especially Bill, who thought I had accomplished great things. I, however, thought there was still more room for improvement.

By that time, I had learned something more about the Germans. It seemed that if one could master the local authorities of the camp, he was free to do as he pleased, provided he did not display any weakness at all, especially when they were trying to regain authority. This was possible for a war prisoner regardless of Germany's might. Within our camp, Germany's strength amounted only to what the *Kommando Führer* and his guards could do; there, face to face with us, what they could do depended on their individual ability rather than their collective strength.

Eight

QUITE often, Bill would suggest that he would be happy to have me come to New Zealand after the war and spend some time, or even stay there. I had to decline Bill's invitations, not because I did not think it worthwhile to go, but because in my mind, the end of the war seemed a long way off, and I was not certain I would survive. So far everything had worked out satisfactorily, but no one could depend on the circumstances; they would very certainly change, especially during the last days of fighting.

By the winter of 1943, everything in the camp seemed well under control. Whatever remained for me to do was routine, something anyone could do, whether he could speak German or not: replenish our Red Cross supplies, and remain in touch with the International Red Cross, keeping them posted on our affairs.

I visited George at the hospital as often as I could get a guard to take me there, and each time I saw him, he was feeling better and happier that the operation was successful. In three weeks' time, he was back at the Klettendorf camp. I told the *Kommando Führer* that he should stay in the camp for another two weeks regardless of the doctor's statement that he was able to work. Living in the camp, however, with nothing to do, seemed a boring life for George, and he became irritable and nervous. At the end of this two-week rest period, he was given a job at the plant — a pushbutton job that required neither strength nor effort on his part. He seemed satisfied that things had worked out right for him.

Because the slave girls at the plant were not Germans and they would be hanged if they became pregnant, I quite often appealed to the men in the camp to refrain from approaching these girls. Bill made the same appeal almost every day, and I was pleased to see that everyone felt the same way.

Four prisoners, however, mainly because of their lack of morals, I think, managed to have intercourse with some of these girls without being caught, and bragged about their feat when they returned safely to the camp. Although I condemned their actions, there was nothing I could do to prevent it, except to renew my appeal that the women be left alone. The other prisoners in the camp condemned them as well, creating for these four an embarrassing atmosphere. They blamed this on me, and they decided that they should raise complaints as to the legality of my appointment over a British soldier. All four lined up in my office with the threat that either I quit within two days, or something unpleasant would happen.

"Don't bother to answer them," Bill remarked.

The Geneva Convention gave me the right to take disciplinary action against all four, but the difference in our nationalities caused me to abstain from using that right. Regardless of Bill's suggestions, as well as those of others that those four be punished for their behavior, I considered them soldiers, like anyone else. They felt that because the sergeant major in Goerlitz should have appointed a British subject in the first place, I should ask the central Man of Confidence to relieve me of my duties, and I decided this was the best thing to do, though in my heart I was deeply hurt.

Bill, however, reported the incident to the central Man of Confidence, while at the same time he completely neglected their protest. A few days later all four were recalled to the main camp by the Man of Confidence for disciplinary action. Everyone seemed happy when they were taken away, except Bill and me.

The sugar campaign was nearing the end. With Red Cross supplies enough to cover a period longer than the one the prisoners were to spend there, it seemed to me that Bill was capable of handling the situation himself for the remainder of their stay in Klettendorf. At the same time, I entertained the thought that perhaps somewhere in Germany soldiers of my own nationality were receiving the worst kind of treatment from the Nazis and that if I joined them, I could in some way devote my efforts to their welfare as I had done in our present labor detachment. With these thoughts in mind, I let Bill know that I was planning to ask for a transfer.

I remembered for a long time Bill's expression. In the remaining four days that I spent in this camp, he did everything in his power to convince me that it was important for me to stay.

"What will happen to us after you leave?" he kept saying, as if he were ready to admit the worst.

I didn't quite agree with his views. I did not see why he could not do exactly what I had done. On the other hand, there was very little left for Bill to do and he could always visit the central camp, if at any time he needed guidance or help. The central Man of Confidence was there for that purpose.

Very much reluctant and still pleading that I stay, he endorsed my request to the central Man of Confidence for relief. I mentioned that George wanted to be transferred with me. The answer came four days later when the *Kommando Führer* notified both of us that we were to be moved to Stalag VIII-B in Lamsdorf (later changed to Stalag 344) near the Polish border; the guard would be ready to take us there in the morning.

Bill realized there was nothing more he could do when I told him that the order for my transfer had arrived. He seemed very much in despair, something that surprised me, as I expected more courage from him. But under the circumstances, despair and fear were the only natural reactions on the part of any man.

The *Kommando Führer* also was surprised to learn of my transfer. Only George seemed happy with the news. The idea of a change made room for new hopes.

I was busy that night getting addresses, as most of the men wanted me to write to them after the war, if I had the opportunity. I was somewhat reluctant to leave, because I had spent all my years in captivity with them up to that time, but there was nothing more I could do for them. Each time I looked back at the situation in the camp I found the same answer: there was no further reason for me to be there.

With my transfer finalized and the trip scheduled for the next morning, Bill and I spent the rest of the night talking about postwar plans and aspirations. Those days seemed far away, and we hoped we would meet again, but we knew that Klettendorf would be the last time we would live together.

One of the most disheartening things in a prisoner-of-war camp was a transfer. When the time came to leave, all of that world so far known within the camp belonged to the past and all human ties established there were cut. New friends and a new life were to start where the old ended.

Late that night before my departure, I tried to get some rest, as I anticipated a hard day ahead. By morning, the guard was already waiting at the *Kommando Führer's* office to take us away. All I took with me from Klettendorf were my clothes and a box of sugar, as did George. It seemed useless to take anything else, as it would very likely be confiscated in the search when we entered the new camp. Bill went with us to the *Kommando Führer's* office, and when we were ready to leave, he shook my hand, trembling, and wished me the best of luck. I knew that this wish was one he had meant with all his heart.

The train was late that morning. George and I had to wait a few hours, stamping on the frozen platform, while the guard was rubbing his hands as he walked back and forth trying to keep warm. Klettendorf was hidden in the snowstorm. Every now and then the whistle of the small locomotive hauling the trucks laden with sugar beets to the plant broke the silence of the remote village station.

"Heaven knows what comes next," George murmured, gritting his teeth.

"Nothing worse, I hope. One can never tell in this miserable world," I said, as I kept looking in the direction of the tracks.

"Any idea how long it takes to get to Lamsdorf?" George asked again.

"Oh, I suppose something like four to five hours, maybe a little more. We should be there by evening."

The train finally arrived past noon. We took our seat in the *Dienstabteil* — the workers' compartment. The guard closed the door, stretched his legs over to the opposite side, and laid his rifle between his body and the door.

"*Einsteigen!*" the train-woman shouted for the last time, as the train began to move.

I watched the station fade out of sight through the window. In the midst of the snow-covered fields, huge piles of sugar beets were waiting to be taken to the plant. A small forest of evergreens, all covered in white, interrupted the view every now and then.

"We have to get off at Oppeln," the guard shouted. "The train doesn't go any farther."

I kept watching outside. Everything seemed quiet and peaceful. No barbed wire around you, no guards to point their bayonets the minute you approached the gate. No threatening *Kommando Führer*. Out there, just a few feet away, everything was the same as back home. And yet between those few feet and you there was an invisible wall that kept freedom out of your sight, out of your reach. Just four words could tear that wall to pieces. Four little words — "the war is over" — could chase the darkness out of your mind and bring the sunshine back into your heart. Yet, you had to realize that those four words were a far-away dream — a dream that had to come true, somehow. In this land of human suffering and pain, any relief seemed to be a distant reality. Yesterday, one of your friends was the victim. Tomorrow it may be your turn. Who knows what those Nazi maniacs were planning for you? The war would be over someday — naturally. But would it make any difference to you? Would you be there to see it?

Yesterday it was the women and youths of Poland, France, Belgium, and Italy who had to dig their own graves before they died. But how could you know that tomorrow it would not be you? To the Nazis you were just a prisoner who had to withstand every torture and pain, and die if you dared raise a complaint. To them you had already lived one day too many. You had made their government spend one dollar extra; you had taken one more German soldier out of the front. You could not possibly hope the Nazi government would tolerate your existence much longer.

As I sat by the window gazing outside, I could not help but realize how unfortunate I must have been to find myself in a situation like this.

And yet, in spite of every proof I had so far that as a prisoner I was no longer a living being, I dared oppose their plans and condemn their actions in Klettendorf without being afraid of being killed. Why?

I was by no means brave. Still more, I was fully aware of what it meant to even hesitate to obey a German order at the instant it was given. But I had not only hesitated to obey their orders, I had also made them carry out my own. I kept asking myself *why*.

Then I began to see for the first time that the Nazis were a different type of criminal. Unlike the ordinary criminal, the Nazi was a psychopath who committed crimes to disguise his own weakness and incompetence in solving, or even understanding, human problems. Consequently, he directed his crimes against persons whom he considered much weaker than himself, while at the same time he maintained some sort of respect and admiration for those who defied his will, those whom he felt to be stronger than himself.

The war prisoner is a "weak person." Having lost his freedom and rights, and being at the disposal of the detaining power, he assumes instinctively the attitude of *enduring* every injustice rather than *protesting* it. The Nazi, unable to understand the reason for the prisoner's attitude, considers him weaker than himself, failing to realize that his armed superiority causes this reaction in the prisoner. A Nazi would shoot a prisoner because his clothes were made out of rags and he was unable to stand on his feet, without comprehending that if the prisoner was poorly clad, it was because the Nazis had refused to give him clothes, and if he could not stand on his feet, it was because the Nazis had refused to give him food.

This realization threw some light on the cause of my luck. I was pleased with my reasoning. If this were actually the case, I was much safer fighting them than giving in to every type of injustice they might engineer.

Under the light of such a discovery, I began to find hope and courage, and where before I could only see danger and peril, I began to see some guarantee of safety. I realized that my only chance for survival rested in my ability to maintain the position I had assumed during my stay in Klettendorf — proving to them, through every one of my words and every one of my actions, that I was not afraid of them, in spite of their might. From then on, the Nazis seemed to me more like psychopathic cripples than trained killers or criminals.

I felt happy as I drew these conclusions. George noticed a smile on my face and wondered what had happened.

"Oh, nothing," I said. "I was just thinking."

After changing trains in Oppeln we arrived finally at Lamsdorf late in the evening. The camp was five miles away near an ammunition depot.

Upon arrival, we underwent the usual search, but managed to get the boxes of sugar through by letting the guard have a small part. We were locked in Block F-I, a transit compound, and the next morning, after going through the fumigation process again, were allowed to enter the main camp.

Stalag 344 was unusually large. Its internal arrangement was much the same as the camp in Goerlitz — two main roads dividing three sets of compounds. At the extreme end of the camp were the barracks where Greek prisoners were kept. The guard from Block F-I followed both George and me to the entrance of this compound, and told us it was where we were to stay.

I felt relieved that George would finally have many friends with whom he could communicate, thus ending the need for me to look after him.

Although the sleeping and living accommodations provided by the Germans in previous camps were by no means flattering, the barracks where I was placed now was the worst I had seen. Used originally as a jail for prisoners convicted by camp officials for offenses against Nazi authorities, it had nothing left except its walls and ceiling. Door and window panels were gone, water pipes had been removed, and the beds lacked the ladder-type baseboard. Instead, some wires were nailed on, which sometimes broke loose, and the prisoner landed on the ground.

In one corner of the barracks, some bags sewn together were hoisted to form a partition for what was intended to be an office for the barracks commander. I pulled aside one end of the curtain and stepped in. A sergeant was lying on the top of a three-story bunk, while a short man with a dark brown moustache was sitting on the bench beside the table arguing with some prisoners. Upon seeing me enter, he turned his attention to me and, in English, asked what I was doing there. I answered in Greek, and as soon as I did so, he seemed to realize that I was a new man, just brought in.

"I'll show you to a bed," he started to say.

I didn't give him a chance to go on. I was much disheartened with the conditions they lived under, thinking they had probably lived in the same place all the years since the fall of Crete. I could not see how they had managed to find relief from the cold and dirt, nor could I see how they had endured this without voicing a protest or complaining to the protecting power during the past years of captivity.

I kept gazing around the room trying to answer those questions for myself. The barracks commander seemed to anticipate what I was thinking. He pulled me gently by the arm.

"Let's go out," he said, indicating he wanted to talk to me in private. "Can you speak German?" he asked.

"Yes."

"Then you speak English, too, I take it?"

I nodded again in the affirmative with a grin. The commander let out a sigh of relief.

"What is the object of this?" I asked, although I had already suspected the reason for his curiosity.

Without answering my question, he went on to say that I did not have to sleep with the rest of the prisoners in the barracks. I could take the bottom bed in his office. There were a few things, he said, he and I could work out together. He wore no insignia, so I asked him what his rank was. He told me his name — Joseph Kavroudakis, a sergeant major in the infantry.

To me he looked like a regular soldier whose life had been spent in army camps. He seemed old, because of the hardship he had undergone, for the most part, in prisoner-of-war camps, and I was very much surprised to learn that he was only 24.

It was getting cold outside so I suggested that we carry on the conversation inside — as if the inside were any warmer. The sergeant major kept twisting his moustache; it appeared that this act of nervousness was helping him concentrate.

"I need a man like you badly," he said finally, as we started to walk back into the billet. "For three years now I have wished someone like you would turn up."

I wondered what he meant, although from what I had already seen in Stalag 344, I gathered that he was having difficulty in his duties as barracks commander. He knew very little German, and not much more English, in a camp that was inhabited entirely by English-speaking prisoners. I did not say anything of my experience in Klettendorf. I was glad to be out of there and for once free of the tension and danger I had willingly assumed. I felt I would be much more at ease if I had no more responsibilities to carry out. Yet Joe's suggestion and my bewilderment over the living conditions in that block induced me to help him do "some things" he felt would benefit the welfare of the men in his barracks.

"All right!" I said finally, while we both pulled the curtains aside and stepped into what supposedly was his office.

"This is Sergeant Thomas," he went on to introduce the man on the top bunk. Thomas, a rather tall fellow with an equally glamorous moustache, got up on his bed and stepped down to shake my hand and join in our discussion. But we had to cut the conversation short when the German Block *Führer*, the compound leader, rushed into the billet, yelling at everyone to get out — we were going to have a search.

This meant that all the men in the barracks were to take their belongings outside and wait until German guards searched every inch of the billet — for some five to seven hours. Similar searches were carried out in Camp 57 in Italy, but this was the first time I had seen one carried out in mid-winter for so many hours.

What the Germans were looking for were small radio sets that prisoners had bought from the Germans before. These radio sets, which consisted of a pair of earphones and could get either London or Moscow, were our means of information about the war from Allied sources. During previous searches many such sets were found, resulting in the prisoner's punishment; but soon after the search, they were sold back to the prisoners by business-minded Germans for the price of one bar of soap.

Nine

I spent most of the time during the search talking with Joe, the sergeant major, trying to find out why they had endured such conditions.

"You think I haven't tried everything?" Joe asked in a sad, desperate voice. "You should have been here in the early years, '41 to '42," he continued, as if he didn't expect any answer. "Then you could see what the dogs did to break down our morale. Everyone had to give in to their treatment."

"I don't know what it was like in the camp then," I said, as Joe searched in his pocket for a cigarette, "but it's got to change now. I am going to try, starting right now."

Joe looked at me with surprise. "Don't be a fool!" he nearly shouted. "You are only going to get yourself shot. Others had the same idea before. You know where they are now?" He looked at me again as if he expected me to ask, then proceeded to tell me anyway. "In the cemetery," he said, "a few kilometers from here."

The sergeant major remained silent for a few seconds. I wondered if the reason he was trying to discourage me was not just a test to find out whether I had meant what I said. Then again I wondered if he had expressed this pessimism because of his past experiences in Lamsdorf, or because he was afraid that my attitude against the Nazis could have disastrous results for the prisoners as a whole — something which he wanted me to consider before I embarked on my adventure.

By this time the search was over, the guards and German officers had left the Block taking away the hounds they had brought in the morning, and we were free to go back into the billet.

"Let's go inside," Sergeant Thomas suggested. "I'm getting cold out here."

While sleeping quarters looked miserable, the Red Cross picture was somewhat bright. The prisoners had been receiving parcels regularly since 1942 — one food package per week per man. They did not, however, receive any clothes. They were still clad in their original uniforms, though a few things had been donated to them by other British prisoners in the camp, who had been receiving clothing from the Red Cross and their relatives at home. Joe seemed extremely pleased, though I could not understand why, from the grim prospects he had pointed out during the search. I was not happy at all. Furthermore, I was not only disgusted, but also desperate, not knowing what to do. It was very deep into the night when I decided to get some sleep.

I had to be up at five o'clock for the first roll call of the day. I noticed that along with the German Block *Führer* came a South African sergeant in charge of the neighboring Block. He walked in front of the column, counting the men in fives. He showed his count to the German and went into the billet to find the remainder of the prisoners. When he came out he called Joe, the sergeant major, but Joe sent the South African to me with the proper introduction. This sergeant, by the name of Beste, a thin, middle-aged individual, complained that too many of the prisoners were staying inside during roll call, when they should be out like everyone else, unless they had a written excuse from the doctor.

"The Germans won't like that!" he warned.

I was very much surprised to find that a war prisoner was so preoccupied with what the Germans liked. I could not help laughing at

Sergeant Beste's warning.

This was the first time I began to get an idea of what had brought about those conditions in Lamsdorf. I began to see that it was mainly the fault of the agents appointed by virtue of Article 43 of the Geneva Convention, who confined themselves to receiving and distributing collective shipments, while at the same time using the privilege of representing the prisoners as a means to gain friendship with the Germans and make their own lives secure by complying more than necessary with their whims. According to the spirit of the Geneva Convention, such an attitude was not entirely out of place. Remembering, however, the cold fact that as soldiers we were expected to oppose and fight the Nazis under any circumstances, to me it seemed degrading.

I laughed at Beste's complaint because I could not see the reason for his concern over the Germans's problems. Furthermore, I was witnessing the cheapest behavior on the part of a soldier who undertook to fight for the same cause as I had. I told him that the next morning everyone would stay in bed and that he could let the German Block *Führer* worry about it.

Because Beste had displayed such authority while in no different status from me, and with a purpose no different from mine, I asked him how it happened that during the three years he had been in Stalag 344, as he had stated, he had endured seeing 300 men live in a billet that had no protection against the cold, no sleeping facilities except the floor, and no sanitation except a little water one had to suck out of a pipe drop by drop. Beste was embarrassed at this question and looked for a minute in the direction of the sergeant major, expecting Joe to agree that my questions were out of place. Not finding any understanding in Joe's expression, he walked out of our Block, taking the German with him.

After the daily soup was served, I told Joe that I was going to take a walk around the camp.

"I'll come along with you," he said.

I was curious to find out the details about the situation in the camp. I had not been far from the truth in my suppositions, but I needed to be convinced that I was absolutely right.

"Where are we headed?" Joe asked, when he noticed that we were walking toward the main gate.

"I want to see Goodie, the Man of Confidence," I said. "There are some things I want to find out from him."

Joe attempted once again to convince me that there was nothing to gain by such an interview. "There isn't a man in the camp who doesn't think Goodie ought to be court-martialed."

As we approached the gate, I noticed some trucks unloading bales of clothing into a storage room isolated from the rest of the camp.

"What's that over there?" I asked.

"Red Cross clothing," Joe answered. "They have been coming in quite regularly. So far, in spite of my requests, we have not been allowed to have any. They are only intended for the British — that is what I was told," he said.

"But the clothes come from the International Red Cross, don't they?" I challenged Joe.

"Yes," Joe replied. "But it doesn't make any difference."

"Did you talk to the Man of Confidence?"

Joe nodded with a dejected look. "It's no use asking him any more," he said.

I knew very well that ethnic prejudice existed without restraint in the camp, and a hostile attitude of the British prisoners toward those of Continental Europe was aggravated by the fact that only the British were fighting the Nazis on an organized front. But I could not believe that a man with the responsibilities of the Man of Confidence would assume such a bias among prisoners without realizing that he would have to account for it at the war's end.

We bypassed the sentry at the gate joining the road to the clothing store. I approached one of the noncommissioned officers, who was holding some sheets of paper in his hand, standing at the rear of the truck. Talking with him, I learned that he was in charge of clothing distribution to prisoners. He was a sergeant major in the British army, but he said firmly that he had no instructions from the Man of Confidence, and neither did he have permission from the Germans to issue clothing to the men in my Block.

We left this section and kept walking, trying to find a way to get clothes for our men without any misapprehension on the part of the British. From prisoners who were caught in the Middle East and were now in Lamsdorf, I had learned that the Greek government, exiled in Egypt, had managed to save the treasury deposit in gold and was paying its due contribution to the International Red Cross for the purchase and delivery of food, clothing, and medical supplies to Greek prisoners of war in German camps. Thus, I did not think the Man of Confidence was justified in his position, nor did I believe that it was the Germans alone who had restricted the issue of clothing to British prisoners of war. If the Germans were causing this hardship, I felt I could settle the matter as I had done in Klettendorf, but first I had to make sure that I blamed the right group.

Only a few minutes had passed after our return to the billet when the German *Lager Offizier* walked in to make an inspection of our living quarters. Another prisoner called my attention to this as the *Lager Offizier* was already on his way out, apparently feeling that everything was well.

"Wait a minute!" I shouted as I pulled the curtain separating the sergeant major's office from the rest of the billet.

The German officer turned around, surprised at my tone.

"Are you the *Lager Offizier*?" I asked him.

"*Ja*," he replied. "What of it?"

"How does this pigpen strike you?" I asked.

"*Alles ist in Ordnung*!" the German said, as if he was blind to the conditions that actually existed.

"Come with me for a minute," I told him.

He followed me into the washroom where I showed him the pipe from which we had to suck water drop by drop, and asked him if that was what he called "in order." He became embarrassed with this display, and started to swallow the words he had intended to speak.

As I took him around and showed him the windows where the wind was blowing through and the floor where the prisoners slept, the officer's earlier remark and the sight of the misery reigning inside forced me to lose control of myself, and I began to shout at him. At first, he was amazed, but eventually he promised that something was going to be done about improving the conditions in the billet.

The remainder of the prisoners who had gathered at my shouting smiled grimly when I told them of the German's promise. Still, I didn't believe he was actually going to do anything about it; neither did the sergeant major.

The same afternoon two more German officers came in to make an inspection. In my exasperation over Nazi failure to provide even the elementary basis for survival and the indifference of the prisoners themselves, who would rather endure the cold, dirt, and misery than raise the slightest objection, I used every word and every means I could muster to make it clear to the Nazis that *whether* we lived or not made no difference, but it made a great deal of difference *how*. The rest of the prisoners understood what went on before them as each one expressed his support, contending that I had done the right thing.

Circumstances are altogether different when one lives inside the barbed-wire fence, dominated by the feeling of being lost and forgotten. His own leaders are of no importance to him anymore. Discipline is a ridiculous thing. Self-respect is a lost property. The only one he considers is the armed guard, because he knows that his entire existence depends on the guard and his decisions.

Somehow my opposition seemed to bring back a stronger sense of self-respect, something the Nazis had tried mercilessly to destroy and had succeeded in doing, to a certain extent. It was not very difficult to revive this feeling. Though numbed for years by pressure and intimidation, self-respect could spring up at the first sign of encouragement. Aside from attempting to improve the physical conditions existing in the Block, I was also aiming at bringing back this feeling of self-respect, as I believed we could be more content and the atmosphere in the Block a great deal brighter.

It was lack of dignity, I believed, that had caused war prisoners within the camp to become selfish, irritable, and greedy, willing to deprive anyone — stranger, friend, or brother — of anything he possessed or was entitled to possess, so that they might have it instead. It was the lack of self-respect that made man display his animal nature under the circumstances that existed in Stalag 344 on December 20th, 1943. There, in an alien world — deprived of all material possessions, reputation, economic and political strength, naked of all external masquerades, personal identity abandoned — all that one possessed was an instinctive desire to preserve his own life at the expense of everyone and everything else.

This was perhaps one of the most important things I have ever learned. I discovered at Lamsdorf for the first time that anything tangible or superficial can be taken away from a person. What cannot be taken is what a person possesses in his heart. Seeing the extent of man's inner will for self-preservation, I realized that nothing could uproot this instinct, except a long, persistent culture and education, beginning from the time a man's inner world is formed.

Yet there were men like Joe, the sergeant major, in Stalag 344, in whose hearts this education and culture had tempered the primitive instinct of self-preservation. Although they had lost everything else, like the rest of us, there was something that neither the Nazis nor the circumstances they forced upon us could take away. This thing was within them and I believe it could have only been the result of a culture that had shaped them after the image of eternal values.

I caught the first glimpse of Joe's inner self through his confidence in my actions when he completely overlooked the fact that I had only arrived at the camp the day before, that he knew nothing of my background, and that he had no reason to believe my nationality and past. What is more, he had no reason to trust me without first obtaining some information in the same manner that the British did, through their Secret Service.

Although I didn't know the reason why the sergeant major had trusted me so far, I was glad to see that in Joseph Kavroudakis I had found not only a capable and conscientious soldier, but also a trustworthy and genuine friend. He seemed well educated, in spite of the fact that he had spent most of his life in army camps and was trained for no other duty than that of a soldier.

One of his outstanding qualities was his ability to understand the ultimate objective of any movement that the Nazis initiated at its very beginning, and his ability to cope with dangerous situations — as proved later — was a result of quick action on his part at the instant an idea was conceived. By virtue of these qualities, he managed to maintain such discipline among the prisoners that it reminded them of the days they had spent in their regimental camp, where discipline was the main feature of the day. Everyone respected Joe as a brave and honorable leader. His confidence in me was something I could not have done without. In times of danger, he was always there to remind me that he was still my most valuable friend.

My second day in Lamsdorf turned out to be the worst for Sergeant Beste. His willingness to comply with German wishes, in order to buy his own safety, was what infuriated me the most. I could not believe that anyone, knowing the reason for which he had undertaken to fight the Nazis, as a soldier, would behave in the way Sergeant Beste did.

I was expecting that after the embarrassing episode that morning, he would leave all matters to me and the sergeant major, seeing that we were both willing and determined to cause difficulties in the work of the

Nazis — something that would bring him into a rather precarious situation.

To my surprise, however, Beste showed up again with the Block *Führer* for the evening roll call. In the same way he had done that morning, he reported to the Block *Führer* the number of men in the Block both inside and outside the barracks, complaining to me about men being left inside without permission from the doctor. He pointed out that he had not specifically mentioned this to the Block *Führer*, thinking he had rendered a service on my behalf.

"Let me worry about the sick or those who stay in the barracks," I said. "You can tell the Block *Führer* anything you want. Quit worrying about me!"

Beste seemed enraged. "I'm supposed to be in charge of this Block," he said.

"I've seen more people in charge of this Block," I whispered to myself, "than in charge of a regiment."

"You are making my position difficult," Beste complained. "Stop doing it! It's an order."

This was another mistake on his part. I could not agree that one man's safety was more important than the safety of the other 300 men, so I told him that if he showed up in the same Block again, with or without the Block *Führer*, I would throw him over the fence. He raised his head back a couple of times, bounced back and forth, and walked out in a hurry without waiting for the Block *Führer*, as he usually did.

After dismissal, Joe reassured me again that I was free to take any steps I though necessary to improve the welfare of the other prisoners in the same Block, and that he endorsed my actions completely. He warned me, however, that I should be more careful, as no one could tell what the Germans would do if they found me battling them too often.

Ten

THE next day became one of official visiting. First the **Lager Offizier** was back again, then some German officers from the **Kommandantur**, and, finally, the division commander and the colonel commanding the camp, accompanied by Goodie, the Man of Confidence — a man much disliked. Each one of these officers, including Goodie, seemed very much surprised to find that such adverse conditions actually existed. No one seemed to have known of the circumstances under which the prisoners in our Block had lived for nearly three years, and this was the first time they had found out about it.

As I realized their cunningness, I burst into threats, shouts, and any other means of expression for my anger, without concern that I was letting myself go too far. I could not control the anger as I stood there looking at the conditions inside the barracks on one hand and the Germans's surprise on the other.

If there was any man in those three years whose duty was to call those conditions to the attention of the German authorities, that man was Goodie, and even now he was hesitating to say anything, for fear that it might embarrass the camp officials. As Goodie stood shaking his head in an affirmative nod to German promises, I broke in emphatically and pointed out that unless something was done to fix the building's water service, beds, and everything else needing repair, I was going to inform the protecting power of their failure to do so. Then one of the German officers nodded for me to go along with him as soon as the general left.

To my satisfaction, he let me take out of the storage room the glass that was needed to fix the windows. The next day the repair squad arrived — the beds were put back into shape, the window and door panels were fixed, the water service was restored, and we began to get coal for use in the stoves. The curtains concealing the sergeant major's office were replaced by wooden partitions, but we still lacked clothes, something we badly needed.

Meanwhile, Beste, seeing the improvement he had failed to bring about because he simply was afraid to ask or risk asking, began to feel uncomfortable, now that someone else had accomplished what he should have done. Moreover, he realized that the sergeant major had even more confidence in me now. But mainly, the prevailing attitude of the camp administration up to that time — that prisoners can benefit only by complying with the Nazis's wishes — had been proved wrong. That is what hurt Beste and his associates the most, and one night he called a mediator and expressed to him that he had every respect and esteem for the sergeant major, but many complaints against me. Joe, however, assured the mediator that anything I had done was with his full approval, and that if there was one soldier in the camp he could trust without fear or suspicion, it was me.

When Beste learned of the sergeant major's response, he informed me through Joe that I was required to see the Man of Confidence, Goodie, for some matter of importance. He led me himself to Goodie's office through a barricade of assistants, and left. I was curious to know the reason for this invitation — something which I already suspected — and Goodie immediately began his methods of intimidation that he had used against other prisoners in the past who had dared criticize his policies or get in his way by severing his relations with the German camp officials.

"I brought you here to warn you," he said, "that unless you stop assailing the Germans, I shall have to get rid of you."

I was not surprised by this threat, as many of the other prisoners had already acquainted me with Goodie's nature and character. He was liked by no one and had a very bad reputation, even among his own countrymen. It was obvious to me that he could depend on the Germans completely to help him maintain discipline along the lines that the Germans had prescribed.

He could very easily have gotten rid of me as he had threatened; all he had to do was ask the Germans. His threat was quite real and possible except for one thing: he could not overlook the fact that I was doing my duty as a soldier while he was not. I told him that when he was ready, he knew where to find me. Meanwhile, I was going to continue fighting the Germans for everything the prisoners in my Block needed to survive.

I left his office and returned to the billet. Joe seemed worried over the cause of this arraignment and heaved a sigh of relief to see me back. He was glad to see that I had realized the other dangers within the camp linked to my efforts to bring about bearable living conditions in the Block.

In the days that followed, I managed finally to convince Goodie that we were entitled to receive clothing from the Red Cross like everyone else. I secured his permission and even cooperation, after threatening to report his activities to responsible Red Cross officials during their next visit. Realizing that I was not joking, he had to grant this permission, and as the Christmas week drew near, our barracks became clean, warm, living quarters with an excited and content crowd.

In the evenings or afternoons, many would gather around the tables provided and play a game of poker; others would spend their time reading books, borrowed from the camp library, while Tom, Joe, and I spent most of our days seeking more improvements in order to maintain what we had already accomplished.

I was gratified to see, and so was the sergeant major, that many of our men began to make friends with the British in the other compounds. Many of the British at the same time began to frequent our barracks and associate with us, creating an atmosphere of mutual trust and friendship.

Under such conditions, Christmas Eve 1943 arrived. I did not feel the way I used to at Christmas time, but I was far from being unhappy. Even though we were still prisoners, at least a way was found in which a number of small comforts could be obtained to make life bearable — to some degree at least — inside the barracks where the shouts and firing of German guards could not be heard, in surroundings peopled by men like Joe and the others with a common background, a common purpose, and a common future.

I was thinking of the last Christmas I had spent at home, of the war that eventually would engulf me, of the friends I had made from the British air force — Jack Bassett, especially. I wondered what had happened to him since he was moved to Rhetymo after the Germans had landed. He could have been killed or successfully evacuated somewhere in Egypt, or he could be in England now with the rest of his squadron.

I left the billet and kept walking in the compound toward the gate, thinking of all that had taken place since that Christmas — especially of Jack, who was on the same convoy with me, but on a different destroyer the night of the evacuation of Heracleion, and Basil. I wondered if I could obtain information from the Red Cross; such things seemed possible, although it would take quite a while, and the war might be over by the time I received the information, so I gave up on the idea of writing. The prospects of receiving an answer to any of my letters in a prisoner-of-war camp were dim, because of the time required for a letter to reach the camp.

I crossed the main road and, walking through Block-II, I came into Block-XI across the second main road. The two billets in this compound were inhabited by airmen. From curiosity rather than any other reason, I entered the first of the two billets. The blue uniforms with stripes and wings and the RAF badges reminded me of Jack, but I was hoping he was anywhere but there. I went through the billet and entered the second.

As I stepped through the threshold someone bending over the fire preparing tea stood up suddenly to wipe the smoke from his eyes. The face looked familiar, but I couldn't believe it was Jack. I went closer. He seemed to think my face was familiar, too, as he kept staring at me.

"Pardon me," I said. "Were you in Crete in 1941?"

"Tasos!" Jack exclaimed, grabbing my hand.

"Jack?" was all I could say, shocked with regret to see him there.

"How in the world did you get here?" he asked me.

"How in the world did *you* get here?" I replied.

"It's a long story."

Jack offered me some tea, and we each took a cup made from food containers and moved to his bed, still amazed to have found each other. I learned that Jack was captured one day before I was, but on Crete. He had been in Stalag 344 since, and for some time he had been in a working camp. He had gone there during the one-year purge of the prisoners in Lamsdorf, following an alleged story that German prisoners had been found drowned with their hands tied, after the British commando raid at Dieppe. Prisoners were hung upside down from the ceiling by the Germans.

We spent most of the evening talking about past experiences. I suspected that Jack knew nothing of what had happened to Basil. It was past midnight when I decided to return to my compound.

"You can stay here for the night," Jack said. "I'll tell the barracks commander."

I declined, unaware that the sentries had orders to fire on anyone crossing the fences between compounds after twelve o'clock.

Since the gates were all closed, I had to jump over a series of fences and walk through several other compounds before I reached mine. I saw the searchlights, which the sentries turned on to illuminate the camp now and then. However, not knowing that they would fire if I were seen, I paid no attention to them and got back to my compound without being noticed.

Joe was much surprised to see me get in that late; he wondered where I had been.

"Over in Block Eleven," I said.

"You fool!" Joe exclaimed, jumping out of his bed. "Don't you know that you could get shot crossing from one compound to another after midnight?" he said.

"No," I answered. "I don't. But I am here now."

The Christmas Eve celebration was still going on in the billet, as we were permitted to leave the lights on all night because of the occasion. On other nights, lights had to be out by ten o'clock and everyone sound asleep.

"Let's play a game of poker," Joe suggested, still shaken over my luck in crossing through the fences. I realized how fortunate I had been. Joe told me how another prisoner a few days before I arrived had been caught in the daytime jumping over the fence from the main road into Block-VI. A German patrol spotted him as he was trying to free his clothes from the barbed wire, and the sergeant leading the patrol shot him before he had time to get away from the fence.

"Well, let's play poker," Joe said, and we moved down to the corner in the billet where Joe spent his time playing cards with other prisoners from Crete. Playing poker on Christmas and New Year's Eve is a custom among Greeks.

In this corner of the billet the men had arranged their bunks to form a small closed space heated with a stove near the window. A table stood in between at the center of this square. The bottom beds were used for seats, being very close to the table, and as the top beds were very near the ceiling, it looked more like a private room inhabited solely by Joe's personal friends — something that gave the company a much more congenial appearance. I would later frequent this same corner many times, whenever I wanted to get away from the complicated and risky life of the Block leader. The carefree attitude of the residents of this little country club and their concentration on a poker game formed a warm, relaxing contrast.

I finally got tired watching the game and went to my room to sleep, with mixed emotions about this exciting day. I went to bed feeling that another day had gone, and that we were that much closer to the end of the war.

Early in the morning a German guard showed up with a note in his hand, looking for the sergeant major. Joe handed the note to me and the guard added that he needed 20 men to go outside the camp for work. Being Christmas, the Germans did not want to spoil their holiday by working, and had decided they could use the prisoners instead. Upon hearing this request, Joe became furious and told the guard in the few German words he knew to "Get the hell out!"

I was wondering what might happen next, and soon got an idea when I saw headed for our compound the German *Lager Feldwebel*, who had shot the prisoner trapped on the barbed wire. He walked inside, asking for Joe, the *Stabsfeldwebel*. Not finding him there, he entered Joe's office. He led the sergeant major out and asked him, in the presence of the rest of the prisoners in the billet, to provide 20 men for work outside the camp. Joe showed him the exit.

"*Raus!*" Joe shouted at the German, his hand pointing to the door.

The *Feldwebel* pulled out his pistol immediately and pointed it toward Joe as he screamed with fury, "I'll give you five minutes to get these 20 men together."

Joe turned around and went back into his office with an indifference and calmness that surpassed imagination. Two minutes passed and the *Feldwebel* had not yet seen one man show up for work. I was sitting at the table in the same office, waiting to see what the end of the German's count would bring.

There was one minute left; but Joe didn't seem to care. Some of the men who could understand a little German had grasped the *Feldwebel's* threats. Seeing that the sergeant major was not doing anything to carry out the *Feldwebel's* order, with less than a minute remaining, they started to come down from their beds, indicating they were willing to go out by lining up. I believe they did this because they suspected the Nazi would go through with his threat and would shoot the sergeant major this time.

Joe's attitude seemed justified; the Nazis always picked holidays to remind us that we were still prisoners. Joe had felt that it was either going to be Christmas Day, as he told me later, or the last day he lived, and between the two, he had made his choice. Joe didn't know that the guard had been directed there by Goodie, and even if he had, Joe plainly didn't know the meaning of fear. I was to find this out later.

Eleven

*A*S *the days went by and the New Year came, incidents like the one on Christmas Day continued to occur with either me or the sergeant major involved each time. The talk about our defiance of German orders gradually spread through the camp, surprising other prisoners. The continued improvement of our living conditions, our morale, and our self-respect, upset every theory so far maintained, which claimed that only submission to German will and treatment was a means of survival. Eventually, even the Germans showed respect, and this was best exemplified on the day of March 25, 1944 — National Greek Independence Day — when the German commandant of the camp provided a garrison of honor, which kept the* **Lager Feldwebel** *and all other Nazis away from the compound for that one day, letting the* prisoners feast.

Such results greatly embarrassed the prisoner administration of the camp, as more prisoners began to wonder why, for instance, Goodie, Beste, or the "clique," as Beste described the administration of the camp, could not do the same. The shame was aggravated as the days went by, and in some way I suspected that Goodie's "clique" could not tolerate the situation much longer without taking steps to curb the enthusiasm and approval with which the prisoner greeted Joe's actions and mine.

The opportunity for Goodie to retaliate presented itself without any effort on his part, when the German camp officials informed me and the sergeant major that we were to be repatriated to Greece and that our complete home address and next of kin were required for that purpose. This was the time I began to see that Joe could smell danger long before he could see it. There was a possibility that the Germans might have meant what they said, as they were at the time occupying Greece, and they could afford to set us free. However, I and a few other prisoners in my barracks had been captured either en route to Egypt or during the German campaign there, and I was certain that repatriation would be carried out only for those who were captured in Greece and had failed to show any tendency for active warfare after its fall to the Germans.

The most probable conjecture was that the Germans did not really intend to carry out our repatriation, but instead intended to transform our group of war prisoners into political prisoners, and finally into civilians, with the obligation to work in German war industries or accept the same fate that befell those in other concentration camps for refusing to do so. Similar prisoner-of-war transformations had been carried out before with Poles, French, and other Continental prisoners. It was quite possible to do the same with us. Joe suspected that this was the case, while every man in our billet wishfully believed they were really going home.

There was no way of finding out the real aim behind this Nazi move, and the time left for action on our part was limited. Our only source of protection was the International Red Cross, through which we could transmit information on the Nazi plans to our government in the Middle East. Of course, we still had a choice between working for the German war industry or walking into the butcher camps. The latter seemed our alternative if we failed to get any protection from the Red Cross. We were fortunate, however, that Red Cross representatives had accidentally visited the camp in early March 1944, on which occasion Joe managed to send a message describing recent German intentions toward us. These representatives promised to have quick action taken by the Allies to stall the Nazi drive.

About the middle of March, 200 of us were ordered to leave the camp for an unknown destination. Joe and I were on the list. No mention was made of the reason for our move, something which the Geneva Convention specifically required for war prisoners.

While I packed my clothes, I tried to figure out, by going over the information the Germans had provided in regard to our movement, some way we could discover what the next few days had in store for us. There was nothing to go on, and my suspicion, as well as Joe's, about our possible fate seemed to be the only reasonable conclusion. A friend of mine from New Zealand, by the name of Bill, a member of the British Intelligence Service, dropped in to tell me goodbye.

"Keep your chin up," he said, and shook my hand. "Don't give up hoping."

"We still have a choice," I said. "Maybe, they'll have to bury us instead."

Bill seemed to understand completely that I meant to continue my resistance, and he tried to convince me that this was a very unwise thing to do.

"There is one thing I will never do, Bill," I said, "and that is to look upon the Nazis any differently from how I have so far. I joined the British to fight them, and when I can't fight them any more, I am not going to let them use me as a means to achieve their ends."

Bill realized that there was very little he could do to persuade me otherwise, and he left, wishing me luck and that God might be with me.

We departed the next morning in cattle cars, and two days later we were unloaded by an airfield in Poland called Udetfeld. We marched through the air force camp to a lonely wooden billet by the airport hangar.

We were settled in this billet after being told that it was just another working camp. A garrison of Germans had been provided with a sergeant as the *Kommando Führer*. However, I still regarded this as the first step in separating the prisoners from any source of protection, until it would become practicable to attempt our "conversion" to political prisoners. That we were told this was another working camp meant very little.

This was the ordinary manner in which prisoners were converted into civilians or sent into extermination camps. They were first separated from the main camp and denied any contact with the Red Cross authorities. If the Red Cross failed to inquire, or even if the Red Cross inquiries failed to indicate the whereabouts of such prisoners, the Germans would proceed with the conversion. This was the way in which a half a million Poles had disappeared as civilians or as victims of gas chambers in concentration camps.

With Continental prisoners, the Germans claimed that the Red Cross had no authority to interfere, as Germany was occupying their lands; they prevented every Red Cross effort to protect such prisoners. To avoid such a fate, basing my conclusion on suspicion rather than facts, Joe and I induced the *Kommando Führer* to acknowledge that the sergeant major and I were to represent the prisoners in their relations with the Red Cross — Joe in his capacity as the senior noncommissioned officer, I in the capacity as assistant *Vertrauensmann*.

I was much relieved to learn from him that our labor detachment was Camp E.745, Udetfeld, part of Stalag VIII-B in Teschen, Germany, another British prisoner-of-war camp, and that the conditions that existed in other British labor detachments were to continue in this one also.

The first day was always the busiest and most difficult one, because Joe and I had to make the new German garrison understand that we were not going to submit to any treatment different from the one described by the Geneva Convention. The *Kommando Führer*, however, seemed almost the same type I had met in Klettendorf. He was very cooperative in granting us every facility I requested. Joe was more worried about the location of the camp. It was next to the airfield, and getting bombed was a constant danger.

The cooking facilities consisted of a field kitchen, and the toilet facilities were poor. We knew nothing as yet of the food situation, but waited to find out the next morning.

In spite of our fears, however, about the German intentions behind this transfer, Camp E.745 was the first place where Joe and I were free to organize the camp to the degree of efficiency we desired and to the standards we thought appropriate for a military establishment.

Immediately that first night we convinced the *Kommando Führer* that a trip for the sergeant major and me to Teschen was necessary. Our first objective was to acquaint the central Man of Confidence there of our suspicions. Our second was to arrange for Red Cross supplies.

Having done everything possible the first day of our arrival in Udetfeld, I waited until the next morning for the remaining arrangements. We needed a kitchen staff, a barber, a *Sanitäter*, and a responsible individual to take charge of the kitchen supplies, which we anticipated would be small, having to be provided by the Germans. We had to know the nature of the work intended, something we had not yet been told. Being near the airfield, it seemed we were to be used for work connected directly with warfare, and this worried me, more so when the *Kommando Führer* said he didn't know — though he promised to find out soon.

The following day was a busy one, but a number of details were settled. The sergeant major appointed George Karaolanis, one of the noncommissioned officers, to take charge of the kitchen, with two cooks to do the kitchen work. We were fortunate to have a medical man in our group who handled the sanitation duties. We also had a barber, and a shoemaker, who, together with the rest of our staff, were excused from labor outside the camp. Joe acted as the Man of Confidence, but I replaced him in cases where he expected I would get better results.

Our trip to Teschen was to come two days later. No specification had been made yet as to the type of labor.

About noon the same day, the *Kommando Führer* informed me that the man in charge of the kitchen, a couple of others, and I had to walk to the *Verpflegung* (ration) office to get our daily allotment of food. Joe wanted to come along, curious to know what our provisions would be. A guard accompanied us to the air force barracks where the *Verpflegung* office was. We were to receive the rations from the store after we had first obtained from the ration officer a statement of the allowances made to us, on the basis of the number of men in the camp.

The ration officer was located in the middle of a long narrow hut. Two other offices adjoined his. One was occupied by a sergeant in charge of food shipments, the other by two women, from whom we were to get our ration statement.

We were all taken into the office, which the women occupied. As we walked in, the two attractive women provided a pleasant sight, in contrast to the surroundings we had been accustomed to. I had seen a girl every now and then during the first months in Germany, but never, during the three years of captivity, had I been within talking distance of one. The sergeant major started to curl his moustache as he watched George trying to say a word in German he had forgotten — the only German word he knew. George paced back and forth, glancing at the girl nearest him every now and then. Finally, he drew a packet of cigarettes from his pocket and offered her one. She declined politely, and George lit one for himself.

"Will you do me a favor?" George said to me. "Find out her name, will you, please?"

Seeing George's eagerness to get acquainted and knowing how useless it was to entertain such a thought, at a time when the chance of seeing her again depended entirely on whether the German took us to the same office or not, I offered to get the information for him, but thought he was being foolish.

"*Ich heisse Johanna* (My name is Johanna)," she answered, smiling. Meanwhile, George recalled that he knew a few words in French.

"*Parlez-vous Français?*" he asked.

"*Oui,*" she said laughingly.

It seemed for a moment that George had found the means for conversation, but his French didn't go much farther than his German. Johanna was much amused as George tried to get together all the French words he knew. She spoke fluently, which made me think that her knowledge of French was more than happenstance. She said that she had learned the language in school.

The other girl by this time had prepared our ration statement, and it was time for us to leave, so we had to break up the scene and move on, mainly because the guard was already rushing in to find out the cause of our delay.

I soon rid myself of the feeling that the sight of the two women had stirred. Joe and the others didn't say any more about them either, realizing that this was no time to fool with girls. George, however, did not. I could not understand why he did not have the willpower to forget them, especially when he knew that the closest he could get was one or two steps, and the most he could do was talk about the ration statement. Joe kidded him during our trip back to the camp, but while George would not admit that he was aroused, neither could he conceal the fact that he was.

We returned to the camp with our rations for one day as George insisted that we get them each day, hoping that he would have an opportunity to see Johanna, whom we called "Joan." These were much the same as the rations we were allotted by Germans in previous camps, but for this day, at least, there was no reason to worry, as we still had food left from the last issue of Red Cross parcels. There was no reason to think we should not succeed in getting new Red Cross supplies in time.

As the day drew to a close and further activity inside the camp was forbidden, the sergeant major and I were retired to our room to plan the next day. Joe and I had been allowed a separate room near the front entrance of the billet, which we used as a bedroom as well as an office. A two-story bed with blankets and mattresses was placed in one corner of the room near the fireplace, which we kept warm with coal supplied by the Germans.

It was in this room that I was to make a most difficult and dangerous decision. I learned that once I had set out to fight the Nazis inside the barbed wire, unarmed and unprotected, I had to go all the way without making mistakes, without showing any trace of fear, even at times when I felt nothing but fear. It was in this room that I learned the value of the cause I was fighting for.

I was not depressed. Neither was the sergeant major. The fact, however, that the future was obscure left little room for joyful spirits. Still, from our previous experience, we both felt that although we didn't know what the future held for us, a certain degree of hope was there. We were willing to try to make conditions bearable, regardless of what might be asked of us, and we knew that we had the determination needed for success.

George Karaolanis, who seemed to have enjoyed his first day in three years, dropped in our room for a chat. He did not feel like going to bed. There were certain things I liked about George, especially his cleverness at cards. He was one man for whom the saying, "He who wins at cards, loses in love," did not hold true, because George was winning in both.

There was some degree of happiness in his demeanor that night, which to me seemed beyond belief as I thought of the dangers facing us, especially that of being converted into civilians or sent to extermination camps. Joe had the same feeling. The fact, however, that George had made some progress with Joan was enough to give him hopes, but to me and the sergeant major, George's optimism seemed out of place.

We spent nearly half the night planning things for the next day. We had to turn the lights out at ten o'clock, but we could go on talking all night if we wished, as long as we were not heard by the guards outside.

Both entrances to the billet were barred at midnight. They were to open again at five o'clock in the morning. Barbed wire was nailed over the glass windows, something I could not understand, but always believed it was there to remind us that we were prisoners.

Arrangements for our transportation were made within two days. Joe and I were escorted by a guard, which the *Kommando Führer* had provided. We boarded the train at Udetfeld, and after changing at Tarnowitz, Kattowitz, and Bielitz, we arrived in Teschen the following morning.

By comparison, Teschen seemed very different from other cities that I had seen in Germany. With a population partly German, partly Czech, Hungarian, and Polish, and the culture of each race shown in the building architecture, house decorations, and commercial establishments, it seemed more of an international city than an ordinary German town. A river that went through the city increased the attractiveness of this beautiful little town and at the same time separated it from Stalag VIII-B.

We found the central Man of Confidence, Read, in his office, and he welcomed us with a strong handshake. He was altogether different from Goodie, the central Man of Confidence in Stalag 344. Read was a conscientious man with great courage, something that induced him to give us his assistance in solving our problems despite the difficulties involved. I told Read of our suspicions and emphasized that although there was no clear-cut indication of such danger at the moment, if later these suspicions came true, it might be impossible for me or the sergeant major to contact him or the Red Cross. I suspected that when such a move was to be undertaken by the Germans, communication between our camp and the protecting power would be made impossible.

Read, who accepted our suspicions without doubt, agreed to visit our camp within a month, feeling that should anything develop or should we be prevented from contacting him or the Red Cross, he would be there to learn of the situation. If he were forbidden to visit, he would be convinced of the situation just the same, and would report it to the Red Cross.

That day, Read arranged for clothing shipments to our labor detachment as well as Red Cross food packages, which were to be shipped from the central depot in the city of Sosnowitz.

By the time we were ready to leave Teschen, we were convinced that in Read we had found a sincere and honest Man of Confidence, with a remarkable sense of duty — completely different from the characters I had met in Lamsdorf. I believed all his promises, and I had no doubt in the least that he would try to carry them out to the limits of his ability. Thus, partly satisfied with Read's assurance of an intervention on our behalf later, we left Teschen.

We arrived at Tarnowitz later the same afternoon to pick up from the labor camp there enough parcels for one issue, until the depot in Sosnowitz began to make their shipments, but we had to wait for a truck in order to bring the Red Cross packages with us. Our guard went to E.745 while we stayed in the labor detachment in Tarnowitz for the night. He returned the following morning with the truck on which we loaded Red Cross supplies sufficient for two weeks. In the meantime, shipments from Sosnowitz were to begin arriving, and the Red Cross parcel situation seemed to be in order.

Twelve

IT was a Sunday morning when the situation suddenly changed. Along with our **Kommando Führer**, a new German came, accompanied by a captain and a couple of new guards. Being used to the old **Führer**, the men were slow in lining up for the roll call parade. The new German rushed into the billet, bayonet in hand, howling, yelling, and kicking in an effort to get everybody out within a few seconds.

"*Raus! Tempo! Tempo!*" he shouted as he saw the men coming out of the door reluctantly. There was something peculiar in his voice, something nearer to a lion's roar than the sound of a human voice. When he saw me he gave me a cold stern look for a moment, and his eyes shrunk into a fiery, angry stare. When no one paid attention to his shouting, he became infuriated and began to push the men out.

"*Ruhe, Mensch!* (Be quiet!)" someone yelled back at him.

The German, already wild because the prisoners were not moving fast enough outside, rushed at the man who had shouted. He hit him hard between the shoulders with his bayonet, and it seemed that he would kill him as he swung again with greater fury. But although he had started to lower the bayonet toward the prisoner's head, he suddenly calmed himself and let it hit the prisoner's back hard enough only to cause a grimace of pain. The others who saw this were shaken out of their slackness, as though they had realized suddenly that this new German was much more dangerous than any they had seen before.

"*Lass die Schweinehunde mal raustreten!* (Get the bastards out!)" he ordered me, waving his bayonet and still shouting, "*aber schnell. . . . Raus! Auf mein Lieber, ich mache keinen Spaß!* (Don't mess around!)" while his guards duplicated his performance throwing out everybody and hitting with their rifles those they found still in bed.

I paid no attention to his threats. "Relax," I said. "You've got the whole day."

He did not say anything. He growled, as if he felt the sound of his voice was sufficient warning.

When finally everyone was out on parade, the old *Kommando Führer* told me what this was all about. This German was to be our new *Kommando Führer*. The officer with him was the captain of his company.

I looked at the right hand of the new *Kommando Führer*. He was wearing the Nazi emblem — a skull crossed by two bones in the form of an X — engraved on a ring. His name was Fritz Rinke and his rank was corporal. As he was introduced, he came forward and asked that we stand at attention, while he introduced his captain. Rinke, however, was the only one to click his boots and raise his hand for the Nazi salute. The captain was irritated at this.

"I want more obedience from the prisoners!" the captain yelled.

"*Jawohl, Herr Hauptmann!*" Rinke answered quickly. "*Es wird sich alles ändern* (Everything will be changed)," he said, anxious to impress his captain that there was nothing to worry about, now that he was going to be in charge.

The men felt relieved when this bunch of Nazis retired to the guard room, 150 yards outside on a little hill overlooking the camp. Joe and I, however, did not feel the same. Rinke, his captain, and the guards were inside the camp for an hour that morning, but their nature was apparent from the moment they walked in. We knew what lay ahead of us, but there was nothing Joe and I could do to stop it.

"Damn our luck!" I said angrily.

Just then a guard came rushing in.

"Come on to the *Kommando Führer's*," he ordered, lowering his rifle with the bayonet facing me. He walked around and placed himself behind us. "*Na, los!*" he shouted.

The captain was leaving as we entered the guard room.

"*Pass mal auf!* (Watch out!)" Rinke warned with the same growling sound. "Everything is going to change," he howled. "You are our prisoners. You are going to learn not to speak up to a German soldier. I'll show you! I'll . . ."

"Don't lay a hand on a prisoner again!" I said sternly. "We are soldiers!" I shouted, shaking from anger. "Just remember that we are."

Rinke stood up. He raised his hand, taking a step back. Then swinging his bayonet before my face, he growled, "*Macht doch keinen Spaß, mein Lieber! Pass mal auf!*"

"Let's go!" Joe said. We left Rinke standing there, pale with fury.

Not satisfied with our reaction to his threats, Rinke came back in the camp later to repeat the morning's performance. As I felt his bayonet, I made no move, but Joe diverted his attention by telling him that he was not dealing with Russians and that there was plenty to fight about if that was what he wanted.

"*Wart'e mal! Wart'e mal!* (Just wait!) *Es wird sich alles ändern*," Rinke began to shout again, promising that everything was going to change gradually since it had failed to change in one day.

Everything, indeed, began to change a few days later when Rinke came in to tell us that the administration staff of the labor detachment would be reduced to only me, Joe, and the kitchen chef, and that all others would be employed outside the camp, warning me that this order better be carried out, as he said, "At a time when Germans are slaving to meet the production needs Hitler has set forth, prisoners in our hands can't stay in the camp doing nothing."

"That is your funeral," I said. "Nobody asked you to start a war."

"*Verfluchter Kerl!* (Damnit!)" Rinke growled, hearing my remark. "*Ich werde es dir schon zeigen!* (I'm going to show you!)" he said, as he moved forward to hit me with his bayonet. But to my surprise, again he refrained from hitting me. Instead he threatened that he would kill me some other time, which made me suspect that Rinke was trying to force the staff of our labor detachment to work on his own initiative, and he did not want to be discovered acting without orders from his superiors.

The three guards with him kept looking alternately at Rinke and me, waiting to come to his aid if necessary. The fourth, a slender, tall German about 22, gazed at me with a faint smile, as if he wanted to show a hidden satisfaction over Rinke's embarrassment.

"I want to see those men go out to work in the morning," Rinke said as he placed the bayonet in its scabbard and started to walk back to the gate.

"Polland," he shouted at the young German who was still grinning, "make sure tomorrow morning that they go with the rest."

"*Jawohl, Herr Unteroffizier!*" The young German answered promptly.

I noticed that he wore a half-shoe on one foot, limping as he walked.

"We'll see what tomorrow brings," Joe said with a sigh of relief on seeing the Germans leave.

"Probably nothing!" I said.

"He hasn't given up," Joe insisted.

"I think he has," I said. "Otherwise, he would not have left it to his guards."

Joe smiled, placing his arm on my shoulder. He was pleased and proud of my actions.

"We have a long way to go," I said with some embarrassment over Joe's praise. "We are still prisoners. Rinke knows it, too."

We had much struggle ahead, indeed. Rinke seemed to have given up for the moment, but he was apt to come back with something else. He was not the type who would be satisfied to treat the prisoners according to the laws of any authority, but would follow his own method of persecution and hatred. Every other rule had to conform with his or he saw it as being against the "interest and safety" of Nazi Germany. He seemed to think he was the only one who knew how prisoners of war should be treated. The authors of the Geneva Convention, the German authorities of Stalag VIII-B, or any other decent German did not. This is what he thought, and that is what he practiced in the following days.

I gained a clearer impression of the new garrison of our labor detachment and especially of the guard named Polland, who was employed by

Rinke as a clerk. The direct opposite of Rinke, this German seemed friendly from the first day, and clever in leading the *Kommando Führer* to believe he was treating the prisoners according to Rinke's instructions.

It seemed that once the *Kommando Führer* laid down a policy regarding the prisoners in the labor detachment, the guards had to endorse that policy wholeheartedly, and even to a greater extent than Rinke himself, if they did not want to be accused of neglecting duty and be sent to concentration camps for showing leniency toward prisoners. With Rinke as the *Kommando Führer*, it was wise for everyone to look out for himself and to forget his own feelings and opinions, because the one thing Rinke would not hesitate to do was punish Germans friendly toward us while Germany was collapsing under the Allied might. For these reasons, Hans Polland seemed a clever individual. Being the clerk of the detachment, he had full knowledge of the plans concerning our treatment as prisoners, and his mild and humane attitude encouraged me to believe that he was inclined to offer the prisoners all the help he could.

During the many months I had spent in German prison camps, I had gradually learned how the German people were being tricked into continuing the war. Paul Joseph Goebbels, Hitler's main propagandist, and his staff initially had indoctrinated the Germans with war ideas using the slogan "*Kraft durch Freude* (strength through pleasure)." This form of deceit was successful in the early years of the war, when the German forces were winning. But in the later years, when the German military began to retreat, and it became apparent to some that the war had been lost, the slogan was changed to "*Kraft durch Furcht* (strength through fear)." To convince the Germans that their only alternative was to keep fighting, Goebbels harped that the whole world hated the Germans and that the Allies would have no mercy if Germany collapsed. The only way they could maintain the hope of surviving was by fighting the armies massed against them.

This sort of propaganda gradually created the fear of suffering an injustice if the war ended with an Allied victory. The Germans believed Goebbels's threat that their freedom and lives would last only as long as they kept fighting. As a result, the Germans looked upon war prisoners and any other aliens inside barbed-wire fences as part of those forces of destruction that threatened their survival, and they wreaked vengeance on any prisoner or civilian within Germany at the first opportunity.

Rinke was exemplifying this. He kept the influence of "*Kraft durch Furcht*" propaganda alive within our labor detachment, and his guards assumed an attitude similar to his, making the task of safeguarding and maintaining even the existence of the prisoners in our camp very difficult, if not impossible.

In contrast to this was Hans Polland, and the fact that he could make a judgment of his own convinced me that his sentiments toward the prisoners were motivated by human decency and justice, rather than any weakness. I began to build some faith in his cooperation, uncovering loopholes in the criminal Nazi machinery of destruction, whose chief operator in our camp was *Kommando Führer* Rinke. For a while, however, I continued to be cautious of Hans, because I feared he might at some time or other give in to the other Germans.

It had only been a few weeks since Rinke had taken over the post of *Kommando Führer* at E.745. In this short time, however, the number of incidents like those during the first days kept increasing. Nevertheless, none of the prisoners showed much trace of fear or intimidation. Joe's life and mine became much endangered, as Rinke realized we were both standing in his way, and that if he were to have any success in carrying out his objectives, he had first to dispose of us. Once we were gone, the remaining prisoners might be willing to submit to his treatment. The captain had told Rinke that by his next visit, he expected Rinke to have everything according to his plan.

Spring of 1944 was nearing its end. Warm weather had replaced the cold stormy days, and nature seemed to project a bit of brightness into the sullen world inside our camp. I was standing by the gate one day — a habit I had picked up in the earlier years of my imprisonment to gaze at the free spaces beyond — when the sentry approached me with a grin on his face.

"Are you the Man of Confidence?" he asked.

I answered him with a "*Ja*," somewhat curious as to the reason for his inquiry.

"You can trust me," he said. "I'm on your side."

I thought he was one of Rinke's stool pigeons at first, trying to get friendly with prisoners so he could carry to Rinke information of prisoners' plans for escape or other situations.

"I am a member of the Intelligence Service," he insisted, when he saw that I hesitated to believe him. "If there is any message you want to send away, I will be available any time."

I did not believe him. I told him that there was no message I had to send anywhere, and I started to walk back into the billet.

"Wait! Just one minute!" the German called. "I am telling you the truth. You can depend on me for any service you need."

I paid no more attention to the guard. I went back to my room to find George Karaolanis waiting there for me.

"Will you write me a short message in German?" George asked. "Just one or two lines. It won't take long."

"That depends on what it is," I said.

"I want to make a date with her."

I could not understand how George could possibly have a date with Joan when the Germans were just waiting to catch someone with a German female and hang him. But because George insisted, I wrote the short note he wanted, and as I finished, Joe came in from another room. He was very depressed and almost desperate, as he anticipated that our time with Rinke promised to be dangerous. He shook his head in disappointment.

"I doubt that any of our efforts will succeed," he said.

"It seems that way sometimes," I acknowledged.

We were still talking when the same sentry I had spoken with earlier dropped in to the room with the excuse that he was suspecting something. In the few minutes that he spent inside, he tried to convince me that he was, indeed, on our side, and that I had no reason to distrust him. Then he went on telling me that I was depriving the other prisoners of a service destined to help their well being by refusing to give him my confidence.

"What does he want?" the sergeant major inquired.

When I told Joe of the guard's pretenses, Joe was angry and shouted. "Tell him to get out!"

"Why is the sergeant major swearing?" the guard asked.

"*Raus macht!*" Joe yelled.

The guard did not say anything further. He went out, back to the gate.

The captain came for his promised visit, accompanied by a major and a general. They walked into the camp while Rinke led the way, kicking the prisoners to make them stand at attention before his superiors, as if he wanted to show his respect for them by having the prisoners salute.

He introduced me to the major, while he stood to attention himself. "This is the *Vertrauensmann*," he said.

I stood there holding my hands in my pockets while the real reason for the general's visit tormented me, when the captain suddenly went wild because I had kept my hands in my pockets instead of greeting the German officer. Joe had approached the scene in the meantime, and was asking me what all the noise was about. I told him that the captain did not like my posture.

The major, the general, and Rinke went through the billet, with Rinke standing at attention each time he had to open a door and show the rooms. Before leaving, the general inquired as to what nationality we were, and Rinke promptly replied that we were Greek.

"Greeks?" said the general with surprise. "How does it happen that we still hold them prisoners?" Then he continued, "They are not entitled to any Red Cross care, are they?"

"They receive Red Cross parcels and clothing," Rinke said.

"Where do they get these?" the major asked this time.

"From Stalag VIII-B in Teschen," Rinke informed him.

The captain broke in then, saying that they occupied Greece at this time and that he could not see why the Red Cross had anything to say about us. They moved outside and carried on their conversation a few yards from the barbed wire fence so that Joe and I could not hear. Finally, the captain, the major, and the general left in their car, while Rinke returned to the guard room.

The sentry, who had been insisting all morning that he was a member of the Intelligence Service, again approached me while I was standing near the gate with Joe, wondering what the Nazi officers were talking about. He offered to convey to me their conversation. He could not make it all out, but he said he heard the captain say that being members of the Greek army with Germany occupying Greece, we were no longer under the status of prisoners, and that the Germans had full authority to assign us to whatever industry they found necessary. The captain also suggested that it had been a mistake to allow us to contact the central Man of Confidence, and that the Red Cross packages that we had so far received should be returned to the British camp. The sentry said the major and the general did not seem to disagree with the captain's views.

"Why was he mentioning these things?" the sentry asked when he had finished retelling the conversation he had overheard.

I did not acknowledge him, but I knew why the captain said what he did. The fear I had concerning our conversion into civilians had started to become a reality.

I explained to the sergeant major what the guard had said. Seeing that I was impressed with his information, the guard went on again, insisting he was really on my side and that I could rely on any service I wanted him to do for me.

He told me that his name was Frank, that his ancestors were Polish, and that because he lived in Germany, he was drafted in the *Wehrmacht* — the armed forces — to escape the fate of concentration camps, where he said he had already spent some time. He insisted that he had no sympathy for the Nazis.

This additional information about him shed some light as to the type of person he actually was. I had no doubt that he belonged to those who, at the outbreak of the war, when Germany won all the battles, hastened to place themselves at her service, as though she had already won. When the tide had begun to turn, they realized their mistake and were trying to change again to the winning side. This type of person — not rare at that time — offered me very little assurance that I could place any confidence in him, especially when his past behavior was so clear. I refrained from saying anything to him, but I used his information just the same.

The time had evidently arrived for the worst to happen — choosing between working for the German war industry as civilians or the fate of the extermination camps. There was nothing I or the sergeant major could do to prevent it, except hope that Read would arrive in time.

If Read showed up as he had promised, Rinke would realize that the move he was planning to carry out was not possible. As for sending back the Red Cross supplies, Rinke was not worried at all. He could simply distribute these to his guards, avoiding any suspicion that Read might have upon seeing them turned back. By the time Read suspected our fate, there would be nothing that he or the Red Cross could do.

Never in my life had there been a moment when I found myself more helpless than that afternoon at Udetfeld. What if Read did not show up? What if he were unable to do anything? All he could do would be to tell the Red Cross. But once we were gone, the Red Cross could not change the situation. Those were the things Joe and I were thinking as we walked around the billet, trying to find hope.

George came along to tell us of his meeting with Joan, and in the courtyard, the men had set up a volleyball net, supplied, along with other sports equipment, by the Red Cross.

"Come on and join us," one called.

"Some other time, fellows," I said, but the men insisted at least one of us join them. The lot fell on me.

Thirteen

THE *following morning I went with the sick to visit the doctor, as I had done each preceding week. The guard detailed for our escort was Frank, the same one who, the previous day, had been trying to convince me that he was a member of the Intelligence Service. Because he had been a divinity student, I usually referred to him as "The Deacon." On the way to the hospital, he kept telling me of his service to the Allied cause, insisting again that I should place faith in his willingness to serve me. To get rid of him, I told him that I needed detailed maps of Germany and that he could get them for me, since he was so eager to help. He said that such a thing was difficult as all maps were military property, but he would try to get what I wanted the next time he was home on leave.*

The hospital was located near the **Verpflegung** *office, with* an air force *Sanitäter* and a doctor as the only staff, and could only handle minor injuries. Chronic diseases or major injuries were treated in other hospitals near Udetfeld. During my earlier visits to this hospital, I had gathered the impression that the personnel there were a much finer group of Germans, and I had realized that in general, Germans — except those directly in charge of prison camps — were not familiar with the mistreatment of war prisoners. Rinke and other *Kommando Führers* were summoned each week by the captain and given instructions concerning the treatment of war prisoners outlined by the German High Command.

Because the *Sanitäter* and the doctor were unaware of these instructions, they treated us with the same degree of humanity as they did their own air force personnel. The doctor in particular, a young man around 30, well educated and of mild nature, had been extremely considerate toward the prisoners who had reported sick in the past weeks. He was excited at the opportunity to use his limited knowledge of English, and sometimes, in the presence of other German officers, he would talk to me in English instead of German, trying to show that he knew more than the others.

If it is true that doctors are to treat a patient according to his illness without regard to his nationality, status, or financial condition, without prejudice or malice, the young air force doctor at this hospital was a perfect example of such a principle. He made no distinction between prisoners and Germans. He treated no one with less care than his ailment required, and sometimes he recommended prisoners to hospital care simply because the prisoner wanted such care, though his illness could be cured with a few pills.

I asked the doctor if he could pay a visit to our quarters, so that he could get an idea of the conditions there and recommend sanitary steps. He promised to do this, and when he asked whether the *Kommando Führer* permitted such a visit, I told him it would be altogether useless to consider such a step unless it was carried out in spite of Rinke's objections. I was certain Rinke would not allow anyone to know of the conditions within our quarters, not even the doctor, in spite of his rank of lieutenant.

The doctor winked his eye as I finished and said, smiling, "I'll come there as soon as I get a chance."

I was returning to the camp when I saw the sergeant major, George, and a couple of other men heading for the *Verpflegung* office to receive the ration statement. Joe looked at the sick register, which the *Sanitäter* of our group was carrying, and grinned when he saw three more men recommended for return to Lamsdorf. He expressed the desire to meet this doctor, so I asked my guard to let me join the sergeant major's group, to introduce him to the doctor as soon as we received the rations from the store nearby. The guard consented without objection.

As usual, we were first marched into the *Verpflegung* office and walked into the room occupied by Joan and the other lady, whose name I never found out. Joe referred to her as "Potato," and this was the name she went by within our group. The visit gave George the opportunity to see his sweetheart for a few minutes at least.

From there we walked to the ration store. George, by this time, had become familiar with the personality of the ration store sergeant. I saw him push a packet of cigarettes into the sergeant's pocket to receive a whole leg of beef, which the sergeant threw into our cart with several extra bags of potatoes.

"These Germans!" George exclaimed. "They will trade anything for cigarettes."

I thought George's trading interest was limited to kitchen supplies, but I discovered the same day that he had exploited the trading nature of this German sergeant in order to see Joan alone in the store while the German guarded the door against any approaching danger.

Finally, we started for the hospital. We found the doctor still examining patients, this time Polish civilians.

Although the Polish employees in the air force barracks were the last to see the doctor, they received the care they needed. In their conversation with the doctor, they were frank about their complaints and felt free to ask for any treatment they believed necessary, which the doctor rendered without hesitation as far as the hospital facilities permitted. He recommended those needing better care to the military hospitals in Tarnowitz.

Upon seeing me and the sergeant major walk in, he raised his head and greeted us with a smile. He could not understand why Joe was curling his moustache. He started to imitate Joe's gesture, but having shaved every hair from his face, he found nothing to curl, so he burst into genuine laughter.

When I introduced the sergeant major, the doctor seemed interested to learn how the labor detachment was run. I explained the sergeant major's role and mine, as recognized by the International Red Cross and defined in Article 43 of the Geneva Convention. Upon hearing the words "Geneva Convention," the doctor became interested in knowing more details. I showed him the copy I had with me, and he asked if he could keep it and return it to me the following visit, when he had read it through.

I gave it to him, mainly because I wanted this German to know of the treatment that the prisoners deserved and to learn it the way it was outlined by the authors of the Convention, instead of by the Nazi High Command. I suspected that sooner or later Rinke would poison the doctor's mind, as he had done with most of his guards, by advocating the barbaric treatment he had been taught by his captain.

Even if Rinke attempted to give his views, I felt certain the doctor would soon realize the injustice and brutality in Rinke's behavior. Thus, I hoped I would not need to explain very much to the doctor to persuade him to contribute to our welfare.

We left the hospital and returned to the camp. I headed for Rinke's office to find out when he was intending to carry out the doctor's instructions on returning the men recommended to Lamsdorf for medical care. He said he could not do anything unless the company made arrangements for their transfer.

"Then why the hell don't you let the company know about it?" I asked him, angered over his idleness to make the necessary report.

The Deacon — Frank — who was in the guard room, overheard my shouting, and Polland, who was sitting at Rinke's desk, tried to divert my attention by handing me the mail that had arrived the same morning. Rinke gave in by promising to let his captain know of the doctor's recommendation.

When I walked back into the billet, the sergeant major called my attention to one prisoner isolated in a room and holding a big wooden pole in his hands. He was threatening to kill anyone who got within his reach. No one dared walk inside the room. The guard who had brought him into the camp from work told me he had been acting strangely all morning. I demanded to know exactly what had happened. Then some of his friends who had been working with him told me that for some weeks he had been interested in a girl working in near them. Having no way of approaching or even talking to her — because of the danger of being caught — he had started to act odd. That morning he had attacked the girl and had torn her clothes off. His act was unusual enough to convince the guards that he was out of his mind, and without protest they refrained from any punishment and believed the prisoners' explanation that the man was crazy.

"So we brought him here," the prisoner said, "but couldn't get the pole out of his hands."

This unfortunate creature, who had enough strength to lift four men with his hands, kept walking like a gorilla inside his cage, carrying the pole and threatening everyone, but making little sense. Rinke, who had been notified in the meantime, rushed in.

"I'll make him get his mind back in a minute!" Rinke shouted, thinking the man was pretending. As he got close to the door, however, and saw him waving the pole, he quickly backed away, convinced it was a hopeless case.

I got Rinke to sign the transfer of the prisoner to Lamsdorf, on the grounds that his presence threatened the safety of the other prisoners. He definitely needed to be isolated in the mental ward at Lamsdorf, even though I knew that once there, the attendants would finish him off. His transfer was quite a difficulty, and Rinke, after a long argument, agreed to let two of the prisoner's friends accompany him on the train to keep him under control and avoid any disastrous incidents.

Fourteen

THE Red Cross food supplies rolled into camp E.745 at Udetfeld, in spite of the efforts of Rinke's captain, and the prisoners continued to receive one food package every Saturday. The cans of food, however, were punctured, so that we could not store them for purposes of escape.

The men went to work in the morning under the supervision of guards provided by the **Luftwaffe** — air force — and returned in the early afternoon. Their work consisted of digging drain ditches around the barracks and the highways nearby. They were thus able to contact Polish civilian workers on the same job, and gradually they discovered ways to trade with them. Almost everyone exchanged items from his Red Cross parcels, such as bars of chocolate or cans of oatmeal for chickens or rabbits, both of which were abundant in those Polish villages. For cooking facilities, they used the stoves in each room; they did their own cooking most of the time. Rinke did not suspect such exchanges and never bothered to search anyone returning to the camp. In this manner the food situation in our camp improved considerably, and as far as the men were concerned, aside from five to six hours of daily labor, there was no other hardship imposed. Whenever Rinke made his appearance in the camp or at the site where they were employed, they felt uncomfortable, but as soon as he was gone were at ease again.

Joe and I were in a different situation. We were still waiting for Read's visit as the only hope to save us from the planned murder through our delivery to extermination camps. We were definitely opposed to being converted into civilians, to be eliminated gradually as the last drop of energy was drained away for the benefit of German war production. Although Rinke's plan was still in the works, it would not take long before it was put into action. Our chance for survival rested on the ability to kill that plan. This made Read's visit all the more urgent.

I was much relieved the following day when I saw Read arrive. He was led inside by his escort, who then retired to the guard room. I was at the gate to welcome him and so was the sergeant major.

"Glad to see you, Sir!"

He shook my hand. The rest of our staff gathered around, surprised to see him. Joe and I didn't want them to suspect the reason for his visit, lest it panic them unnecessarily, so I asked Read if we could talk in private, using our office. I took the kit bag hanging on his shoulder, and led him into our quarters.

Read sat on the chair, stretching his arms to relax himself from the long trip. He laid his cap on the table and kept gazing around the room. Joe stepped outside the room for a minute to ask the shoemaker, who was also an excellent cook, to prepare something to eat with the rabbits that were brought in the day before.

"What's new?" I asked the central Man of Confidence.

He did not say anything, as though he meant it was no different than what it had always been inside a prisoner-of-war camp. Joe returned and tried to open a conversation, curling his moustache in his habitual manner. I told Read of the general's recent visit and the guard's information concerning their talk outside the camp by the car.

"I feel certain," I went on, "this is what the Germans are planning to do. I don't see who could stop them, especially when Greece is under their control, and they are desperate for working manpower. A prisoner of war is a liability to them, because they have to let the Red Cross interfere and, in some cases at least, they have to consider the Geneva Convention. But a civilian is an asset, since they can use him for any type of labor without having to provide any specific amount of food and care. If they decide to dispose of a civilian, they are not bound to make excuses of any kind to the protecting power."

Read kept listening with much concern, although I really had no right to involve the central Man of Confidence with a situation that I suspected, but could not prove. However, under conditions of captivity in Nazi Germany, the only chance for survival rested in the prisoner's ability to stop the Nazis before their plans took root, without waiting for full evidence of their intended action. While in a number of instances, the prisoner's suspicions might have been completely unfounded, if in only one instance his misgiving was true and no measures were taken in time, there would be nothing anyone could do to save the prisoner.

"You need not worry," Read remarked, interrupting me. "I am going to do all I can to stall such a drive by inducing the commandant of Stalag VIII-B to withdraw from Rinke's captain any authority that he might feel he had in devising such an arbitrary plan. I will also report the situation to the protecting power, so that the camp commandant will be convinced he has no other choice but to carry out my request."

I didn't tell Read anything more; it seemed clear he had understood our situation completely, but I felt reluctant to believe the German camp commandant could have very much influence on Rinke's captain. He was a conscripted soldier, while Rinke and his captain were both members of the SS — the *Schutzstaffel* — the elite military force of the Nazi party.

Joe had told me of similar lack of authority at Lamsdorf, where the *Abwehr* (defense) *Offizier* with the rank of captain had overridden decisions of the commandant of the camp, a colonel, because of the authority the captain held as a member of the SS. He disregarded the colonel's decision that a convicted prisoner's life be spared and shot the man anyway. It could happen that Rinke's captain would disregard any order opposing his plans, even if it came from a superior, such as the commandant of Stalag VIII-B. I did not feel the commandant's intervention was going to be much of a guarantee of our safety. Nevertheless, it was a step that could do no harm, and maybe it would work.

"I am going to tell Rinke," Read said, "that I am advising the British government of these German intentions and that anything they might do to you could result in reprisals against German prisoners in British hands."

It was getting about noon. The cook showed up and informed us that he had finished preparing dinner. Read was very much surprised with the quality of our provisions. Then Joe explained how we managed to get this type of food, something which Read thought was a wonderful idea. We didn't want to let him go until the day was over, or possibly the next day, if he wanted to stay overnight, but Read insisted that he must leave, as there were other duties he had to attend to the following morning in Teschen.

So we were contented with his stay throughout the afternoon. He looked over our living quarters, learned the nature of the work that the men were doing, and saw our medical accommodations and Red Cross supply stock. He got an idea, too, of Rinke's personality and character.

Although he was a prisoner like the rest of us, his presence seemed a source of comfort to me. I couldn't tell whether this security was real or the result of wishful thinking, but I was glad he had visited the camp on that day.

The escort came for him at the gate late in the afternoon, and he left the camp, after talking for a few minutes with Rinke in the guard room. I didn't know what he told Rinke; I was not going to find out until my next visit to Teschen, but I hoped Read had succeeded in scaring Rinke out of his plans.

At midnight, Hans Polland walked in the camp to lock the doors of our billet and bar the windows. I was strolling in the courtyard when he walked in. The Deacon was guarding the main gate, gazing suspiciously at Polland. Hans came into my office for a few minutes to tell me of Rinke's reaction to Read's reprimand.

"Maybe I should keep the *Haupt-Vertrauensmann* here and put him to work," Rinke had said sarcastically after Read left.

I expected such a response from Rinke, because to him it made no difference if German prisoners in Allied hands were to be punished for his acts of cruelty against us. And it made no difference to Rinke what anyone ordered him to do outside of his own captain, whom he obeyed faithfully.

Any success Read might have depended on how his intervention could change the views of Rinke's captain.

Fifteen

SINCE our arrival at Udetfeld, we had been permitted to take a shower once every week. The shower room was located in the airport hangar. Each time, guards were detailed to take us there in groups. Most of the employees in the hangar were Polish, with the exception of the foremen, who were German.

One day in early June 1944, I went along with the second group. The Deacon was one of the guards.

"I am going home on leave for a day," he said. "When I get back I will have the maps you asked for."

"You do that," I said. "Make sure you bring me the right maps."

The hangar was about 500 yards away from the camp. A number of airplanes were inside undergoing repairs. Although this was the only airport I had seen in Germany, I got the impression it was the one doing the most repairs. Each day, two or three German planes crashed because of failure to take off or other troubles, such as sudden stopping of the engines, loss of a wing, or sometimes loss of the plane's tail. More airplanes were under repair than were available for flight.

I walked into a small cabin to undress for the shower.

"*Kamerat!*" somebody called behind me.

I turned around to see one of the Polish employees in a machinist's uniform trying to approach me with caution, as if he feared that he might be seen by the Germans. He entered the cabin, closing the door behind him. Then in his broken German he told me of the news we had long been waiting to hear.

"They have landed in France," he said. "This morning."

I was afraid this might have been another rumor, because many other "landings" had turned out to be nothing more than commando raids. I asked him where he got his information and how big this landing was.

"It came over the radio this morning," he said. "Hundreds of ships have taken part in the landing. This is it! The second front we've been waiting for. The German newspapers have published the news." Then he pulled a newspaper out of his pocket and handed it to me.

One of the guards was walking in my direction. I came out of the cabin taking the newspaper with me, still partly dressed, pretending that I was going to wait until one of the shower rooms was empty. I did not glance at the folded paper for fear that he would see it, so I waited anxiously to return to the camp and read the news. I did not expect the German newspaper to give a true account of the situation. By this time, however, I had found a way to read between the lines and learn of the actual situation from what little news the Germans gave away.

I pulled the paper to the side of my pocket just enough to read the headlines:

"*DER FEIND IST AUF DER SEINE MÜNDUNG GELANDET* (The enemy has landed at the mouth of the Seine)."

I could not conceal my joy over the news. I was partly convinced that this time it was really the "second front." The others in the group noticed the change in my expression and wondered what had happened. I told them, and they took my information as authentic. In a few minutes it became difficult to quiet them down, in order to avoid episodes with the guards.

I returned to the camp an hour later. The Deacon wanted to know the reason for the prisoners' enthusiasm.

"They feel happy after a shower, of course," I said. "It feels nice to be clean."

I went straight into my room. Joe was getting ready to leave with George Karaolanis and the kitchen staff to get the rations for the next day. Now that the danger of being seen had passed, I took the paper out of my pocket and began to read. It contained only a short communiqué of the German High Command, which mentioned that a full-scale Allied landing had begun at the mouth of the Seine. The last part of the communiqué dealt with the usual news of *Terrorangriffe* (terror raids) over western and central Germany. It made no comment on the situation at the Russian front, because it was a special bulletin issued on account of the landing.

A wave of enthusiasm soon spread through the camp. For the first time in three and a half years, the chance for liberation had started to become a reality. Many predicted that we would be free within weeks. Others, grown weary from previous disappointments, felt that the second front would not bring our liberation in less than two years, at the least. I did not share either opinion, although I was confident the war would be over soon. I maintained this attitude knowing the tendency of the Nazis toward us. Rinke was much closer still than the second front, and I did not believe he would be content to let us survive while it was still within his power to make our liberation impossible.

"You want to come along?" the sergeant major asked me.

I wanted an opportunity to talk over the news with him, so I went. Joe seemed happy, but thought as I did — that if we were to benefit from an Allied victory, we had first to remove any threat of extermination that Rinke might engender before the Allied troops could reach our vicinity. With the Russians closer than the Western Allies, it seemed improbable that the British and American troops were going to be our liberators. Consequently, as we mulled over the situation, we ended up with the same conclusion — that as far as we were concerned, we still had to fight Rinke.

The news of the Allied landing in the west was soon followed by the news of an all-out Russian offensive in the east. In Poland, General Bohr had staged an upsurge with his underground troops in the capital city of Warsaw. In Germany, an assassination attempt was made against Hitler, but, according to Goebbels, "divine providence" had once again spared the life of the "beloved *Führer*" for the benefit of the *Vaterland*. "A proof of this miracle," he wrote in the official Nazi newspaper, *Das Reich*, "is the fact that although [two] generals . . . who were standing farther from the bomb, were killed, Hitler, at whose feet the bomb exploded, suffered only minor bruises." News of the hanging of 30 prominent non-Nazi German officers who had been linked with the plot followed, freezing the enthusiasm of those who had wishfully believed that an overthrow of the Nazi government by the Germans themselves was possible.

Knowing of the Nazi tactics when Hitler first ascended to power, I wondered if the assassination plot was not something that the Nazis themselves engineered to eliminate those high-ranking officers in the *Wehrmacht* who were already willing to surrender. I could not see the logic in Goebbels's reasoning, and could not believe that it was possible for Hitler to escape death when others farther away from the bomb did not. If the so-called assassination attempt had been made by non-Nazis, then Hitler would be dead; if Hitler was still alive, then the plot had to have been orchestrated by the Nazis themselves to create the grounds on which to prosecute those Germans who had already accepted defeat.

At the Udetfeld airfield, the German air force group was ordered to carry out raids against the insurgent troops of General Bohr in Warsaw. Caught without sufficient ground crews to load and repair the planes, they decided to use the prisoners of our labor detachment. Airplane crews rushed to the locations where the prisoners were being employed and marched everyone to the ammunition depot near the hangar where the bombs were stored.

Realizing why they had been brought there in such a hurry, the men made no effort to obey the air force crews driving them with bayonets and machine-guns toward the trucks, on which they were to load the bombs and haul them to the planes. In their haste to get the planes loaded, and with the prisoners refusing to obey, the air force crews began to beat the men with whatever they had in their hands. The commandant of the base rushed in with additional guards, and ran through, beating the prisoners with the butt of his revolver, yelling and screaming over the failure of the crews to get the planes loaded, swearing over the delay of their mission. This hell of screams, shouts, and glittering of smashing bayonets lasted well over half an hour until finally the prisoners, beaten and exhausted, were unable to stand on their feet. They lay there where the Nazi fury had burst, bleeding from their wounds, but still smiling, because the Nazi planes had failed to take off.

"You fools!" one of the prisoners managed to tell the commandant of the base. "Don't you know that you can't make us load the planes, even if you shoot every one of us?"

Having failed with the prisoners, the Germans began to round up every civilian they could in the area. But their planes remained grounded throughout the day. In a small measure, these simple heroes had given a lesson to the enemy — perhaps a reason for its eventual defeat.

Our men were brought back into the camp late at night. They seemed happy, in spite of their wounds, that they had made their small contribution to the war effort by forcing the German *Luftwaffe* to stay aground for one day at least, thus saving the lives of others who were destined to become the target of those bombs.

I was standing by the gate, bewildered at their condition. Joe was also there, watching their faces bleed, without saying a word. I called the *Sanitäter* to bandage their wounds, while I tried to find out what exactly had taken place. George Karaolanis and the rest of our staff gathered around, asking them what had happened.

"Let's go inside," I suggested, when the men finished telling us everything they had gone through that afternoon.

"Who do you think authorized the air force crew to use prisoners for loading bombs?" Joe asked as we walked back to our room.

"I don't know," I said. "I think Rinke did, or maybe the commandant of the base decided on his own."

Joe kept curling his moustache. "Find out tomorrow," he said. "I can almost swear it was Rinke."

"It could be either one."

The following morning, Rinke came in for the roll call parade. It was Sunday, and everyone was in the camp. Rinke pretended that he didn't know anything about what had gone on the day before.

"How did they get hurt then?" Joe asked him, angered by his denial. Joe had always found words to communicate when he was angry.

"They probably fell down," Rinke replied, pleased with the sight of bandaged faces; he seemed to enjoy seeing the prisoners hurt.

"If I had been there when they fell down," he continued, "I would have kicked them till they got up again."

Joe was enraged. "I'm going to do the same thing to you!" he shouted.

"I want to see the base commandant," I said angrily. *"Na, gehen wir los, Mensch!* (Let's get going)"

"What do you want to see him for?" Rinke asked, with some concern.

"Are you taking me there or not?" I asked. He did not answer. Instead, he followed me to the commandant's office.

"Unteroffizier Rinke meldet!" he shouted at attention as we walked in.

"What does the *Unteroffizier* wish?" the major behind the desk asked, suspecting from my presence it had something to do with the prisoners.

"Der Vertrauensmann," Rinke said, pointing at me.

I asked the major directly who was responsible for the incident. At first, he was incredulous, but he eventually gave in and admitted it was Rinke.

"What did you want to know that for?" Rinke inquired as we stepped outside.

"Because I am going to make you learn the Convention by heart," I said, "and make you remember it for the rest of your life."

Rinke didn't seem to believe I could do such a thing, although the major's admission of Rinke's responsibility in the previous day's episode had him so worried that he took off the same afternoon for the company office to confer with his captain over the consequences of such an incident.

"We can take advantage of this episode," I said to the sergeant major later.

"How?" Joe asked.

"We can report the incident to the protecting power," I said, "and ask for their investigation in the matter. We have grounds for such a report."

"Are you kidding?" Joe asked with surprise. "Do you think that the Germans are going to let that report get to the protecting power? In the first place, they will throw the letter in the wastebasket, and, in the second place, they will get after you and me for sending such a report."

"I wasn't thinking of sending a letter," I said. "Next month, we are due for another visit to Stalag VIII-B. There will probably be disabled British prisoners there awaiting repatriation. We can send a message with one of them. Once they know what it is all about, they can write to the protecting power in Geneva as soon as they are out of German hands."

"What if there are no such prisoners?" Joe asked.

"We can tell Read," I said. "He may be able to send the message through the British Intelligence Service."

"Do you think the Nazis will let the protecting power interfere?" Joe insisted. "Or do you think that the Red Cross will bother to get involved just because a few prisoners were beaten up here? As far as you and I are concerned," he kept saying, "all depends on what we can do here — ourselves. We have to fight Rinke alone. There is no hope from any other source."

I wondered why he was reluctant to use the information now, when he wanted to find out who was responsible for the incident the day before.

"Then I'll make the report," I said.

"Listen, Aslanis!" Joe shouted, angry over my insistence. "You may have your own opinion in the matter, but you are still a private, and as long as I am your sergeant major, you will do as I say. Remember that when we go to Teschen next month."

"Don't you think it is foolish to worry about rank inside the barbed wire?" I asked, and walked out for some fresh air.

It was dark already. In the sky above, the stars were shining. I kept asking myself: Why would Rinke be in such a hurry to see his captain unless he was afraid of something? I could see the sergeant major's point. But somehow I hoped that if we raised an objection to the protecting power, something might come of it. If we kept quiet, there was nothing to expect at all. It was true that with millions of other prisoners inside concentration camps the fate of 200 men might not be a significant motive for action on the part of the Red Cross, especially when the Nazis were trying to save their own skin. But while the Red Cross had no access to concentration camps, so far it had been allowed to interfere in prisoner-of-war camps, I kept telling myself.

I walked back and forth inside the camp until late that night when Polland came in to lock the doors of the billet and bar the windows. Seeing that I was nervous, he began to tell me that Rinke went to the company headquarters because he was scared of the consequences of Saturday's incident, which had been entirely the result of his initiative.

I didn't say anything, although I welcomed his information. To my surprise, he put his arm around my shoulder and said in a friendly tone,

"Don't give up hoping! Keep fighting Rinke. Many Germans would be on your side if they had a chance."

"I wouldn't trust those Germans," I said.

"Maybe you wouldn't," Hans replied, "but your courage defying Rinke has won you friends among the Germans just the same. We admire you for that."

I leaned against the window panel. I don't exactly recall how I felt then, but I remember that hearing one of the enemy admit his admiration as boldly as Hans Polland did that night was something I had never expected, and for quite a while afterward I wondered if Hans was only pulling my leg. Nevertheless, it made me realize for the first time that the feeling of human decency was not completely lost from the hearts of at least some Germans.

"Incidentally," Polland said after a few minutes of silence," my parents and my fiancée are coming to see me tomorrow. I talked to them about you when I was home last, and they expressed the desire to see you — that is, without letting the other Germans suspect anything."

I knew Polland was hinting to me about escape, and that his family might help me. "As long as my friends here need me," I said, "I am staying with them. Together we make a good team. With me all by myself or with them abandoned in the hands of Rinke, we would be open to the vultures."

"Anytime you decide to," Hans said, "you can stay with my parents until the war is over. The Germans will never find you there."

"Thanks!" I said. "I'll let you know if I change my mind, but for the present I am staying with my friends."

"What did Polland want?" the sergeant major asked, when he saw me walk back into the room.

"He was trying to get me to escape," I said. "He thinks I can stay at his home until the war is over."

"Do you know how to get there?" Joe asked.

"Hans drew me a map of the part of town I need to know. I have memorized the streets from the railroad station to his home, once I get to Gleiwitz."

"Well, are you going?"

"No! I am staying here, with the rest."

Joe came closer to me, with an expression of regret. "I'm sorry," he said. "I didn't mean what I said to you this evening."

"You were within reason," I said. "You don't need to apologize. Let's get some sleep. I'm done for the day."

Rinke returned from the company headquarters the following afternoon. He seemed happier than the day before, indicating that the captain had endorsed his brutal action against the prisoners. He came into the camp a few hours later to tell me that his *Hauptmann* had told him there was nothing I or the sergeant major could do to him because of Saturday's episode, and that the captain did not think the Geneva Convention was important.

Hearing Rinke talk like an ignorant child, Joe began to tell him that it was not right to treat prisoners that way; they were still human beings entitled to their honor and dignity, like Rinke himself.

"I am going to kill one of you," Rinke said. "I don't know which one yet. I am waiting for my captain to decide."

Rinke spoke with such naiveté that he made me wonder whether he was not suffering mentally.

"Suppose you were in the prisoners' place," I said. "How would you feel if you were treated this way?"

"You would probably do the same thing to me," Rinke said. "If I were your prisoner, you'd probably kill me just as soon. You should anyway."

"There is Hitler's master race," I said to Joe. "Nothing but criminal psychopaths, living in a world of confusion and fear."

Rinke kept gazing at the horizon, as if we were not there, lost in the midst of some mystifying dream. When he finally realized that he was inside the fence, he unlocked the gate and began walking toward his office while Joe and I stood there wondering over his peculiar behavior.

I was ready to return to my room when I saw the doctor driving toward our camp. He had kept his promise, it seemed, and he was coming to inspect the conditions in our labor detachment.

"What are you cooking?" he asked the cook, seeing the field kitchen in the courtyard.

"*Suppe!*" the cook replied, while the doctor stirred the contents of the boiler with a big wooden ladle.

"*Es schmeckt gut!*" he exclaimed, helping himself. Holding a bowl with one hand and a spoon he had borrowed from the cook in the other, he toured the billet first and then the rooms.

"You could use some disinfectant," he said, after he finished the inspection. "I'll see that you get some tomorrow when you come to the hospital."

He gave the *Sanitäter* some other instructions regarding the cleanliness of our first-aid room, and promised to see that we received additional medical supplies.

"What is *he* still doing here?" he asked me, when he saw one of the sick he had recommended for hospital treatment.

Rinke, who had rushed back upon seeing the doctor, searched for an excuse. "We are waiting for the company to make arrangements for their transfer," he said. "They will be shipped out to Lamsdorf as soon as arrangements have been made."

"When I recommend a man for the hospital," the doctor said angrily, "I expect my recommendation to be carried out right away."

"*Jawohl, Herr Leutnant!*" Rinke agreed. "They will be in the hospital as recommended."

"You better see that they are," the doctor said, partly satisfied with Rinke's promise.

"By the way," the doctor said to me, turning around suddenly, "here is the book on the Geneva Convention that you gave me. I read it through. Interesting, indeed!" he said, handing it to me.

Rinke gave me an angry look, suspecting that I had something to do with the doctor's visit there. He did not say anything, however, in the presence of the doctor, trying to avoid any further embarrassment.

"Let me know of any sanitation problems you may have in the future," the doctor said to me as he was getting ready to leave.

"There are some things we need right now," I said.

"Like what?" the doctor asked, turning back.

"Like the toilet, for instance. We can't use the one here now. It is wide open, and the flies keep circulating everywhere. We need a small kitchen to protect the food from those flies, and a new toilet with better sanitation facilities."

"Why haven't you done anything?" the doctor asked Rinke.

"The captain said it wasn't necessary," Rinke mumbled. "It would hurt the war effort to go through all this expense just for war prisoners."

"I'll see that you get what you need," the doctor said to me again.

"I would like to see the captain when he is here again," he told Rinke. "These things they ask for are quite essential."

"*Jawohl, Herr Leutnant!*" Rinke promised. "I'll tell the captain you wish to see him."

The doctor winked his eye as he stepped out of the camp. I grinned at his gesture, feeling content that he had given us the cooperation we needed.

The war news continued to improve every day. The Allies in the west had occupied Cherbourg and had broken through Saint Lô. The German forces in the east were in full retreat. Udetfeld became an advanced airport, making the possibility of an attack on the airfield more imminent.

Rinke told us we were to dig an air raid shelter for protection against Allied bombers, but we soon found out it was only to help the Germans guard the prisoners more closely during air raids, because the shelter that we made could not serve as protection at all. Bullets could pass through the scant earth covering of the ceiling, and the first day it rained, the ditch filled with water. Rinke enjoyed throwing everyone in the muddy drain, kicking those reluctant to lie in the mud, waving his pistol at anyone who still happened to be in the billet at the instant the air raid alarm had sounded.

The German garrison of our labor detachment was increased from 9 to 25. Another *Unteroffizier* was added to Rinke's staff, which by then consisted of Rinke, Polland, and the new *Unteroffizier* Hans, whom we later nicknamed "The Rat." Of the new guards, some were friendly toward the prisoners, especially one whom we referred to as "The Berliner," because of his conceit with regard to his place of birth. He was more concerned with sex than the war, which he seemed to think was somebody else's business. Successful adventures with girls, he believed, were the exclusive property of Berlin natives, and he took a great deal of pride in the nickname he was given. His important feature, however, was his mild character, which rendered him completely harmless, and sometimes useful, to prisoners.

Another new guard, whom we referred to as Alex, seemed friendly toward the prisoners at the start, but proved to be of more help to George Karaolanis, as he arranged and safeguarded meeting places for George and his sweetheart, Joan.

The doctor made good on his promise, and work on the new toilet and kitchen building began at the expense of the air base command. Elderly Polish civilians were used for construction; the younger Poles were conspicuously absent, most likely killed in Nazi death camps. Under Rinke's watchful eyes, the Poles strove painfully to dig the foundations for the two buildings and waited for the end of the day to return home and eat. We felt pity for those poor creatures, and often attempted to give them food. Rinke, however, spotting this through the window of his office where he could see without being seen, made them pay a bitter price for having dared to eat. He beat the old Polish civilians with his pistol, causing them to fall, threw the food we had given them on the ground, and made them work until they gave up caring.

I had to tell our men to refrain from any generosity, because it always ended with the Poles suffering the same fate. And I told Rinke that if I ever got out of the prison camp I was going to make him pay for every single act of cruelty he had so far enjoyed, but he assured me that no such thing was going to happen, because he was not going to let me get out alive.

"What I've done with these Poles should give you an indication of what I'll do with you," he said one afternoon, when he had finished beating the civilians.

I was ready to jump on him, enraged over the threat — which I didn't believe he had guts enough to carry out, except against weak, old, harmless civilians — when the sergeant major broke in to find out what time Rinke intended to issue the Red Cross parcels.

"Don't ask him for anything," I told Joe. "I wouldn't even spit on a beast like him."

Joe, however, did not seem to agree. "His day will come," he said. "He can't go unpunished for what he is doing. Go back in the room and play a game of cards," Joe told me, placing his arm around my shoulder. "You are more useful alive," he concluded, trying to calm me down.

I didn't say anything. Instead, I walked back in the billet, nervous and disgusted for having to put up with Rinke. I joined a group of our men who seemed to be in good spirits. They had obtained a bottle of liquor, which the Poles had made from sugar beets, but none would drink it — it contained around 90 percent alcohol.

"Give me that bottle," I yelled at the man who was displaying the powerful liquor to the rest, betting that no one would dare drink it. It was a small bottle, the size of a soda, but I swallowed half the liquor in it before a concerned sergeant quickly grabbed the bottle from my hands and hid it.

"Are you out of your mind?" he shouted. "You want Rinke to find out?"

"Oh!" I exclaimed with amazement over the sergeant's fear. Then remembering Joe a few minutes earlier, I said in a dramatic tone, "Maybe if I am drunk I won't be sensitive to reason. Now, are you giving me that bottle or not?"

"You won't be sensitive to anything if you drink the rest of that liquor," the sergeant said, trying to give the spirits time to catch up. My eyes had begun to feel heavy. The sergeant still seemed worried that Rinke might find out.

"I don't care what happens," I mumbled and started to walk back to my room. "I just want to lose sight of the barbed wire around me for a while."

I went to my room and lay on my bed. Polland dropped in the room to tell me that he and *Unteroffizier* Hans were to supervise the parcel issue.

"Count me out of the roll call," I said, with my eyes half closed. "I have a stomachache."

Polland grinned at my excuse. "Don't let Rinke suspect anything," he cautioned.

Joe came in to find out what had been holding up the parcel issue for so long. As soon as he learned the reason of my ailment, he told everyone in the room to clear out and leave me alone. I turned on my side and went to sleep.

When I finally woke up the next day, I was still feeling tired, and the liquor had given me an awful taste. I headed for a cold shower, and Joe reminded me that we were scheduled to visit Read in Stalag VIII-B the following morning.

"All right," I said. "We will talk about it as soon as I finish."

Sixteen

I was still discussing with Joe the details of the visit to the central camp, when Polland dropped in to tell us he was to be our escort for the trip.

"That'll be fine!" I said, thinking the trip would not be much of a strain with him as the guard. I wondered why Rinke had decided to send Polland instead of one of his loyal watchdogs.

"I had something to do with his decision," Polland said, anticipating my queries.

Joe started to curl his moustache, when I told him that Polland was to be our guard. He chuckled, as he always did when he was pleased.

We boarded the train in Udetfeld early in the morning, taking with us the parcel we had been issued the Saturday before.

Everything around was still asleep. Most of the way between Udetfeld and Tarnowitz, our next stop, I kept leaning on the window with my head outside, watching the train race through the flat plains. It felt good to see that we were moving away from Udetfeld, even if it was only for two days. We made good connections all the way, until we reached Bielitz, the last station, where we had to change trains before arriving at *Manschafts-Stammlager* VIII-B.

"When is the next train to Teschen?" Polland asked the ticket agent, as we stepped into the crowded waiting room.

"The earliest will not leave here until six o'clock," the man informed us. The clock on the wall showed 2:00 p.m.

"I guess we'll have to spend the time waiting here," Polland remarked.

We walked into the crowded, noisy bar, and sat at the only available table in the corner, while the others, mostly Czechs, looked curiously at us.

A stranger on crutches greeted us with a warm, friendly smile from the smoke-filled corner of the room. He left the counter and came to place himself at our service.

"Wait until you see his sister!" Joe said. "She's really something!"

We had been in Bielitz twice before. Both times, Joe and I were always with each other, under the watchful eye of the guard. It was a mystery to me how Joe knew of this man's sister.

The stranger walked to our table. "May I?" he asked, looking alternately at Polland and us.

"He is harmless," I said.

He let himself down slowly into the chair and placed his crutches inside his arm. "Some beer?" he asked. "I lost my leg in an accident," he said when he saw me looking at his amputated side.

"There she is!" Joe exclaimed.

I turned and looked in the direction where Joe had pointed. The woman he had described as the bartender's sister was serving drinks to the customers at the counter. Upon hearing Joe's exclamation, she looked our way with a soft, genuine smile. Her mildly swollen breasts showed pointedly above the counter. Her pretty round face seemed to recognize us. Her eyes, sparkling and clear, gave me a feeling I could never forget. I thought a soft cloud was gently lifting me up into the sky.

"First we drink," the stranger said. "Then you make love to her." He motioned with his hand for his sister to bring us four glasses of beer. Polland offered to pay for it.

"No," the stranger said. "The drinks are on me."

The boldness of the man's suggestion surprised me. It also began to stir in me a passionate desire which, up to this time, I had kept restrained. Hardened by the cruelty of war and the sterility of prison life, the thought of making love to this beautiful woman gave me an unforgettable feeling of happiness. It seemed as if the chains of captivity had been removed, freeing my soul from the weight of oppression and suffering, which I had thus far patiently endured.

While at first I hesitated to take advantage of the situation, the ease with which the bartender's sister behaved, and the suggestion of the bartender himself, soon began to weaken my resistance to the invitation. I became impatient, burning with a desire that up to then I had never known.

Polland seemed embarrassed. "I'll be caught," he protested.

The young lady brought four glasses of beer. When I got a closer look, she seemed more beautiful than I had thought at first.

She winked at me and smiled, as she set the glass of beer on the table. I smelled her fine, soft perfume when she leaned and let her hair touch my face. It seemed like a dream, hearing a beautiful creature like her trying to find an excuse to converse, while under the table she pressed her warm leg softly against mine. I felt uneasy for a minute, but she smiled politely and winked again as she turned and walked back to the counter.

The others in the bar kept glancing suspiciously in our direction. The bartender refilled our glasses while his sister went upstairs.

"She'll be back," the man assured me. He seemed happy over the Allied successes on every front, and took for granted that Joe and I were his friends, since we all were on the same side of the fence.

"Here is to victory!" he proposed, raising his glass.

"Here is to freedom!" I said.

In the course of an hour, the bartender, Joe, and I, developed into a very happy and friendly group, while Polland was ready to fall asleep, under the influence of seven huge glasses of beer.

"Don't be afraid to ask my sister for anything," the bartender suggested, when he saw her return. She went behind the counter to serve the others, but every now and then she glanced in our direction with the same soft, smile.

Suddenly, a Nazi officer walked in.

"It's a shame," he shouted at Polland, "for a German soldier to sit drinking beer with damned prisoners!"

"*Jawohl, Herr Leutnant!*" Polland said with embarrassment, standing to attention.

"I ought to take your name and have you reported to your commanding officer!" the Nazi shouted. Then, apparently satisfied with warning Polland, the officer went and sat at a table, which terrified patrons hastened to vacate.

The bartender's sister did not leave the counter. Her warm inviting smile, her penetrating startling eyes, seemed to have a language of their own, relating feelings that words could never express. I saw her walk slowly away toward the back of the counter. There were tears in her eyes, at the harshness of the Nazi officer. I felt I had known her for years.

"Some day," I said to Joe, who was curling his moustache with disgust, "this war will be over. It'll be a beautiful world after that day."

The bartender's sister did not come back into the room any more that day. I never saw her again, but I thought of her many times, standing behind the counter, smiling like she did that afternoon.

Read gave us a cordial welcome to his office when we finally arrived, late in the evening. He seemed eager to know the latest developments in the labor detachment.

I told him that we had been having some difficulties with Rinke, but it was my feeling that we could take care of the situation for a few more months. I did not mention the incident of the bombs at the airfield. Read told me of the steps he had taken in the meantime to destroy the Nazi plans for our conversion to civilians.

"There is nothing to worry about now," he said. "The commandant of the camp is a good German, and he has given instructions to the captain of Rinke's company to withhold any initiative from your *Kommando Führer*. He is an old soldier, not one of Hitler's enthusiasts."

I could not very well see how this step solved the situation, but I contented myself with the thought that Read knew what he was doing.

"If Rinke gives you any more trouble," Read suggested, "just let me know. I'll fix him up. We have the colonel on our side."

When we finally took care of all matters related to the labor detachment, Joe and I decided to take a walk around the camp. A German sergeant was amusing himself with a group of Italian prisoners. He had them all lined up outside their billet. Shouting and waving his pistol, he made them line up in threes, but as soon as they did, he shouted because they had not lined up in fives. He made them run near the barbed-wire fence, and as soon as they reached it, he began swearing again because they had not stayed near the barracks. In their panic and confusion, the Italians failed to see the German's purpose and added to his amusement by running all over the compound, falling over one another, while trying to get where the German had indicated before he began to fire.

I felt sorry when I saw them, pale and starved — some screaming and crying, not knowing when the German sergeant would decide to stop his game. That kind of thing went on unchecked with the Italians, because neither the Germans nor the Allies were on their side — much less their own government. They didn't have one.

The following morning we left Stalag VIII-B to return to the labor detachment. We stopped again in Bielitz, but the bartender's sister was not there this time. Our next stop was Sosnowitz, where we had to make arrangements for additional Red Cross supplies, because the parcel depot for the entire camp was located there, at another labor detachment. I was very much surprised to see that this garrison consisted only of an old man, a member of the German militia, who could hardly stand on his feet.

"Don't they guard you when you work here?" I asked the Man of Confidence.

"The Germans do the work here," he replied, grinning. "We've got them pretty well trained."

We were late getting back to the railroad station. The next train to Kattowitz was scheduled to leave in six hours, so we walked into the bar and tried to pass some time. A waitress came, asking if we wanted anything to drink. Unlike the one in Bielitz, the bar in the Sosnowitz station was almost deserted. A few passengers now and then stopped at the ticket office to inquire about the next train, then, taking a look at the clock, they walked out of the station to return home. We ordered a glass of beer, hoping to drown the bitterness of our fate in the inebriating effect of alcohol.

Joe kept eying the waitress. "What do you think about some fun with this girl here?" he asked.

"I don't care, Joe!" I responded.

"Why not? We'll probably never see another woman."

"Ask her," I said, giving in. "See what she thinks."

"You talk to the girl at the ticket office," Joe insisted. "I'll talk to the one here."

"You go ahead!" I said.

Polland suspected what the sergeant major was after, and volunteered to get the girl to agree. We spent almost two hours there while Polland exhausted all forms of persuasion.

"I can't leave here for two hours yet," she insisted.

"We have lots of time," Joe hastened to assure her. "We can wait here for weeks."

"All right," she consented finally. "As soon as I leave here, you follow me."

"We can't all go together," Polland interrupted. "You leave first," he told the girl. "They will follow from a distance. I will be last, far behind."

We followed her as Polland suggested, when she left the station to walk home. German officers looked at us suspiciously, seeing our guard far behind us, but they did not understand what we were doing. We had walked almost a mile when she finally entered a house on the side of the street. We thought this was where she lived, and hastened to get there. I reached the house first and started to walk in, when I saw a group of Gestapo officers coming to the stairs from the hallway above. Through an open door at the top of the staircase, I saw more officers smoking casually while talking to someone behind a desk.

"This is a trap!" I shouted, as soon as I realized where the young female had led us. "Keep walking, and pretend you don't know anything," I told Joe, doing the same myself. A quarter of a mile past the house I turned back to see if the officers were following us. They were still outside the house, waiting for us, without suspecting that we had already passed. I noticed a streetcar coming toward us.

"Let's get on it!" I said to Polland, who had already caught up with us.

"They'll stop it when we get to the house," he cautioned.

"Come on, we can't stand here and wait, keep moving!" I insisted. We got onto the streetcar, headed for the station. To our luck, the Gestapo officers were still expecting us to arrive from the other direction, so they did not bother to stop the trolley. We arrived back at the bar without getting caught.

"We were lucky to get away!" Polland remarked.

Our train was there at ten. When we arrived at Tarnowitz late at night, the train for Udetfeld had already left. We had no place to sleep except the floor in the waiting room, so we decided to spend the night in an empty passenger coach, abandoned on the railroad tracks.

"Suppose somebody couples this coach behind a locomotive while we are asleep?" Joe asked. "We might find ourselves in Breslau by morning."

"Don't worry, there is plenty of barbed wire there, too," I said.

Joe laughed at my remark, but I didn't feel any inclination to joke. Now that everything around us was peaceful again, the memory of the few hours I had spent in Bielitz the day before returned.

Joe wanted to cheer me up. "She is only a woman," he remarked. "There'll be millions of women when we get out."

"You mean *if* we get out," I said.

"Let's get some sleep!" Polland said. "I'll probably be in your shoes in a few months. And to think I didn't even want to be in the war!" he protested.

"How did you get into the *Wehrmacht*?" I asked.

"I was living peacefully in Gleiwitz," Polland said, "when Hitler came to power. They told me I had to join the *Hitler-Jugend*, or my parents would be sent to concentration camps. My parents urged me not to join, but I could not stand to lose them. When the war broke out, they put me in the *Wehrmacht*. They sent me to the Russian front a year later. I was wounded there and brought back to a hospital in Germany. As soon as I was able to move again, they sent me to join Rinke's company. But I don't think I'll be there much longer. As soon as I have the opportunity, I am going home and I intend to stay there until the war is over.

"I didn't know what the Nazis were like until I joined the *Wehrmacht*. I saw them murder hundreds of innocent people and then brag about it. No pity or mercy. I remember those murders every time I see Rinke treat you the way he does. I feel ashamed to wear the German uniform anymore. You are not afraid of Rinke, are you?" he suddenly asked me.

"I don't know," I said. "I just believe in something that Rinke doesn't."

"He's upset that he can't break you," Polland said.

"Let's get some sleep. I'm tired," I said, stretching my body over the long wooden seat on the side of the compartment.

We were back in camp E.745, Udetfeld, the following morning. "So long, fellows," Polland said as he left us inside the camp and went to report to Rinke the cause of our delay.

George Karaolanis came out of the billet, anxious to learn how our trip had turned out, and to let us know that everything in the labor detachment was peaceful during our absence.

"Did Rinke give you any trouble?" I asked him.

"He wasn't here at all yesterday. He went to Beuthen."

"I almost forgot that Monday is the day he visits his captain," I remarked.

George, the sergeant major, and I walked into our room. The shoemaker offered to make some coffee for us.

"Play some records!" I told George, as I sat on the sergeant major's bunk to relax from the trip.

"Which one do you want?"

"You know the one — what's the name? . . . *Return of Sorrento*, that's the one."

"Oh, the record made by the Italian Benjamino Gigli," George replied, in an effort to display his knowledge of music.

The shoemaker came in with a pot of hot coffee. "Get your mugs ready!" he told us as he set the pot on the top of the stove.

I got up to get my cup, which was hanging by the window facing the gate. I was surprised to see Rinke walking toward the entrance of the camp, with the expression that he always used whenever he had found somebody on whom to vent his fury. A prisoner was standing near the gate, waiting for Rinke to enter. I sensed trouble and raced outside as fast as I could, but Rinke had begun to hit the prisoner with his bayonet before I could leave the room.

"*Was ist los, Mensch?*" I shouted at Rinke.

"He told me that I am crazy," Rinke explained, enraging himself with his own words.

"That's impossible!" I said in disgust. "The man can't speak a word of German!"

"He made a gesture with his hand," Rinke said. "He rolled his finger on the side of his forehead, like that!" he added, and raised his bayonet again.

"Leave him alone!" I shouted. "He wasn't far from the truth," I thought to myself, although I didn't believe the prisoner had meant

Rinke in particular, but rather Nazis as a whole.

"*Pass mal auf, mein Lieber!*" Rinke cautioned the man, and placed his bayonet back in the scabbard.

Joe had by then reached the scene. "I'm going to make you regret this," he warned, "as much as you enjoy doing it now. You've got no right to beat a man!"

Rinke was surprised by the sergeant major's threat. "I am a German," he yelled. "I can do as I please!"

"Not with my men!" the sergeant major shouted. "You can beat your own guards, if you want, but when you lay hands on my men, you are going to regret it."

Rinke refrained from saying anything more. Instead, he walked out of the camp and returned to his office.

"I hope he doesn't lay a hand on me," George said with a sound of warning. "I'll cut him to pieces if he does."

I did not think George had meant what he said, until a few days later. The next Saturday, as on every other Saturday afternoon, we were issuing Red Cross parcels, while Polland and *Unteroffizier* Hans supervised. As always, all canned food had to be punctured. The prisoners were allowed to do the puncturing, while the Germans checked to see that there was a hole in every can taken away from the distribution counter. George was one of the prisoners doing the puncturing with a sharp-point kitchen knife. The Rat — Hans — was checking the contents of each parcel, when he came across a can he thought had been purposely left intact.

"*Du verfluchte Sau* (Damned pig)," he began to swear at George, but that was as far as he went. George knew the meaning of the expression. He had heard Germans swear at Polish civilians before. Realizing that he had become the victim of this vulgarity, he jumped over the counter almost instantly. His fist landed on the *Unteroffizier's* face while, with his other hand, he was ready to make use of the long kitchen knife.

"You think I am going to stand here and take it?" he yelled.

I grabbed George's arm just in time to stop him from killing the German, but George struggled to get free.

"I'm not going to let a little rat swear at me!" he kept shouting, still struggling to get his arm away. Polland stood in front of the *Unteroffizier* in an attempt to bring the fight to a close. I took the can about which the German had complained, swept away the paper trimmings covering the hole, and threw it in the hands of the *Unteroffizier*.

"Here is your can," I said.

The *Unteroffizier* realized his mistake. Overtaken by George's assault, and feeling his punch, he tried to regain his composure.

"That'll teach him!" George commented, and resumed his work, while Joe reprimanded him for causing the incident, in spite of the German's guilt.

When Rinke learned of this dispute later, he made no effort to get even with George. Instead, he began to ridicule the *Unteroffizier* and the remainder of his guards for letting the prisoners do as they pleased. He seemed to like seeing his guards take a beating from the prisoners. This apparently gave him the assurance that he was the only one whom everyone else feared and obeyed. His own valor and bravery, he believed, thus remained undisputed among the prisoners and Germans. He did succeed in gaining prestige among the German civilians in the area and the guards in the camp, and for many he seemed to have become the outstanding soldier and hero in this locality. But Joe and I knew what he really was — a sadist and a coward.

"You may be the hero for everyone else," his guards insisted, "but you can't make the sergeant major and his friend believe that."

"*Wart'e mal! Wart'e mal!*" Rinke kept promising. "Just wait! I'll show them!"

So everyone, prisoners and Germans, waited to see if Rinke would carry out his promise. The Deacon, still attempting to gain my confidence, brought to my attention all the gossip between Rinke and his guards, and Polland kept me informed of every instruction that Rinke received from his captain regarding the prisoners in the labor detachment. Joe and I simply gave up the thought of ever walking out of E.745 alive. For the two of us, Udetfeld was the end of the road. In this remote Polish village, we were to stay for good, as Rinke promised, unless we both gave in.

Meanwhile, Rinke started his "*Kraft durch Furcht*" propaganda campaign, in an effort to get every German in the area to treat the prisoners as he did. One or two of his guards followed his example. Most, however, did not. He learned this after his next visit to the company office.

Seventeen

IT was not long after the failure of the assassination attempt against Hitler that the consequences began to be felt by those Germans who had opposed the Nazi regime through failure to register with the party. In the civilian ranks, the Nazis were given complete authority over the lives of non-Nazi Germans, while in the ranks of the **Wehrmacht**, the SS was authorized to punish by death those German soldiers who showed any reluctance toward carrying out the duties prescribed by the Nazi High Command. In prisoner-of-war camps, the SS troops were given the power to hang or to send to concentration camps those German guards who refused to be brutal and savage in their treatment of war prisoners.

Rinke was summoned to the company headquarters for specific instructions on the prisoners in our camp. As soon as his train passed by, heading for Beuthen, and the guards located Rinke sitting by the window, they felt certain he was on his way. They spread into the camp and wandered around the rooms, hoping someone would offer them a cigarette or start a conversation. This would give them the opportunity to show that they and Rinke were two entirely different kinds of Germans — that they were really on our side of the fence, but they could do very little for us when Rinke was present, because they feared for their lives. In this, I think they were completely honest.

Although Rinke had failed to intimidate the prisoners, he had succeeded in frightening his guards by beating them or threatening them with internment in concentration camps, or — what seemed worse at the time — by suggesting to the captain that they be sent to the Russian front. Living under constant fear and dominated completely by Rinke, with their complaints against his undignified behavior toward them rejected every time by the captain, who completely endorsed Rinke's actions, the German guards hoped even more than we did for his replacement. My own and Joe's defiance of Rinke, as a result, had led them to believe that we could bring about such a thing, feeling that as prisoners, we had a better ground on which to halt his relentless sadism and terror. They expressed this wish directly to me, especially The Deacon, who volunteered to cooperate with us in any way. He even began to stand at attention whenever Joe or I passed by, presenting arms in the German military fashion, embarrassing everyone, including himself.

While Rinke was away, Hans Polland dropped into my office to acquaint me with the latest of Rinke's plans.

"You should hear the things he said about you," Hans said, waiting for some degree of surprise or agitation on my part.

"What did he say?" I asked.

"If he does to you everything he has promised for the last few weeks, there will be nothing left of you," Polland answered. "You'd better watch out."

"If one could carry out every threat he voiced behind another's back," I said, "they would not be voiced. He would have already carried them out."

Polland gazed at me for a few seconds and then lay down on the sergeant major's bed. "I'm tired," he said. "I'd rather lay here for a few hours. I wish the war was over," he whispered as he stretched his legs in an effort to relax.

I walked into the adjoining room where Joe was playing cards. It had become a habit with Joe and me to frequent this room, because we both wanted to be in the company of our men and spend time listening to their problems and their experiences at work. Joe did most of his listening playing poker. I played the records we had received from the Red Cross. Music seemed the sweetest thing one could hear in this atmosphere filled with threats. George was leaning against a bunk, trying to talk the shoemaker into letting him play a hand.

"No!" the shoemaker said, shaking his head.

"I'll tell you what I'll do," George said. "I'll let you see my cards. How's that?" he asked.

"NO" was again the shoemaker's answer. "I don't want to see your cards."

"I'll let Joe check my hand," George continued, "to see that I don't cheat."

"I won't play," the shoemaker insisted. "You couldn't be honest in a game of cards even if you wanted to."

George kept teasing the shoemaker while a couple of guards were standing, grinning at his gestures.

"Get Rinke to play cards with you, when he gets back," the shoemaker suggested.

"Ah, ha!" George exclaimed, laughing. "I just thought of something that will scare the daylights out of Rinke. When he comes in to turn the lights out, I'll hide behind the door and appear as a ghost at the moment he turns around in the dark to close it."

"Just how do you think you can do that?" the shoemaker asked.

Then George went on to demonstrate. He borrowed a sheet from the infirmary, then covered himself with it, bent forward, raised his arms like a vulture trying his wings, making a roaring sound.

"*Lieber Gott!*" one of the guards exclaimed, not knowing what George was doing.

"*Ich, Rinke.* Boo!" George tried to explain, clawing his fingers like a vulture.

"He'd scare me all right," the other guard murmured. "*Verfluchter Kerl! Er sieht als ein Übel aus* (He looks like a devil)."

We burst out laughing. We were free from the pressure of Rinke's presence, and the feeling of relief had given everyone the disposition for jokes and laughter, including the German guards.

"How about a game of volleyball?" one of the sports-minded prisoners suggested loudly.

"Yeah! How about it?" some others inquired.

"How about playing the Germans?"

George explained their plan to the two guards standing at the doorway. The guards hesitated for a moment, then agreed to get a team ready for the game to which Joe and I had to consent, seeing that everyone else had welcomed the idea.

I was a regular member of the team, so I joined them while George and Joe stood on the side watching.

We had won the first two games when Joe suggested that I get some war news. I called Polland out of the game and we walked to the guard room. A few of the men were cleaning their rifles, and as we went into Rinke's office, they looked up curiously to see what we were doing. Hans turned on the radio to get London, and after a few seconds, the English commentator gave a summary of the news.

At first I couldn't hear what he was saying, but the sound cleared as he announced that the liberation of Paris was near, and the Allied forces in the south were racing toward Lyon, while a U.S. column from the north had reached and bypassed Bordeaux, heading for the Spanish frontier. The Germans had continued shooting V-2 rockets into England, but the attack had lost its fury because of the deep Allied advance in France. I was still listening to the broadcast when The Berliner dropped in, returning from guard duty.

"*Bist du verrückt, Mensch?* (Are you crazy?)" he shouted, seeing Polland and I had dared listen to an English broadcast.

"So long as you keep *your* mouth shut," Hans said, "nobody is going to know anything about it."

"*Du brauchst keine Angst haben* (You don't need to worry)," The Berliner affirmed in changing tone. "I won't say a word." Then, as if he wanted to convince both of us that the war was completely out of his concern, he walked cautiously to the bunk where The Deacon was lying sound asleep, nodding that we both keep quiet. He opened his cupboard, avoiding the slightest noise.

"No wonder he is so skinny," The Berliner whispered. "Look what he's got here!"

In the cupboard was a month's supply of bread and jam rations. Suspecting that this strange creature had probably done other funny things, The Berliner opened quietly the small suitcase at the foot of The Deacon's bunk, to find a pressed uniform of the type worn by priests, which he apparently had received while a divinity student. The Berliner undressed himself completely, then jokingly put on the uniform he had found in the suitcase. He was still trying to put on the garment when The Deacon woke up.

In an attempt to remove the uniform from The Berliner, The Deacon tore away the front part when The Berliner pulled himself back, leaving the front of his body completely naked, with a strip hanging over his back. The Deacon stepped down from his bed, but The Berliner had already raced outside, and a long chase began in the fields. When The Berliner was passing by the guard room again, another guard, waiting with a bucket full of water, emptied it over his head from atop the roof. Polland was looking at the scene with surprise, while the rest of the guards tried to make things more interesting by adding their abuses to those of The Berliner, bursting into wild laughter.

This display of disrespect and contempt for the uniform of a priest left me more bewildered than Rinke's brutal belief in the eventual annihilation of the prisoners in his hands. I had no respect for The Deacon as a man, since I could hardly conceive of him as one, but perhaps without realizing it, he did represent a bit of Christianity in this forsaken wilderness. I saw nothing amusing in The Berliner's fun, and I was left with little doubt that the Nazi character was, at heart, barbaric.

Neither The Berliner nor The Deacon were men of integrity. The Berliner, on one hand, was the type of person who maintained that a man was entitled to force himself on any woman within reach. Women had only one function, he maintained, and as often as possible he tried to prove his point. The Deacon, on the other hand, was a homosexual, falling in and out of love with any handsome young male, prisoner or German. He was extremely dangerous because whenever prisoners refused his advances, he would spur Rinke into acts of violence and cruelty toward the prisoners.

He appeared to have been very embarrassed by the fact that I had witnessed this whole scene. When The Berliner and the other guards finally came back in, they were still laughing wildly.

I took this opportunity in the guard room to go to Rinke's office to search through the papers in his desk. Among them I found small booklets bearing the title *Behandlung der Kriegsgefangenen* (*Treatment of*

War Prisoners), issued by the *Oberkommando der Wehrmacht* (Army High Command). I glanced through them quickly, trying to finish the search before any of the guards suspected what I was doing. One paragraph was interesting:

> *Dem Kriegsgefangenen sollte bei jeder Gelegenheit klargemacht werden, daß er dem Deutschen untergeordnet ist. Der Lagerkommandant hat sich daran zu kümmern, daß alle Gefangenen in seinem Lager zum Widerstand unfähig sind....*
> *Die Kriegsgefangenen ununterbrochen daran erinnert werden, daß ihnen keine menschliche Behandlung zusteht....*

At every opportunity it should be made clear to the prisoner of war that he stands below the German, and the camp commandant should see to it that the bulk of war prisoners in his camp are rendered incapable of resistance....
The prisoners should be continuously reminded that they are not entitled to any humane treatment....

As I looked anxiously around to see if any of the guards were coming, I saw Rinke entering the guard room. I shoved the papers back into the drawers in a hurry and leaned against the desk facing the entrance to the guard room, trying to look indifferent. I tried to give the impression that I had just dropped in. Polland fortunately came to my assistance, saying that he had gone into the room a minute earlier to buckle on his bayonet, according to Rinke's instructions that every guard should be armed in the presence of a prisoner.

"So, there is no mail for us today," I said.

"No, there is nothing," Polland replied, as if in a hurry to turn his attention to what Rinke had to say.

I pretended to express some disappointment over the lack of mail while I walked out, heading for the camp. All the guards had managed to clear out of the camp, spreading in all directions, except one who couldn't find a way to return to the guard room without raising suspicions. Rinke spotted him from the window of his office, and came rushing into the camp where the guard was trapped. Then, grabbing his rifle, he beat the guard, who took the punishment as a natural consequence, while protesting amid tears and cries that he was not the only one who had taken advantage of Rinke's absence.

Eighteen

RINKE took the names of all the guards who had been associating with prisoners that day and had them all replaced, with the exception of The Deacon, Polland, and the guard Alex. Rinke was extremely pleased when he learned that one of the new guards had shot two Polish civilians the following day for trying to trade food with prisoners. But he was not too pleased when later in the same week he finally discovered that two of the prisoners from the labor detachment had escaped.

"They won't go very far," he said to me when he found they were missing. "They won't get back in the camp alive; not while I am here."

Joe and I had managed to cover their disappearance for four days, hoping they would have the opportunity to get far away from camp E.745. We both foresaw their fate if they were ever returned to the camp. The escape was discovered by their foreman, who did not see them return to work after continuous absence, and reported this to Rinke.

I was getting ready to go to bed one night when Polland came in suddenly with some urgent news.

"You're moving away from this camp the day after tomorrow," he said. "At least, this is what Rinke is going to *tell* you during roll call tomorrow afternoon.

"Nobody but the captain, Rinke, and I know that this is a fake. What will really happen is that after you are taken outside, they will conduct a thorough search of you and the camp, confiscating everything except a day's food supply, a set of underwear, and your uniform. You will then be brought back to the camp again."

"The order for your departure will come by telephone from the captain tomorrow morning. No one else outside of Rinke and I are going to know the truth. Even the guards will think you are moving away."

Joe summoned one man from each room and conveyed the information Polland had brought.

"Don't let any of the guards suspect that you know the truth," he cautioned. "Pass the information to the rest in your rooms."

Everything developed according to Polland's information the following day. Rinke gave us the news of our "move." His guards started to pack for the trip, but we spent most of the night hiding everything we could in the top of the ceiling and in the ground beneath the floor.

I gave Polland all my papers and the maps that The Deacon had brought me, so that he could hide them.

The next morning, we were taken outside the camp. A train was already waiting at the station to take us away, but, of course, we did not go.

The Germans searched our camp throughout the whole day. They found some of the stuff we had hidden in the ground, but no one thought of looking above their heads in the ceiling. They did not suspect we knew the truth.

As soon as The Deacon realized that the whole move was a fake, he felt a great deal of remorse because he did not know in time to warn us. I still did not trust him, so I concealed the truth.

"What did you do with the maps I gave you?" he asked me anxiously.

"That was the first thing Rinke found on me," I lied. "I didn't know all this was going to happen! How could I know? You hadn't told me anything about it!"

"I didn't know myself," The Deacon answered, looking at the ground.

Polland returned the papers and the maps to me the following morning. The Deacon came in later to take George for the rations.

"That Polland!" he shouted. "He knew the truth all the time, and yet he never told you," he kept saying. "I don't think he is worthy of any trust at all."

"You are quite right," I said, keeping him in the dark. "Just think what would have happened if you had known the truth, instead of Polland. You could be the clerk!" I suggested ironically.

He seemed to want to make up for not knowing about Rinke's plan. "I'll do anything you want me to," he said, touching my hand.

"I don't want you to do *anything*," I said imperatively.

At that, he began to get belligerent. "You *do* want to help your friends, don't you?" he asked, suggesting that if I accepted his advances, he would do all he could to help the other prisoners.

"On your way!" I said, pointing toward the gate.

He jerked the rifle away from his shoulder.

"Do you know that I can kill you?" he said, hoping to show me he was still in charge.

I was getting ready to shove him out of my way, but he hurried outside when he saw me moving toward him.

I waited there for George and the cook; Joe came out of the billet to see what the shouting was about.

"That Deacon again," I said. "He's getting worse all the time."

When the summer of 1944 finally was coming to an end, Rinke decided to have the prisoners plant flowers around the guard room in their spare time, after their regular day's work. I refused to let him use any of the men, but some volunteered to do the work, to save me from the trouble Rinke was looking for. The Deacon, in the meantime, turned out as I had suspected — a dangerous liar, trying to get Rinke to make me pay for my rejection of him. I paid very little heed to this, however, as I did not believe Rinke was foolish enough to let The Deacon persuade him into any acts of violence for which he might have to pay himself.

I was engaged in a game of volleyball one afternoon when The Deacon came in to tell me that Rinke wanted two men to water his flowers.

"He can let two men stay in the camp, if he wants them to work in his flower garden," I said. "Or else. . . ."

Before I had finished, The Deacon was already on his way to tell Rinke of my refusal. A few minutes later, Rinke hurried into the camp, armed with his pistol on one side and bayonet on the other. He came straight to me, pushing a bullet into his pistol, readying himself for an assault.

"Did you tell my guard that if I want water for my flowers I can come and get it myself?" he asked.

"I told your guard," I said calmly, "that you can hold two men back from work in the morning if you want them to work in your garden. There is no reason why they have to do this in their spare time."

Rinke was confused for a minute, probably because he did not believe The Deacon, or maybe because he was afraid to attack me. Whichever might have been the case, he was content to caution me.

"I respect you," he said. "You can show me respect also."

It was the first time that he spoke of his respect for my position. His actions in the past and his promises to the guards, however, overshadowed his admission, and I always believed that Rinke restrained himself from attacking me because he was not quite sure of himself. He seemed to hesitate every time he had the opportunity to kill me, as though he was afraid of the act. This made me feel that he was bluffing, even at times when he was deadly serious.

Almost a month had gone by since the two prisoners had escaped from E.745, when we received the news of their capture. Rinke expected to have them in his hands within a few days. Everyone waited to see whether Rinke would kill them, as he had threatened, or bring them unharmed into the camp. I tried to see that the latter happened, but I soon knew that I could not convince Rinke.

Every prisoner in the camp was watching near the fence when the two escapees were surrendered to Rinke that evening. The two were standing outside the guard room dressed in civilian clothes, waiting for a fate they had already suspected. Rinke delayed until dark, then took one of them in, tied him to a chair, ordered the other guards outside, and turned the lights out. Then, using a rifle with bayonet fixed on the end, he unleashed his fury on the helpless prisoner for almost an hour, beating him with both ends of the rifle, throwing at him any heavy object that came to his hand, until finally the prisoner ceased to move and leaned forward, unconscious from bleeding and pain, still tied to the chair. The guards carried the prisoner into the camp while Rinke took in the second escapee for the same treatment.

We felt every blow they received and could see the expression of pain on every prisoner's face as the sound reached the camp from the darkened guard room.

Joe dispersed everyone to their rooms as the first escapee was brought inside the camp, and let the *Sanitäter* attend to his wounds to stop the bleeding. The second escapee was brought in an hour later in the same condition. Their bodies were covered with blood and their eyes were still wet from tears, but although they regained consciousness, they stared into the room without life or feeling. Rinke did not come into the camp that night, nor did he insist on turning the lights out at midnight this time. Later, toward morning, the *Sanitäter* managed to get a few words out of the first escapee.

"No! No!" was all he could say, trying to move away from the bed, apparently thinking he was still tied to the chair. When he realized Rinke was no longer there, he raised his head and looked around, wondering where he was.

I stroked his head, trying to make him see he was in our room.

George, Joe, the *Sanitäter*, and I spent the whole night without sleep trying to get them out of their state of shock, and we finally succeeded in the early hours of the morning. The shoemaker made us coffee, and we did not let any of the other men see them until they could stand on their feet again.

Rinke came into the camp after the prisoners left for work. Finding his victims in our room, he became furious because they had not gone with the rest.

No one said a word. We were trying to decide whether or not to kill him, as we waited for Rinke to make a move toward his victims, who at the sight of him rushed and hid behind Joe and me.

"I didn't touch them," Rinke said.

"How did they get hurt then?" I yelled at him.

"They fell down," Rinke said, unruffled. "I'll prove to you they did." He spoke to his victims directly.

"Come out here," he shouted.

Frightened, his two victims did as he said.

"Did I hit you?" he asked them in the same cunning tone.

"No!" both answered, trembling.

"You see!" Rinke said triumphantly, "I told you I didn't touch them."

"Is there justice in this world?" Joe whispered in exasperation over the sorry spectacle we had witnessed. Our nerves were reaching the breaking point, but we could still remember we were prisoners; there was nothing we could do. The fact that there was no justice in Nazi Germany was nothing new; we were only seeing another example. The only way justice could prevail was to destroy the whole Nazi machinery. But it required the help of millions of others to do a job of this size. Millions of free men who had to see or hear what the Nazis were like, just as we were seeing Rinke.

"I am going to make you Nazis pay for this," Joe started shouting in the little German he knew. "I swear I will, even if it's the last thing I do!"

That was a big statement, but still bigger was the question: how was he going to do this? Rinke didn't seem bothered, as he stood there enjoying his feat.

"*Sie müssen arbeiten gehen* (They have to go to work)," he said as he left the room.

"There *is* something we can do," I told Joe as soon as Rinke was clear of the camp, "if you and I can forget that we are ever going to be free."

"What?" Joe asked, as if he didn't believe what he had just told Rinke a few minutes earlier.

"We can indict Rinke and his captain through the protecting power. We have two counts now, the bomb incident, and this."

"Don't be silly!" Joe cautioned. "The Germans will shoot you the minute you open your mouth. Don't you think Rinke and his captain have thought of that?"

"Maybe they have. But they forgot something."

Joe looked at me in disbelief.

"They forgot there is a God in this world."

"Well," Joe remarked, "if He is seeing these things, why doesn't He do something about it?" he asked angrily. "If *I* can't stand to see it, how can *He*?"

"You and I are going to get it sooner or later," I said. "We have nothing to lose if we get shot, hanged, or burned. I have no family or children, neither do you. How about it?"

"What is your plan?" Joe asked with some interest this time.

"You say the Germans will shoot both of us the minute we open our mouths?"

"Go on!"

"Well, from the time we sign the indictment, until the Germans find out, we have time to get enough evidence in the hands of the protecting power to enable them to carry on the trial after we are gone and prove their cruelties, as if we were there to testify," I said.

"Sounds reasonable," Joe remarked.

I told Joe what exactly I had in mind. There was no doubt that as soon as the Nazis would find out that we had let the protecting power know of their cruelties in the prison camps, they would shoot both of us to destroy the evidence needed to establish the truth in our indictment. It would be a blow to Nazi propaganda if their own cruelties suddenly came to light. An accusation by the prisoners meant nothing, but proof in our indictment did. It would give substance to the rumors about the character of the Nazis and would stir up the concern of those German families whose sons were prisoners in Allied hands. And the Nazis at this time desperately needed the cooperation of every German, Nazi or not, in order to prolong the fighting.

What the Nazis feared most was the reaction of those peoples outside German control, and although thus far they were able to commit crimes at will, they wanted the free world to know nothing of their true behavior within Germany.

My plan was difficult and in many instances impractical, because it depended on whether many assumptions I made were true. Furthermore, it required the genuine cooperation of the protecting power and the central Man of Confidence in Teschen — Read; and part of its success depended on how well I could exploit the services of German authorities ignorant of my purpose, as well as how long I could keep my plan unsuspected by Rinke or his captain.

The same afternoon I drafted the indictment, which the sergeant major and I signed, accusing the German authorities in control of E.745 for violations of Articles 31, 52, 54, and 58 of the Geneva Convention and cruelties against the prisoners, committed by the *Kommando Führer*, Fritz Rinke, at the direction of the captain commanding his company. Polland had given me, at an earlier date, the particulars of the captain and the company's number and identification.

We were fortunate that on the same evening an English doctor being transferred to Stalag VIII-B for repatriation was brought to our camp until arrangements could be made for his trip to Teschen.

On the very first night after his arrival at our labor detachment, he had the opportunity to become acquainted with the *Kommando Führer*, because Rinke came in demanding that the doctor be put to work with the rest of the prisoners in the morning and refused to make arrangements for the doctor's transfer to Teschen. He ignored the directive from the German High Command that the doctor's repatriation had been approved and that he was to arrange for the doctor's trip to Teschen.

I requested that the English doctor write up a medical report, for court proceedings, describing the nature and cause, in his opinion, of the wounds inflicted upon the two escapees, and urged him to deliver it together with the indictment to the protecting power at any cost, even if it meant conveying the information orally. The doctor agreed to my request wholeheartedly, and promised to make sure that the information would get into the hands of the protecting power despite any Nazi efforts to frustrate such a move.

"If you can induce the protecting power to act, Sir," I emphasized, "our lives will not be sacrificed in vain."

The doctor promised to do his best.

To make sure that the medical report was duplicated, I decided to obtain a similar statement from the German doctor at the base hospital. I knew Rinke would try to prevent the escapees from seeing the doctor in the morning, but I felt certain he would never suspect the real reason of the visit.

Rinke came in early the next morning to make sure that the escapees went to work. When he found them both lying in bed, he began to threaten them.

"Either they stay where they are," Joe shouted, "or no one goes to work."

The air force guards were already at the gate waiting to escort the prisoners to their working places. In his confusion, Rinke hastened to get the other prisoners out and gave up on the two escapees.

The sick prisoners were ready to visit the German doctor two hours later. The Deacon was detailed as an escort. Rinke was at the gate to try and stop the two victims from leaving with the others. He kept threatening them, thinking they would be afraid to go.

I told the sick to line up in fours with the escapees in the middle and the guard in front. Rinke pulled his pistol, indicating he would shoot if we made a step farther than the gate. The *Sanitäter* and I covered the two escapees, so that Rinke could not get to them without hitting one of us first.

"Start walking!" I told the guard.

"He'll shoot!" the two objected, certain that he would.

"He won't shoot," I said in German, as we kept walking. Rinke stood there until we were a hundred yards away. He didn't fire a shot, nor did he follow us. I didn't turn to look back for quite a few minutes, and when I finally did, Rinke was on his way back to the guard room.

When we got into the examination room, I told the German doctor what I wanted. I didn't give him any time to make up his mind or ask any questions.

"If you can't make this report," I said, "then I want you to recommend somebody who can."

The doctor raised no objections. Instead, he called his secretary, who registered the details as the doctor dictated, while examining the wounds of Rinke's victims.

"How do you want me to do this?" he asked, when he finished. "You want me to send a copy to Stalag VIII-B?"

"That's right," I answered.

"I'll keep a copy with me, just in case," the doctor added, when he finished signing the report.

"Who did this?" he asked, showing his disapproval for the beating they took.

Then The Deacon went on to tell him the truth about Rinke, for the first time giving us the help we needed. The doctor believed that this was a just case, and that it was his duty to state the facts to the best of his knowledge, regardless of his feelings.

But I did not content myself with the doctor's assurance. I wanted Read to know of the report that was being sent to the commandant of Stalag VIII-B. I also wanted him to make sure that it got there. I felt that if Read knew of the existence of such a report he could direct the protecting power to find it and use it in the trial I was aiming to bring about. Thus I obtained the doctor's identification details and handed them to the English doctor in our camp, with the request that he pass them over to Read.

When the doctor finally left for Stalag VIII-B at the end of the same week, I had given him enough information to convince the protecting power completely of the truth in our accusation. However, I anticipated that the protecting power would have to listen to the German side of the case, and I wanted to have enough evidence to counteract any Nazi denials.

Rinke did not suspect our moves in the least, but a few days after the doctor was gone, he began to fear that some protest on our part might slip out. In his effort to keep his behavior secret, he canceled all future visits to Stalag VIII-B, and, although we had previously been allowed to correspond with Read, from that time on Rinke destroyed every letter from me or Joe that was addressed to the central camp. He thus believed he had frustrated every possible way of communication between our labor detachment and any other person outside. Insofar as the future was concerned, Rinke was completely right. From then on, our voices could not be heard beyond the barbed-wire fence, but they had escaped in time to reach where we needed them to be heard. And that was something Rinke had never anticipated.

We stayed in E.745 for two more days, and then we were moved on foot to another labor detachment in Beuthen, a city 30 kilometers away from Udetfeld. The new camp was number E.757, but it became known to everyone who had been in Stalag VIII-B and Lamsdorf as "Hell Dive" — Rinke made it this during his most thrilling days as our *Kommando Führer*.

The Deacon was conspicuously absent the week of our arrival at E.757 — hanged, it was rumored. Polland was transferred to a Russian labor detachment half a mile away from ours, but I managed to get in touch with him once a week and get the important news. All the others, including *Unteroffizier* Hans, moved along with us, with Rinke, of course, as the *Kommando Führer*. Our work in "Hell Dive" was to dig coal in one of the 60 or more mines in the area. Some of the prisoners were used for construction work in the village of Morgenroth between our camp and Beuthen.

It was almost mid-September 1944, and the weather had already begun to get cold. We had taken the stock of Red Cross supplies with us from E.745; however, some cigarettes had been stolen from the truck, and this provided an excellent opportunity to contact Hans Polland and make the arrangements for our weekly meetings. I had difficulty getting away from my guard, but finally managed to talk with Polland alone.

Our next meetings were to be at intervals of eight days each, alternating in mornings and afternoons to avoid Rinke's suspicion. Rinke had become my personal guard, feeling that he could thus watch every movement I made; he believed no one was as efficient as he was. Still, under his nose, I managed to get to my objective.

Immediately after our arrival at this labor detachment, Rinke jailed the two escapees in the second guard room and forced them into hard labor by making them dig holes in the half-frozen ground, covering up the old one as they commenced to digging the new. We were allowed to give them their German food rations, but they were not to receive any Red Cross parcels. Rinke amused himself by asking them who had broken their ribs. If they refused to answer, he beat them on their wounds, and if they answered that it was he who had done it, he beat them again. He did this mostly in the presence of other prisoners who gradually were aggravated to the point where each had volunteered to kill Rinke, at the cost of his own life.

I felt no differently from the rest, but I tried to convince them that Rinke's life was a very poor price for theirs, when in a few more months they were going to be free.

The strength of the labor detachment was increased to 300 with the addition of British, who arrived during the first week.

Nineteen

AT the end of the first week at E.757, Rinke's captain dropped by to congratulate him in my presence for the excellent job he had done in disregarding completely the prisoners' complaints and drawing upon him the mine director's esteem for his unique cooperation. What Rinke had actually done was to give the mine director and his assistants permission to set a quota of coal tonnage for each prisoner per day, instead of a definite time limit, which he was supposed to do. No prisoner was allowed to quit unless he had dug the prescribed tonnage of coal during his shift.

However, the lives of those prisoners employed in construction seemed somewhat brighter. The area of their employment was surrounded by a barbed-wire fence, but their shift consisted of eight hours' work, and for the time being, at least, they seemed at a slight advantage over those employed in the mine.

We no longer needed to keep a kitchen staff, as the cooking was done by the Germans in the mine kitchen near the Russian labor detachment. Our chef George Karaolanis was detailed with the group on building construction. We no longer had the services of the German doctor in Udetfeld, but I was very much relieved to learn that our new doctor was a Polish civilian, formerly a captain in the Polish army, though I was doubtful whether Rinke would consent to carry out the doctor's recommendations unless they seemed agreeable to the Germans.

I met the Polish doctor on Tuesday the following week, when the sick were taken there for the first time since our arrival at E.757 by Rinke himself and a couple of additional guards. Rinke had gone along to make sure that most of the sick were found capable for work and to see that I did not mention anything about his two victims jailed in the camp. He remained in the examination room until the last prisoner was through, recommending to the doctor his own diagnosis. To help the doctor comprehend Rinke, I suggested the procedure that the doctor in Udetfeld had followed in assigning those very ill to the hospital in Stalag VIII-B.

"*Die Schweinehunde sind alle Arbeitsfähig* (The bastards are all capable of work)," Rinke shouted indignantly over my suggestion. Rinke's temper and opinion of the prisoners let the doctor realize where we stood without my saying a word.

"Talk to me in English, when you get the chance!" the doctor suggested suddenly.

"*Bitte?*" I asked, not believing that I had heard him right the first time.

He didn't say anything, because Rinke was watching suspiciously, wondering what the doctor had said.

"Give me that bandage," he said, this time in German. I took the white paper he had pointed at and leaned near his side.

"Talk English!" the doctor said. "I'll do anything I can to help you."

"Send some of the sick to the central camp," I said.

Rinke was looking on again suspiciously, unable to understand what we were talking about. He thought he couldn't hear from where he was standing, so he came closer.

"*Na, du bist fertig* (You are finished)," the doctor said to the patient. "*Nächster!*" he called, motioning for the next patient.

Rinke seemed satisfied now that there was nothing suspicious about our conversation, so he stepped back again near the door.

"Today?" the doctor asked in English, referring to my earlier question in the same language.

"*Sind sie alle fertig?* (Are they all through?)" the doctor asked in German.

"*Ja!*" I said, nodding with my head to indicate it was the answer to both his questions.

Rinke did not look at the sick register while we were still in the doctor's office. He seemed satisfied that I had not mentioned anything with regard to the two escapees.

I paid a similar visit to the dentist on Thursday that same week. He was also Polish and seemed eager to give me all the latest news as it was broadcast by the Polish underground organization.

"You saw Dr. Tsapla last Tuesday, I heard," he said when I was alone with the patient in the room.

"Is that the doctor's name?" I asked.

"Fine fellow, Dr. Tsapla," the dentist continued. "I see him very often. He lost his leg fighting the Germans in '39 when they invaded Poland. What is the name of your camp commandant — Rinke?" he asked. "I heard you are having quite some trouble with him."

"He isn't very sociable," I remarked.

"It won't be long," the dentist said, raising his voice. I grinned at the dentist's assurance that the war would be over soon.

The visit to the dentist gave me some relief from the oppressed atmosphere of the prison camp. Rinke did not come along this time, as he had been called to confer with his captain in Beuthen the same morning. When he returned in the afternoon, he called me to his office to inform me that a British *Sanitäter* was to arrive from Stalag VIII-B that evening.

"I feel sorry for him," Joe said, when I told him of Rinke's news. "He could have been sent to a better place."

The same evening, the new *Sanitäter* was brought in. He was a member of the British army and a native of Australia. I called him Harry, because it seemed more congenial than using his surname. I soon found out from him, however, that he was sent by Read to tell us that he was aware of every step we had taken to secure evidence for the trial and that our protest had reached the protecting power safely.

"Read wishes you the best of luck," Harry said, "and assures you that he'll do anything he can to get the British authorities to support your case to the end."

Harry's news was the best I had received since I had arrived with the labor detachment. I was glad to see that Read was so clever in his proceedings, something which assured me more than just Harry's report of Read's sincerity and capabilities.

"There is something I want you to do, Harry," I said. "It may be difficult, but it is important. I want you to carry the food tomorrow to the two men in jail."

"That won't be difficult," Harry remarked.

"I know," I continued, "but the reason I want you to do that is because I want you to try and talk to them. That won't be easy, with Rinke standing beside you." Harry listened carefully, while I described the plan.

"I want you to convince them that they have nothing to fear if they report sick. I need them to do that. Once they agree, give me their names in the same list with the others who report sick by next Tuesday. The rest is my job."

Sunday was a rest day for everyone. I was writing a letter on my desk when George came in. He seemed nervous and excited.

"Write me a short note in German," he asked impatiently.

I took out a sheet of paper from my notebook. "What do you want me to write?"

George dictated:

> Come and see me next Wednesday noon. Don't worry about the guards. Alex will let you in through the fence. I will wait for you in the basement of the first building. I love you.
>
> George

I wondered what George was doing. He could not possibly have intended to give the message to Joan. How would she know where he was? Our moves were kept secret from all the Germans. But I was to see exactly what George intended to do with the message. I went outside, curious what he had in mind. To my surprise, Joan was standing outside the fence, trying to locate George. Alex was with her. Rinke was standing in the courtyard in front of his office.

She started to walk around the perimeter of the camp, pretending she was flirting with Alex, who cooperated completely in avoiding Rinke's suspicion, or that of the guards standing in the pillboxes at each side of the camp. At the instant she was on the other side of the billet and Rinke could not see her, George threw the message I had written wrapped around a small stone, outside the fence, fast enough to avoid being seen by the guard. Joan pretended she did not see anything and kept walking in the same direction away from the guard, still joking with Alex. After a few minutes she turned back, picked the message up on the way to the guard room, held it in her fist, then dropped it finally in her bag when she felt sure she would not be suspected.

George was relieved, but still stood near the fence, watching his sweetheart glance at him occasionally with a warm, sincere smile.

On the eve of the next visit to the doctor, the *Sanitäter* gave Rinke the list of the sick. As soon as he saw the numbers of the two escapees he jumped out of his seat. He ordered the guard at his office to bring me in at once.

I suspected why he wanted to see me, so I refused to go.

"If he wants to see me," I told the guard, "he can come and see me right here! I'm not going to his office."

Rinke came in as soon as he learned of my refusal. He tried to argue for a few seconds, hoping I would be frightened into giving up the idea of getting the two escapees to the doctor. Joe was standing by me waiting to see what happened.

"If they want to see the doctor," I said, "I can't stop them, and neither can you."

"I am going with them," Rinke said, then, waving his finger in front of my face, he warned, "Just don't make any mistake and tell the doctor anything!" He turned around and hurried out of the camp.

"Well," I said to Joe, "so far, so good."

Rinke watched me like a dog in the doctor's office the following morning. The doctor could not get anything out of the escapees, although he persistently asked how their ribs had been broken and their bodies bruised so deeply. Rinke answered the questions for them by saying that they had fallen down while they were walking, something which enabled me to get enough courage to tell the truth to the doctor, in spite of Rinke's threat.

"He beat them up after he tied them to a chair," I said, pointing at Rinke with my hand.

Rinke jumped on me, ready to hit me with his bayonet, but soon realized he was only giving away the truth, so he tried to be polite by saying he could not do a thing like that. The doctor, however, was already convinced that he could. I went even further and suggested to the doctor that he recommend they be sent to the hospital in Beuthen for X-rays. It was for this reason that I had planned for them to see the doctor that day. I knew that by the time Rinke's trial began, their wounds and ribs would have healed, so I wanted to have a permanent record of their condition for use as evidence of Rinke's cruelty.

"I can recommend their transfer to Stalag VIII-B for a better diagnosis," the doctor said, but Rinke wanted to have them near him. "Or," the doctor continued, "I can have them X-rayed. I have to do one of the two, as their condition requires a more careful diagnosis than the one I can make with a stethoscope alone."

Rinke seemed to be willing to consent to anything just as long as his victims remained in E.757. He was afraid that if they were transferred to another camp or hospital they would talk about his treatment; if they stayed with him, he knew they would not say a word.

I obtained the X-ray plates the same week and let Dr. Tsapla keep them, with the understanding that they would be handed over upon request only to the protecting power. At the same time, I let Read know of the existence of these records through patients whom I persuaded the doctor to recommend for transfer into Stalag VIII-B in Teschen, instead of Stalag 344 in Lamsdorf, as would normally have been the case.

In this manner I established all the evidence possible for the trial that I hoped the protecting power would bring about. I acquainted Harry and George with the entire case and persuaded them not to hesitate to use my death and that of the sergeant major as further evidence of the truth in the indictment when the representatives of the protecting power arrived for the trial. Thus, I completed all the preparations within my power for a successful conclusion of the trial and waited patiently for the day when the captain of Rinke's company would discover the plot.

The weeks that followed seemed like the longest in my life. There were times when I regretted that I ever made the decision to indict the Nazis and wished the protecting power would refuse to take any steps. There were other times, however, when I felt that it was the best thing I had ever done in my life. I was a prisoner, like the rest in our camp and in other prison camps in Germany, where the only thing possible and reasonable for me seemed to be to take everything in stride in the hope that the end of the war would find me alive. Then the hardships, injustice, and humiliation while in the hands of the Nazis could be forgotten and life would begin again in a free and happy world. Whether now the Nazis called me a *Schweinehund*, whether they beat me for no reason, whether they made me beg for mercy only to receive more punishment were not really important at a time when even my life did not belong to me.

Yet I felt that although freedom needs more than one man in order to exist, dignity is something that a man can retain, even if he has to fight for it alone. I did not mind if I were killed. Being a prisoner, I should expect that to happen any time. But if I were to live a few days, or months, or years, I wanted to live them with the dignity that is due to every human being, prisoner or free.

God had given me the right to a dignified existence. It was my duty to keep this right with me. In fact, it was the only right I still possessed. Everything else I had when free — everything that meant something to me, all those I loved and cherished — were no longer there, but I still had the right to my honor as a man and my dignity as a human being. I didn't think being taken prisoner meant losing or giving up that right. It was all I had and all I could leave behind if I did not survive to see freedom. It was mine to keep under any circumstances.

That is what I wanted to make the Nazis understand. We were not free, we could not protect our lives, but we were still human beings and we deserved to be treated as such. We did not wish to live any other way.

Rinke, meanwhile, began a terrorizing crusade, using everything that came his way. To the mine director and foremen he gave the right to abuse and assault the prisoners, describing them as *Schweinehunde*, *Dreck*, or *Tiere* (manure, animals) and anything that would indicate that they were no longer human beings. He allowed the civilian German workers to keep the prisoners at work until "they dropped dead." He advocated and spread the fear propaganda among his guards, convincing them that we were part of the forces Goebbels had said would destroy Germany. To the Polish civilians in the area, he demonstrated Germany's might by beating anyone who passed him without a sign of respect. To the prisoners, he became more brutal than ever. Very soon he became the most feared Nazi in the area; the Germans were afraid to trust him, and the Polish civilians were afraid to disobey him.

But he became an excellent soldier in the eyes of his captain, and for Rinke that was all that mattered. He did not admire anyone else in the German army. He described the lieutenant of his platoon as a *Schreiber* (clerk) and the guards in the camp as "wet ducks." Rinke was everything in his own mind and in the minds of those who respected him, but he never convinced me or the sergeant major. Rinke knew this better than anyone else, and although he threatened to do almost everything to the two of us, each time he had the opportunity, he restrained himself from losing the lion's skin.

Our willingness to risk his hand tormented him to the limit, and Rinke concentrated his fury on the two of us, hoping to see that we both feared him, instead of despising him as we had so far. Alex and a few more of his guards feared that Rinke was going mad, and began to tell him that he was pulling the strings too far.

"I've been telling him every day," Alex insisted one day, "I've been telling him all the time, 'Stop aggravating the prisoners. You know they are desperate. They will kill you, Rinke. You can't tell what a man will do when he can't control himself anymore.'

"Everyone else is telling him the same thing," Alex continued. 'Rinke is crazy; he can't be normal and act that way.'"

The following week, when returning from the doctor, I decided to see the place where George was working. Rinke escorted me there. Two buildings had been put up already inside the fenced field. The prisoners, split in small groups, were working on the third building, while some of them had started to dig the foundations for the fourth. I looked for George but I couldn't find him.

"He's in the shed," one of the men working there told me.

Since no guards seemed to be around, the *Kommando Führer* went to search for them. He was so mad because of the guards' absence that he forgot he had left me alone. I slipped behind the first building in an attempt to reach the shed before Rinke did. I had a feeling something was going on in there, being surprised myself by the disappearance of the guards. I hid behind the corner, watching to see where Rinke was going, and as soon as I made sure that he was inclined to search anywhere but the shed, I breathed again. At the same time, I heard a light step behind me, and before I had turned around, a soft hand grabbed me by the arm.

"Where is George?" a thin voice sounded.

"Joan! What are you doing here? Have you gone out of your mind? For heaven's sake, leave this place before Rinke sees you."

"No! I won't go away. I came here to find George and I will find him."

"Right now, the *Kommando Führer* is looking all over the place for his guards," I told her. "He'll be here in a few minutes."

Joan was desperate; she did not care what happened. She wanted to see George, she added, as she burst into tears.

I didn't know what to do. I could not convince her to leave, and I could not find George without leaving her alone there. She had grabbed my arm and would not let me take a step unless I took her with me. It took considerable time to convince her that if she would hide herself inside the building I would go and find him.

I ran across the other corner and looked around. Rinke didn't seem to be anywhere. I jumped into the air raid trench. It was a good thing the trench was there, for I got almost three yards away from the shed without anyone seeing me. I heard voices inside. George's "*ja*," sounded repeatedly. I opened the door and rushed in.

What a surprise for me when I saw all four guards sitting around a small table playing cards. A pile of Reichsmarks were heaped in front of George, while a few were left in front of his opponents. Their rifles were thrown at the other end of the shed. A stove was burning in the middle of the room.

"*Wo sind die Kerle?*" a hard growling sounded outside.

All kinds of colors and expressions shaded the faces of the guards when they heard that voice, and a look of fear crystallized in their eyes. They all knew it was the *Kommando Führer*. Before they had time to get their rifles and think of any pretext, he was in. I was expecting his fury to burst on George and me, but instead, he let us go out and closed the door.

"Do you want to bet, George?" I said.

"On what?" George asked, curiously.

I led him to the building where Joan was waiting.

He took her in his arms, and held her — for how long, I don't remember. I noticed he was trembling. He seemed as if he had lost his voice. It was a great shock for him. They were both overjoyed, although they knew that if a German saw them they were both lost.

I left them alone and came back to the shed. A big fuss was going on inside. Rinke was beating his guards.

Twenty

WHEN I returned to the camp, I found Joe chatting with Harry in his room.

"You want to warm your hands?" Harry asked, moving away from the stove.

"No, thanks!" I said. "It's a bad habit, especially if you don't have enough coal to use the stove every day."

"These Krauts!" the sergeant major said. "We live in a coal mine, and yet they don't let us use any coal."

"They must be using it to make butter," I said, grinning.

George came to join our group after he finished washing his hands. He told Joe the news he had heard from Joan, as he handed me the German newspaper **Das Reich**.

"Joan gave it to me," he added.

In it was an editorial by Goebbels, which outlined the plan of the U.S. Secretary of the Treasury, Henry Morgenthau, Jr. The Morgenthau Plan was to completely eliminate German industrial power when the war ended, so that Germany could never rise again.

"What does the paper say?" Harry inquired.

"More lies to support Goebbels's propaganda," I commented. "The same old story. Tell a lie, and there will always be someone to believe it."

"Read it in English," Harry asked, seeing the article.

"Just what the Nazis deserve," he commented when I finished the editorial.

"I can't believe they gave Goebbels a thing like that to support his theory!" I remarked, exasperated that the American official had provided a plan that gave credence to Goebbels's ideas.

"At least we know that the free world is not blind to the extent of Nazi crimes," Joe added.

"Look at the Poles, Jews, innocent women and children they have murdered," George pointed out. "Look at what Rinke has been doing right here. Would you like to see him get away with it?" he asked.

"I was only thinking of the consequences this plan will have upon the prisoners in German hands," I said.

"What do you mean?" George inquired.

"The plan may seem to be the price that the Nazis should pay for their crimes against humanity," I said, "but it helps unite the Germans behind their leaders. They are convinced now that they have nothing to gain and everything to lose if they give up fighting."

"I don't see how that affects prisoners," George insisted.

"I'll tell you in a minute," I said. "But first, listen to what I was thinking about when I mentioned consequences a minute ago.

"So far," I continued, "many Germans have been opposed to the idea of fighting any more, hoping that only those responsible for these murders would have to account for them. The Nazis, on the other hand, who committed these crimes did so because they never thought that they were anything but heroes for murdering people. They were told that by Goebbels, and they believed it. Now they realize what they have been doing because Goebbels tells them that every single one of them is to blame, and that every single one of them is going to pay the same price unless they keep fighting. He tells them now that there is no mercy to expect in surrender or defeat, and that they've got to keep fighting to the last drop. Do you think they will stop murdering prisoners now, when they know that they are not going to live to have to account for them?"

"I don't quite see it," George remarked.

"In plain words," I added, "the Germans will either keep fighting until they are dead or commit suicide if they know they are going to be captured. Meanwhile, they avenge themselves on the prisoners, because Goebbels tells them that the prisoners are part of those forces that are going to destroy them."

George held his head between his arms. Joe was busy curling his moustache.

"Anyone want some tea?" Harry asked.

"I'll get it," I said to Harry. "See if you can warm up some water."

There was enough fire to warm the water, and Harry threw some coal into the stove. "There goes the last bit of dust," he remarked.

I got up to stretch my legs for a few minutes, intending to walk into my room and get the tea leaves. It was just starting to get dark outside. The lights around the perimeter of the camp and in the courtyard were lit. As I turned away from the window, I saw Rinke rushing out of his office to welcome his captain, who was ready to dismount from his motorcycle. He stepped into Rinke's office. A few seconds later, a German *Unteroffizier* came out of the office, heading for my room. I walked over with Joe to see what he wanted.

"The captain wants to see you," he said. "The sergeant major must go, too!" he added. "Get your new uniform on," he advised, and seeing that we were taking our time, he cautioned that we had better get there as fast as we could.

"Well!" I said to Joe, "I guess this is it!"

Joe tried to smile, while he buttoned his coat.

"Say your prayers," I said. "We don't have much time."

"Ready?" the German *Unteroffizier* asked.

We left the room with the German walking behind.

"The captain is waiting for you in there," the guard said, when we came into the courtyard, pointing at the *Kommando Führer's* office. He did not follow us. Instead, he started pacing back and forth in the courtyard.

I opened the door and walked in. Joe followed behind. Rinke was standing at the other side of the large desk in the middle of the room.

The captain was sitting in front near the desk with his back against the wall, facing the courtyard.

"Close the door," he ordered Rinke, who hastened to obey. The captain remained silent for a few seconds, then he asked in his distinct metallic voice, "I hear you have accused the German army of atrocities," he said, slowly but clearly.

"We have only reported what Rinke did," I said calmly, thinking that the captain had other questions to ask. I was thrown off balance by the captain's immediate charge.

"My Rinke?!" he screamed. "You dared accuse my Rinke? Dogs!" he roared. He opened the holster and pulled out his pistol, pushed a bullet in and started to say what Joe and I had already expected to hear.

"*Ich werde euch beide erschiessen!* (I am going to shoot both of you!)"

"You!" he yelled, pointing at Joe. "You dirty little liar. I am going to hang you!"

Joe began to curl his moustache. Rinke also loaded his pistol. Inside the tension-packed room, I said my last prayer. Then I felt my knees weakening. A cold sweat chilled my body.

"We've done our duty," I said, as calmly as I could.

"You stinking liars!" the frenzied Nazi screamed with rage. "Shooting you is not enough. I'll hang you! I'll hang both of you!"

I did not want him to think that I expected mercy. I wanted him to know that we had counted on the consequences. I felt that this was the last chance I had to tell the things that I wanted the court to hear someday, if I survived.

"You damned criminals!" I began, without waiting for his fury to abate. "Because you can kill me, you think you can make me say that I am wrong. But you are not going to. Because I am right, like the cause I am fighting for. You can hang me, captain! But that won't save you. Millions of free men will be coming after you, until they bring you and every other Nazi criminal to justice. You've only got a few days more than me. I am dying as a soldier, captain, but you'll be dying as a criminal!"

I don't exactly remember what the captain did when I finished; I was too confused. All I knew was that it was my last chance to tell a Nazi why I was not afraid of dying, why I was fighting him, and above all my conviction that he could not win. All I expected was to see the captain fire his pistol, and with such a prospect in mind I threw overboard every sense of reason and thought. I was not thinking. I was merely saying something the Nazis had made me learn.

Why I was spared is something I shall never know. All I recall is that I was glad when later on, outside, the cold breeze hit smoothly on my face with a refreshing touch of life. I was still alive, and it was real.

It was obvious that Rinke did not understand either why the captain had spared us. Hearing him yell at me and Joe, calling us liars, Rinke believed that his own behavior was more justified now than before, and from that day on, there was nothing that could stop Rinke from showing what he really was.

"Why do you think the captain didn't shoot us last night?" Joe asked me the following morning.

"I don't know," I answered briefly. "Maybe he was afraid that the protecting power would consider it proof of their guilt."

"I think the captain is trying to throw the blame on Rinke," Joe said suddenly.

"Maybe," I said. "I'm glad he didn't shoot me. It would be awfully cold under this ground here."

"I'm serious," Joe interrupted. "What do you think?"

"I'm not thinking of anything," I kept teasing Joe. "I wouldn't have said what I did to the captain last night if I had been thinking."

Joe began to curl his moustache. "All right," he said finally. "You don't want to talk about it. Let's forget it, then."

Harry showed up at the door of the *Sanitäter's* room.

"You fellows want some hot tea?" he asked.

Joe and I walked in at Harry's suggestion. "Where did you get the coal?" I asked him.

"One of the men brought it in, hidden in his pockets," he answered. "Just enough to boil the water."

Joe stood by the stove sunk in deep thought. "I think the captain is chickening out," he remarked suddenly, as if he had reached the end of his dream.

"So much worse," I contended. "It gives Rinke the opportunity to go wild, feeling he is the only one who knows how to handle prisoners."

Alex walked in, upset over some incident we had not seen.

"I've just been arguing with Rinke," he said in disgust. "That stupid bricklayer; he thinks the captain gave him the right to do as he pleases.

I've spent three years at the front," Alex continued. "That *Verfluchte Sau* stuck his feet out of the train and got frostbite, to avoid going to the front, and he gives me hell because I slept during the two hours I was off duty.

"I'm telling you," Alex kept shouting, energized by his own words, "I'm telling you that man is crazy. *Mann! Mann!*" he went on, "*die verfluchte Sau!*"

I thought Alex was only pleading for sympathy, as I was used to seeing Germans wipe their tears on my handkerchief many times since Rinke had taken over command of our labor detachment. Joe gave him a cigarette.

"He is after you," Alex said to me, while trying to light the cigarette.

"He's been after me since he came to Udetfeld," I said. "I'm still alive and probably will be, for quite some time yet," I added. "Rinke has just been talking again."

Alex seemed surprised that his news did not cause me any concern.

"How come you are only a private?" he asked with some suspicion, thinking I was a disguised officer.

For a minute I did not know what to say. Any suspicion that I was lying about my rank would give Rinke the first opportunity to prosecute me — something he had been anxiously waiting for. I did not trust Alex to keep any suspicion to himself.

"To be an officer in the Greek army, you've got to go to a military academy," I said finally. "I didn't go there."

"How come you are not a corporal or a sergeant?" Alex persisted.

His interrogation aggravated me. "I didn't know I'd be a war prisoner in Germany," I said emphatically, hoping to convince him that I was not disguising my rank.

Fortunately, George came in, returning from the day shift.

"Take him out of here," I told George. "George wants to play cards with you," I told the German.

He followed George outside at his suggestion that he wanted him to do something for Joan.

"They won't even let you drink a cup of tea quietly," Joe remarked.

During the evening roll call, Rinke came in to suprvise the counting.

"The mine director has complained," he said to me, "that the prisoners in the day shift have been late in getting down to the mine."

"How late?" I asked.

"*Na!*" Rinke started to mumble, "the other day they were two minutes late."

"That was the day you went to the mine with them, wasn't it?" I asked.

"*Ja!*" Rinke answered.

"How come, when the prisoners were there a half hour ahead of time, the mine director complained they were two minutes late?" I asked, suspecting Rinke was making up a story of his own.

"They will be awakened at four in the morning from now on instead of five," he said, brushing my question aside.

Joe understood most of the argument, but waited for me to handle it.

For a minute I thought of the reaction of the prisoners who could not be in bed until midnight and would have to be up again at four.

"Why don't you keep them up all night?" I asked Rinke.

Rinke jumped a few steps toward me, drawing his bayonet. Seeing the rest of the prisoners closing in to cover me, he changed his mind and contented himself with threats instead.

"*Wart'e mal! Wart'e mal!* (Just wait!)" he growled. Then, as if he really had discovered a brilliant method to dispose of me, he grinned for a few seconds and continued.

"I am going to nail you inside a coffin and saw you in half. Wait until I get the coffin ready . . . *mein Lieber!* I'll show you."

His threat gave me a sudden chill, like the cold wind that blew from the east that time of the year.

"Is there anything else you want?" Joe asked Rinke angrily.

Rinke ignored him.

"Dismissed!" Joe ordered the men teetering on the frozen earth. Immediately, Rinke reacted as if he was awakened from a dream. George came to join me.

"What was Rinke shouting about?" he asked.

I began to walk with George and Joe back in the billet. "He wants the men to get up at four in the morning," I explained to George. "It won't hurt your group," I added, "but it will hurt those working in the mine. I'd just like to see him try," I said to George. "I'll break his other leg, too."

One of the men came near, showing me a long knife he was hiding under his coat.

"I am willing to lose my life," he offered, "if you just let me cut Rinke to pieces."

I patted him on the shoulder, grinning. "He'll get paid when his turn comes," I said.

Rinke did not construct the coffin for me as he had threatened. In his frenzy to behave like a Nazi, he decided to make one grave for all of us. He assigned one of the rooms in the guards' quarters as an ammunition depot. In there he stored piles of bullets, machine-guns, and hand grenades, enough to equip a regiment instead of just the platoon he commanded. Around the perimeter of the camp he built concrete fortresses with narrow ring-shaped openings facing the camp. He obtained more men as reinforcements for the garrison of the labor detachment, and he toured the local area, arousing every Nazi sympathizer against the enemies of Nazi Germany, among whom he emphasized were the prisoners in "Hell Dive" — with me and Joe occupying the number-one spot. Many Nazi sympathizers believed his sermons, and I found myself in a more dangerous position when dealing with them than in my fight with Rinke himself. One of these Nazis, perhaps the most dangerous one, was the mine director. Others who were dangerous to the prisoners, rather than me, were the mine foremen and workers, including quite a few of the guards in the labor detachment.

At the same time, however, we obtained through his behavior the sympathy and esteem of the Polish population in the area, who offered to supply us with guns and ammunition through their underground organization to defend ourselves in case Rinke went through with his intended mass murder.

After considerable debate on the matter with Joe, George, and the noncommissioned officers among the other prisoners, we decided not to take advantage of this offer. The storage of weapons inside the camp was impossible under the precautions Rinke and his captain had already taken. Furthermore, it would have disastrous results for other prisoners in German hands. If these arms were to be successfully used and at the right moment, it required every prisoner to undergo a thorough training inside the barbed wire and also complete secrecy under the watchful Nazi eye — both of which were appealing but nearly impossible. Joe called me outside, after hearing of this offer of arms, indicating to the rest that he wanted to talk to me alone.

"So far," Joe said, "Rinke blames the necessity for this treatment of prisoners on you and me. His captain justifies this and endorses his policies. If we asked to be replaced, he would either have to treat the prisoners better than he is doing now or take the blame himself, since we would no longer be here to have the blame thrown on us."

I could not see what difference our replacement would make on Rinke's behavior, as I felt certain Rinke would find somebody else to accuse. Nevertheless, I consented to Joe's suggestion and we both walked into Rinke's office.

Rinke seemed surprised by our visit, but I soon told him the reason.

"That's what I've been trying to do for the last two months," he said in desperation, "but no one wants to take your place. Everyone wants to stay away from this labor detachment. I'd do anything to get rid of you," he contended.

"Will you send a message to Read?" I asked.

"I'll be only too glad," Rinke hastened to affirm.

I took a piece of paper and wrote a few lines to Read.

"The sergeant major and I," I wrote, "request this replacement in the interest of safety and the welfare of our fellow prisoners...." Rinke sent the message out the same evening.

Joe and I walked back into the camp. Very soon, the men learned of our decision and gathered in our room to find out if it was true. Never in the three and a half years I had spent in a prisoner of war camp, did I expect the other prisoners to react the way they did that night when they heard us confirm the news.

"Go back to your rooms and get some sleep," Joe suggested, trying to break up the crowd.

"We're not going anywhere," somebody shouted, "until you tell us that you're going to stay."

I helped Joe break up the gathering, pretending that I was angry with their request, although in my heart I knew that the best place for me and Joe was right there with them. Their outspoken reaction to the news was a surprise to both of us — especially for me, remembering that the reason I decided to leave the sugar mill in Klettendorf almost a year ago was so that I could help protect other Greek prisoners.

We succeeded in sending them out of the room, but they must have gathered again in one of the other rooms in the billet, because I didn't see them outside when Joe and I walked over to the *Sanitäter's* room to chat with Harry.

I told him of our decision.

"If you think it is the best thing to do," Harry agreed, "I can't complain."

The door of the room opened and one of the noncommissioned officers showed himself in with a couple of the other prisoners.

"We just had a vote," he said with emotion, "to see how many men want to make you stay, and how many want to let you go as you have decided.

"I am speaking for every prisoner in this camp," he went on, "when I say that we are not going to let you go.

"We know," he continued, bowing his head, "that you were trying to help us when you decided to leave, but I came here to tell you that we are willing to die with you if you stay here. You are and have been our leaders through the worst of circumstances. We want you to know that we don't care what happens so long as you stay with us."

I stood with my back against the top bunk, leaning with my elbow on the bed and biting my fingers from embarrassment. Joe was curling his moustache.

I don't know if any other day in my life has been happier. I don't recall any other time when I felt as I did that cold winter evening, when, locked inside the barbed-wire fence, I heard from others that my presence there had a meaning and that my life, worthless to me, was worth something to others.

They were not the only ones, however, who wanted us to stay. Read wanted the same thing. In his answer to our request, he wrote that he had failed completely to induce anyone else to become the representing agent for E.757, as the news of Rinke's behavior had reached Stalag VIII-B, and our labor detachment was known as the "Hell Dive" to the prisoners in the central camp.

I felt glad about Read's unfavorable reply, as did Joe and our men, who especially welcomed Read's letter as the best news of the year. Rinke was the only one to be disappointed; he had hoped in our absence that he could satisfy much more easily his sadistic hunger at the expense of the prisoners.

Twenty-One

MEANWHILE, Rinke's trial seemed on its way to becoming a reality. The lieutenant of Rinke's company, whom Rinke usually referred to as "**Der Schreiber**," came to the camp and called me in the office to verify our charges against "the detaining power," and to draw up the indictment for the trial.

Rinke did not comprehend the reason for the lieutenant's inquiry. It seemed beyond his understanding that he was about to be taken into court, to account for his actions to German authorities, when he had gone out of his way to safeguard and promote his country's interests along the lines that the **Führer** had described.

He did not for a moment suspect that the lieutenant was doing something more than just writing. The lieutenant always liked to write, he commented to his guards. He could not, however, get himself used to the lieutenant's idea of recording my statements. He kept telling the officer that they were plain lies and inventions of mine. He never gave authority, he claimed, to any air force crew to use the prisoners to load bombs; he never touched the two escapees. He insisted that they simply fell down while walking and hurt themselves. He claimed that he behaved like nothing less than an angel in contrast to my behavior and that of the other "beasts" inside the barbed-wire fence.

At each one of my charges he jumped from his seat trying to hit me, and then claimed that he had never touched the end of my coat, in spite of the fact that he was repeating in the lieutenant's presence the very thing he was trying to deny. The lieutenant became embarrassed at Rinke's display and requested that he refrain from such behavior. "Please, not in my presence," he told Rinke, covering his face to avoid the spectacle of fist fights.

"Why, you liar," Rinke shouted at me, "even the escapees themselves admitted that I never laid hands on them. Bring them here!" he ordered one of his guards.

"That won't be necessary," the lieutenant interrupted, and continued to record my statements.

When he finished, he gave me the indictment. I read through each of the counts he had recorded.

"Please sign here," he indicated.

I signed, and left the office to wait outside. The lieutenant also left a few minutes later. Rinke came to the door, relieved to see him go. He continued to believe that as long as his captain agreed with him, he had nothing to worry about.

"Maybe I should lock the lieutenant in with the prisoners!" he commented to his guards as soon as the officer was out of sight. "He seems to enjoy their company," he remarked, laughing at his sarcasm.

Although the first step toward the trial had been taken, I was not completely satisfied with the results. The fact that the lieutenant was sent to draw the indictment meant that Rinke was the only defendant in the case, and that the captain was freeing himself from the responsibility for Rinke's acts. I expected that an officer of equal or higher rank than the captain would have been sent, as I did not believe that the lieutenant had the authority to indict his own commanding officer. Nevertheless, it was a definite step toward the establishment of justice, and I contented myself with the day's developments. I planned to disclose the captain's share in court. I assumed that when Rinke came to realize that he was betrayed by his captain, he would not hesitate to wrap him in the same responsibility by producing the orders he had received from the captain to act the way he did.

Joe seemed to disagree with my conclusions and hopes. "You can't trust the Germans," he commented. "They may be doing all this just to pull the wool over the eyes of the protecting power."

"Maybe!" I concluded. "Let's hope not."

"Tasos!" Joe whispered while I was seated at my desk writing a letter home, a few minutes later. I walked near his bed, curious to see what he wanted to tell me.

"I received a peculiar letter from my sister," he said. "It is a cryptographic letter. I think I can make out what it says. I've been trying for hours to read it. Listen!"

He started to read to me. I listened carefully, but it did not make sense. I told him to go back to sleep and let me write a letter home in peace for a change.

Joe insisted: "I thought it made no sense, too, in the beginning. But the more I read it the more I think she is trying to tell me that Greece is liberated. Look!"

He showed me the letter, but seeing that I did not go beyond the first two lines he started to read it aloud.

"It's funny," I said, "the German newspapers never admitted that there was any landing in Greece. Well, part of the family at least are free from the Nazis. I wonder how they are," I said. "The last letter I had from home was dated May 1943. I have never received another since I was brought to Germany."

"They are probably all right," Joe remarked.

I was getting ready to finish my letter when Rinke walked unexpectedly into the room. He showed me the sick register and pointed at the POW number, 32201. It was George Vardakos, the prisoner who had undergone the operation in Breslau the year before.

"That number does not need to see the doctor," Rinke growled. "He goes to the mine with the rest of the shift."

I suspected that Rinke was looking for an excuse for trouble, so I refrained from any argument. Joe sent him out of the room.

"*Raus!*" he shouted at Rinke in his limited German. "*Jetzt alle schlafen!* (everyone is asleep!)"

I lay on my bed late that night realizing that for the first time since I was interned in a German prison camp, I felt my nerves relieved from tension and strain. Exhausted as I was, I soon went to sleep, content that Rinke would shortly have to account for every act of cruelty he had committed. I did not know that the worst was yet to come.

I felt no bayonet on my back at five in the morning, although I did hear the morning crew getting ready for work, so I went back to sleep. When I finally woke up, it was eight o'clock. I went into the washroom and took a cold shower. I was very much surprised when I walked outside to find George Vardakos digging a hole in the frozen courtyard in front of Rinke's office.

"Rinke put me to work here," George informed me, crying from anger. "I'll break his neck when he shows up again."

I had no doubt George was going to do exactly as he threatened. I tried to convince him that he could not do a thing to Rinke without risking the lives of all the other prisoners.

"I'm trying to control myself," George assured me, "but I can't stand him. I don't want to do anything crazy."

"What does he have against you?" I asked. "He came into my room last night and told me that you shouldn't see the doctor. You haven't done anything foolish again, have you?" I asked him, thinking of an incident in Lamsdorf when George had beaten up a German civilian with a shovel.

"*He* started everything," George said of Rinke, without explaining what had taken place.

I asked the *Sanitäter* to get all the sick ready and told George Vardakos to line up with the rest. Rinke watched from the window of his office, but did not make any effort to protest George's visit to the doctor. The guard, Alex, and *Unteroffizier* Hans were detailed to take the prisoners there. Seeing George, Hans — The Rat — started to swear at him, and attempted to push him out of the line.

"*Du verfluchter Schweinehund!*" he shouted. "You don't need to see the doctor." George raised his fist and hit the German on the chin, then opened his shirt and thrust his chest forward. "Come on!" he said. "Do it!"

He must have hit the *Unteroffizier* very hard, because the German fell back quite a few steps, lost balance, and dropped with his back on the ground. Alex came to his rescue and started to hit George on the head with the butt of his pistol, hard enough to cause him to grimace as if he were being slain. I grabbed Alex's arm and pulled him away from George.

Rinke raced outside from his office, pale from fury and shaking, embarrassed because he had no choice but to act. I thought he was going to shoot George, as I heard the click of his pistol, but although he tried to get himself angry enough to do it, he contented himself with shouts and yells instead, to the amazement of everyone, including his guards. When George returned from the doctor later at noon, Rinke locked him in jail in spite of the doctor's recommendation that his condition was grave enough to necessitate his return to Lamsdorf.

In spite of the sentry's objections that I could not see Rinke until he consented to let me in his office, I went inside as soon as I found out George was in jail, and told Rinke to let him out.

"If the doctor recommends him to the hospital," I said, "that is where he is going. Not to jail. You can't jail a sick man," I threatened. "I am holding you responsible for anything that happens to that prisoner." He consented finally to release George, but insisted that he would not send him to the hospital.

"You'd better," I threatened again, while I was leaving his office to return to the fenced compound.

I took a casual walk around the camp, but the cold weather soon drove me back into the billet. Harry came into my room to find out what Rinke intended to do with the sick on this week's list.

"Never mind what he intends to do," I remarked abruptly. "They are going to the doctor this time, like any other Tuesday."

"Are you coming along?" Harry inquired.

"Yes!" I answered. "I want to see the men on the construction job on our way. Anyway, it's only Thursday! There are plenty of other things to worry about before Tuesday is here."

Harry was silent for a few minutes, trying to get his thoughts together. "I don't understand," he said finally, "why there have been so many accidents lately in the mine. Every hour somebody is brought back either with his hands or legs hurt. They just don't seem like accidents," Harry concluded.

"I know," I said, my voice reflecting helplessness, "and so does the *Kommando Führer*. Very soon somebody will lose control of himself and bump him off. You'd better get ready to expect the worst at any time."

Joe returned from the mine while I was still talking with Harry.

"Dirty rats!" he exclaimed. "They all behaved like innocent lambs when they saw me down in the pit. No one admitted he ever laid hands on a prisoner. It is always the other fellow who does everything; never the one you talk to. Nothing but a bunch of low-rate criminals that don't have guts enough to admit their own doings, but blame it on someone else."

George Karaolanis came into the room with the usual grin on his face that indicated he had received a letter from Joan. Before he had a chance to say anything, I told him that I could not read his letter until late at night, and George contented himself with that.

"It looks like you've found yourself a job!" Joe remarked.

"It pays to do things for people," I added, grinning, "especially if they are in love."

I sat at my desk and began to record some of the day's experiences in my diary. I did not believe I would live long enough to write anything different from what each day had brought so far, but somehow I wanted to put down the things I saw happen, the way I felt seeing the Nazis torture my friends while I had to remain helpless to restrain their cruelty. I wanted to write about the times I had wished I had spared myself the life of a war prisoner by refusing to accept the enemy hand of rescue the day the *Hereward* was sunk. I wanted to leave behind me something more than my prisoner-of-war number engraved on a flat piece of lead; something that would tell others why I chose to fight Rinke instead of doing what he wanted; something that would lead others to understand why a young farm boy from a rocky island in the Mediterranean Sea believed he had a role to play in this war against Hitler's hordes, which the *Führer* had proclaimed to have released in an effort to "civilize" the otherwise "uncultured" world.

Harry and Joe went over to the *Sanitäter's* room to warm their hands at the stove and make some tea. I left the billet to join them an hour later.

On my way, I stopped for a minute to inspect something odd near the entrance of the coal-mine yard. It looked like three prisoners walking together with a German guard behind them, but as they came closer, I realized the two were carrying a third prisoner on their shoulders. His feet were hanging loose and his head was bent forward, while the two men carrying him were holding his arms over their shoulders to keep him straight.

I told the sentry at the gate to let me out. Rinke came hurriedly out of his office to find out why the sentry had allowed me into the courtyard when he had forbidden anyone to do so without first consulting him.

"But *Herr Kommando Führer,*" the guard protested, frightened, "I couldn't come to your office without leaving the gate."

"*Verflucht!*" Rinke growled at the guard, raising his fist. "You want to argue with me?"

The three prisoners had entered the courtyard as Rinke's fist landed on the sentry's face. The man they were carrying was Peter, one of the prisoners who had arrived from Lamsdorf in September — or rather, it looked like him from where I was standing. I could not see his face, for his head was bent against his body. His clothes were soaked with blood. A number of open wounds on his head were still bleeding, leaving a red trace on the frozen courtyard. I raised Peter's head, but it fell forward again as I removed my hand. He still had a pulse.

Rinke left the sentry alone and came to see the prisoner. At the sight of blood, he stepped back suddenly, covering his eyes with his arm, and rushed into his office, closing the door behind him. I was quite surprised with his reaction.

Joe and the *Sanitäter* were already outside. Harry helped carry Peter in, while Joe and I walked into Rinke's office. Rinke suspected that we did not want to see him for a casual argument. He braced himself and then tried to ask calmly the reason for our presence in his office.

"I want this case investigated," I said, "and the German who beat the prisoner punished. And you are the one who is going to see that my request is carried out."

"Me?" Rinke asked with surprise. "Why me? I didn't have anything to do with that!"

"No?" I said. "We'll see about that."

Rinke laughed. "Maybe that is what I should do with you," he said. "You deserve this treatment more than anyone else."

"I am telling you for the last time," I said. "I am holding you responsible for this, and you are the one I am going to report to the protecting power."

Rinke continued to laugh. He couldn't see how anyone could bring him to justice, and the idea of reporting him to the protecting power seemed to be a very amusing threat. He laughed with indifference.

Joe leaned forward with his fist on the table. "If you don't get the man responsible for this," he said emphatically, "I am going to make you pay for every drop of blood this man has lost."

"No one can make me pay for anything," Rinke shouted suddenly, as if the sergeant major's threat had touched a soft spot in his immune conscience. "I am Hitler. I am Germany. I do as I please."

"We'll see about that," I said, and left his office with Joe leading the way.

We walked together into the *Sanitäter's* room where Harry was trying to dress Peter's wounds. We could not learn what actually had taken place until Peter came to his senses and told us. I suspected that some civilians probably found him alone in the mine and tried to kill him. Joe suspected something similar, but no one for the moment believed that the German who did this was the guard Alex, who only a few days before had been expressing his sympathy and concern over the treatment that the prisoners were receiving in the hands of Rinke.

Peter eventually began to regain consciousness. I did not ask him anything until late at night, when he was able to stand on his feet and walk to his billet. I found him lying on his bed. He raised his head when he saw me enter.

"Hi, Peter," I said smiling. "Feeling any better?"

"I came awful close," Peter remarked. "I hit him a few times," he continued, "but he was armed, and kept hitting me on the head with his pistol. There were five," Peter went on raising his voice, "five against one. Can you imagine that? Five Germans against an unarmed prisoner?" he asked, trying to get up from his bed.

"Now, take it easy," I warned him. "There are no Germans in here anymore," I said, trying to calm him down. "You just stay in your bed and wait until those wounds disappear. Nobody is going to hurt you again."

"I am not going to work anymore," he insisted, with the same agitation. "I tell you," he started shouting. "I am not going to. I don't care if they shoot me. I am not afraid to die. I won't let them treat me like an animal. I am not a dog, I am a man. I told them this afternoon," Peter kept shouting, "that is why they tried to kill me. I told them I didn't want to work for a *Schweinehund* like Hitler."

"Take it easy!" I said again. Then patting his arm I added, "You better take care of those cuts first. I'll see that you are sent to the hospital in Lamsdorf."

I left him somewhat calmer and headed for the door, but as soon as I stepped outside I saw Rinke heading for the billet, accompanied by Alex and The Rat. I closed the door behind me and stood in front of the steps waiting. He slowed his march as soon as he realized there was going to be trouble if he made his way into the room.

"I want to see the man that was brought in this afternoon," he said fiercely.

"You had better ask the *Sanitäter* first," I suggested. "I don't think he will agree with you."

"*Na, los!*" Rinke shouted. "I'll show that *Schweinehund* how to call our *Führer* names again," he growled, while making a step forward to indicate that he was going up the stairs.

I didn't move to let him pass. I kept standing there, waiting for Rinke to make another move.

"*Machen Sie mal Platz!* (Make way!)" Rinke shouted, drawing his pistol from its holster.

I didn't say anything to this new threat; I just looked him straight in the eyes.

"I will attend to him tomorrow," he finally conceded. "I'll fix you, too," he growled, waving his finger in front of my face. "Don't think I am going to let you get away with this," he warned while he turned back with his bodyguards, who were more surprised over Rinke's retreat than I.

I was glad that he had refrained from making any more trouble for the day. Rinke seemed to have been satisfied with Alex's beating of Peter, and considered unnecessary any further intervention on his part.

He was satisfied with the proof furnished by the bleeding prisoner that the other Germans shared his sentiments toward the prisoners, and he was pleased to see that his instigation of the guards and civilians against the prisoners in the camp had begun to bear results. This day was one of Rinke's happiest, one he had thoroughly enjoyed. Things could not have gone any better than they had that afternoon; it was a job well done. Rinke would cite his guard Alex for special mention to the captain for the afternoon's feat and would congratulate the mine director for the cooperation of those civilians who had taken part in the beating.

There would be plenty of time for Rinke to do the same in the morning, when he expected to find the prisoner in bed while his shift was getting ready to leave for work. Rinke would have a real excuse for beating him then, especially if the prisoner refused his order for work. That was why he called it a day and left without going up the steps.

Instead of walking back to my room, I took a stroll around the camp. The cold air was refreshing, and the quiet night seemed a contrast to the world inside me. George Karaolanis came out and joined me for a few minutes.

"When are you going to read me the letter?" he asked.

"Oh, the letter!" I said. "Let's see what it says."

I walked inside to read Joan's letter and write an answer for George. Hers was passionate, sincere, and truthful; she had already furnished astonishing proof of her devotion and love for George in risking her life to see him. George was risking very little. She was the one to sneak through the barbed wire under the watchful eyes of the guards, just to spend a few hours with him. She was the one who had to avoid suspicions for her weekly leaves from the air force post in Udetfeld. Every mile, every turn, every stop on her way to "Hell Dive," Joan had to conceal the purpose of her trip, for one little mistake could end her life and her dream of happiness with George. Her unselfish behavior was unique, and perhaps I consented to do the letter-writing for George because of my own admiration and regard for her.

It was nearly midnight when I finished writing George's letter. The Germans would soon bar the doors. I left his room and walked to the other end of the billet where Joe and I bunked. Joe suspected where I had been, but didn't ask any questions. I picked up my towel and soap and headed for the washroom.

"I don't see how you can bear it!" Joe remarked.

"Just stand there and watch," I said.

"No, thanks," he answered. "It's cold enough as it is. I get the jitters just thinking of you lying on the ice."

I laughed. "I didn't know my sergeant major was afraid of water," I said and walked inside the washroom. The long steel water basin was covered with ice. I kept knocking one of the taps with a hammer until finally water actually started to flow. I lay underneath it, my back against the ice, which covered the bottom and sides of the water basin. The melting ice under the heat of my body made me slide to the other end of the basin, and I found myself sliding down to the same end each time I removed my hand from the long water pipe alongside, which I was using as a brake.

The Austrian *Unteroffizier* appeared at the entrance to the room, and the spectacle caused him to turn around and shut the door; I heard him swear at my idea of taking an ice bath.

When I finished, I went back to the room and dressed in pajamas, which I had just received from a young lady in England. "I have become," she wrote me, "your next of kin through the International Red Cross and I have already sent you some parcels with clothing and cigarettes. . . . Please, let me know just what you need."

The straw on my bed was worn out completely. I could feel the boards of the ladder-type bed frame denting my bones. I was usually allowed to rest on this bed for three and a half hours each night, but I very seldom managed to sleep. Too many things were on my mind.

Since the lieutenant had drawn up the indictment against Rinke, nothing had developed to guarantee that the trial I had sought for him and his captain was going to materialize. So far, Rinke's opinion seemed the correct guess as to the fate of the trial: he had all the aces; I had none.

Whenever the other prisoners looked to me for help, without realizing that I was as much a victim as they, I felt a bitter remorse over this ironic situation. I could not convince them that I had no more rights than they did, that I was a prisoner like them, and that the fact that I was fighting the Nazis did not necessarily guarantee a redemption from the nightmare under which we were living.

To them it seemed that I had brought some hope, and the fact that we were all prisoners was drowned in their desire for a dignified treatment and an equal amount of respect from the enemy.

Many times I believed that they gave me the courage to defy the Nazis, feeling that it was their cause I was fighting for. Each time I had to face Rinke, his captain, the mine director, or any other Nazi, I was thinking of them — how they would feel if they knew I was afraid, and what was going to happen to them if the Nazis carried out their threats.

So, when the men worked, I tried to find ways to remove them from this enforced labor. When they played, I tried to keep the shadow of Nazi terror underneath my own. When they slept, I spent my time thinking of a way to spare them from the fate that Rinke had promised. Rinke's defeat seemed the only possible way.

So far he had succeeded in convincing himself and everyone else outside the barbed wire that there was no penalty for crimes committed against prisoners. His own punishment, if effected, would kill this doctrine, and scare the criminal intentions of those Nazis who believed in his theory. With Rinke out of the way, the other Nazis would be nothing but a group of confused men suffering the effects of their own deception about justice and penalty. For, if justice prevailed right there, where Rinke believed it couldn't, its impact would be strong enough to render harmless the other members of his gang.

With these thoughts in mind, I turned on my side and tried to sleep, waiting for the morning, when I would learn of new surprises and hardships.

The steps of The Rat coming to unlock the doors woke me up. It was already five in the morning; Joe was still asleep. The morning shift crew was told to be ready for work. I got dressed and rushed to the billet where Peter was staying. I suspected that Rinke would be there, seeking an excuse to beat him up.

I found him in the billet with his bayonet ready. He was asking Peter to repeat the phrase he had used the preceding day to describe the *Führer*.

"Leave the prisoner alone!" I yelled, as I stepped inside. Rinke turned in my direction with surprise at my order, then turned his attention to Peter again, ready to hit him with the bayonet if he repeated the phrase.

"I told you to leave the prisoner alone," I repeated, more emphatically this time, walking toward him.

He hesitated for a moment, as if my threat had made him change his intentions. "I'll attend to him later," he promised. Then, heading for the exit, he asked, "Is the day shift ready for work?"

"*Die Leute sind schon alle fertig, Herr Kommando Führer* (They are all ready)," a guard shouted at the door. Rinke hurried to take them into the mine, and in his haste to get them there in time, he gave up the idea of beating Peter. I was relieved later in the day to see that he must have abandoned his intentions completely and considered the incident closed.

In the afternoon, The Rat brought in some mail — the only mail we had received that month. One letter was for me, from my relatives in the United States. I also opened the letter at the bottom of the bundle, which showed the return address of Stalag VIII-B. It said that further Red Cross supplies were not likely to arrive, indicating that we would have to spend the remaining time until the end of the war living on German rations alone.

For a long while I suspected that part of our German rations were used by the women in the mine kitchen to feed the guards. There was no way to check on this, except by letting one of our men work in the same kitchen. Rinke had refused to let any prisoners work there the first time I had brought up this request, claiming he did not have any guards to spare. I did not press my claim any further, as we depended mainly on Red Cross food, which at that time was sufficient. But now that we were left to depend on German rations entirely, the matter seemed quite serious. I gave instructions to Polland during our weekly meeting to check on this suspected racket and inform me of his findings at our next meeting.

Every man in the camp seemed quite disheartened over the news that we were not likely to receive any more Red Cross food. I tried to assure them that the war was nearly at an end, and that in view of the approaching day of freedom, a little more hardship on our part did not matter much. They had their own doubts about the war's duration, but shared for the moment my feeling and conviction for its timely end.

I was not so much concerned with the coming days of starvation as I was with Rinke's promise that he would execute every one of us if he saw a single chance for freedom within our reach. He had already gathered all he needed for the job: 30 guards, armed with machine-guns, hand grenades, and a stockroom of ammunition. Cement fortresses he had constructed were to provide protection for his army during the task. What seemed worse still was the fact that he had created amongst the other Germans the incentive for such an act. Alex was proof.

Although I could doubt the loyalty of a number of his guards, there were many who would not hesitate to follow his orders when the time came. Rinke knew of this divided feeling among the members of his garrison and had already placed the doubtful ones under the close surveillance of those he considered loyal.

These "unloyal" guards promised me and Joe complete cooperation in the event he carried out his threats, and we laid a plan to seize the forts and ammunition depot. This was intended as a desperation move, however, for if there was the slightest chance to escape the fate that Rinke had planned for us, without risking anyone's life, Joe and I were willing to take that chance. At that time, however, our plan seemed reasonable, as it eliminated the necessity of storing arms inside the camp, where they might be found and thus betray our objective, and at the same time it made them available to us when the critical hour arrived. Our aim was to play it safe, rather than engage in any glorifying or history-making adventure.

While we were thus prepared for the ultimate trend of events, we were in no way ready to meet the current developments in the camp. Rinke was out to get Joe and me in a manner than would raise very little doubt in anyone's mind that an assault by the prisoners necessitated the shooting. He had no authority from the captain of his company to do such a thing, but he was very confident that he would find the excuse to show he had not overstepped the captain's authority in any way.

This opportunity came to him on Tuesday morning the following week. I was taking a bath in the washroom when the Austrian *Unteroffizier* came in, dragging along the *Sanitäter* of the camp.

"The *Kommando Führer* wants to have all the sick line up outside in five minutes," he shouted and started back for the door.

"Wait a minute," I hastened to say, wrapping a towel around my waist.

The German stopped, and turned to look back.

"What is the matter with the *Kommando Führer*?" I asked. "Is he crazy? These men are sick; they can't stand and freeze out in the cold just because he wants to see them."

"I think I'll get them out," the *Sanitäter* said, anticipating Rinke's intent.

"You won't do anything of the kind," I interrupted. "If you let him have his way today, you'll have to let him have his way every day," I explained. "You think I enjoy trouble?" I asked the *Sanitäter*.

"Tell Rinke to come here," I told the *Unteroffizier*. "I want to have a word with him."

The German left and the *Sanitäter* remained behind. I finished my bath and went outside to see why Rinke did not show up. To my surprise, I saw all the sick lined up against the fence, while Rinke watched behind the window of his office, laughing. Before I had a chance, Joe came rushing out of the *Sanitäter's* room. Seeing the sick shiver in the freezing weather, he became infuriated.

"Go back to your rooms!" he ordered. They started to leave, but they had not gone far when Rinke came furiously out of his office as he saw them disperse. He was surprised to hear Joe swearing at him.

"You dare give orders without my consent?" Rinke growled, walking toward the fence.

"You dirty, filthy rat!" Joe shouted, completely out of control, moving toward Rinke from inside the fence. "Get in here, you bastard. I'll show you how to entertain yourself at their suffering."

Rinke had become pale, in the meantime, as Joe's words hit him. He thought for a second that Joe had underestimated his power.

"You dare call me names?" he growled again, pulling his pistol from the holster. "I'll show you how to behave. . . ."

"*Schweinehund!*" Joe's voice cut sharply through the air.

Before Rinke had a chance to fire, Joe had already jumped on him, forgetting in his madness and desperation that the barbed-wire fence stood between them. His hands, with fists tight, went through the wires while his body stuck against the barbs of the fence. He was shaking from rage and fury as he realized he could not reach Rinke from where he was. He pulled himself away from the fence and started to walk toward the gate with a peculiar fearful expression on his face. His eyes were red; his face was white; his fists were still clenched. He kept roaring the same words at Rinke, like a lion that craves to plunge its claws into his victim's flesh.

I moved into the courtyard, intending to get Rinke if he fired at the sergeant major. The rest of the guards who had rushed out of Rinke's office, and the sentry at the gate, were overtaken by surprise. Rinke, meanwhile, thinking it was the sight of the pistol that had aggravated Joe's fury, placed it back in its case hurriedly. He did not move, nor did he say anything more. Joe stepped near me. Rinke came closer and tried to speak. His voice was faint. He pointed at himself repeatedly and uttered the word "I" — "*Ich.*" His face was pale and his chin was trembling.

Realizing that Rinke was shocked into fear, Joe began to shout more emphatically that he was the one to be obeyed from now on. "I am going to make you run away from me," Joe kept telling Rinke. It seemed that within a few minutes he had learned all the German he needed to make himself understood.

Rinke followed Joe into the *Sanitäter's* room, still pointing at himself and whispering "I," but without the power to utter the rest of the sentence: "*I* am in command."

He did not remain long in the *Sanitäter's* room, as Joe kept pounding at him, shouting that he was to do as Joe ordered him to. He walked out and returned to his office.

As soon as Rinke was out of sight, Harry grabbed Joe's hand with both of his own and, shaking from surprise and excitement, he tried to whisper a few words. "I want to express my admiration," he murmured. "I have been in many other camps, but this is the first where I've seen something like that happen," he whispered more distinctly.

I patted Joe on the shoulder.

"Well done, sergeant major," I said, myself quite moved. "I was expecting this would happen sooner or later. I'll see you when I get back from the doctor," I said, and left while the rest of the prisoners were crowding the room in an attempt to congratulate their sergeant major.

Twenty-Two

CONTRARY to his custom, Rinke did not come along to the doctor this time. He needed to get away from the camp for a little while. The air there was getting too heavy for him. He wanted to draw some encouragement from his captain and that is exactly where he went.

Dr. Tsapla received me with his usual smile. He was surprised that Rinke was not with me.

"It's just a guard outside," I said, seeing that he wondered whether Rinke had remained in the waiting room.

"How is your medical supply?" he asked, when he had finished with his first patient.

"Not very rich, doctor."

"You see that door?" he said, pointing at the adjoining room on the opposite side of the waiting room.

I nodded, wondering what he was up to.

"My wardrobe is in there," Dr. Tsapla continued.

I looked curiously at the doctor and the small entrance opposite the waiting room.

"Well, doctor!" I asked. "What's the catch?"

"I'll give you a prescription and money," the doctor offered. "You can use one of my suits when you go to the drugstore. No one will suspect who you are. You know how to get there, don't you?"

I thought of the doctor's suggestion for a few seconds. I could pass as a German civilian quite easily. At the same time a healthy man my age walking in the streets of Morgenroth dressed in civilian clothes could easily be taken for a deserter and arraigned before a German military court. Still, I did not want to lose the opportunity to get medical supplies for the camp.

"Thanks, doctor," I said finally, "but do you mind if I use one of my own ideas first?"

"No, go right ahead!"

"I'll take the money and the prescription now."

He wrote a long list of medical supplies and handed me 40 Reichsmarks, the equivalent of $11, with a buying value equivalent to $50. I waited until the medical examination was over.

"*Na, gehen wir ins Lager zurück* (Let's go back to the camp)," the guard shouted when I told him that we were through.

"Not yet," I said. "We are going all the way to the end of the town first."

"What do you want to go there for?" the guard asked with concern.

"You'll find out," I said confidently. "Come on, let's go!"

"The *Kommando Führer* told me to take you straight back to the camp," the guard protested. "*Verflucht mal*," he mumbled, seeing that I was already on my way; he followed behind, still protesting it was against the orders of the *Kommando Führer*.

One block behind the drugstore, I told the rest of the prisoners to wait, while I kept walking toward the small brick house with the sign *Apotheke* hanging above the door. The *Sanitäter* followed me. The guard decided to stay with the remainder of the group.

A beautiful young woman, dressed in a red blouse, smiled from behind the counter. She seemed puzzled for a few seconds over the color of my uniform, but she didn't seem to care.

"What can I do for you?" she asked.

Being used to Rinke's roaring sound, her voice echoed like a slight, lifeless whisper.

"I hope a lot," I replied, smiling. I handed her the doctor's prescription.

A German civilian came in at the same time with a prescription in his hand.

"Would you rather wait for a few minutes?" the young lady asked the new customer. "The gentleman here was first."

"I'd rather wait," I told the young lady.

"All right!" she answered.

As soon as the customer left, she picked up my list again, laid it on the counter and took a pencil to check each item.

"Is your whole family sick?"

I grinned at her remark.

She started to hand me the first items on the list. "*Hm. . . . Augentropfen* (eye drops), *haben wir keine da* (we don't have any), *eine Augenblick, bitte* (one moment, please), *ich werde mal nachschauen* (I'll take a look)," she kept whispering as she came to the next item on the list.

"You live in Morgenroth?" she asked, handing me a small bottle with eye drops.

"No, Godulahuette."

"How long are you going to be there?"

"Quite a few weeks yet, I'm afraid."

"Is Dr. Tsapla a friend of yours?"

"Just my doctor."

"Are you on leave?"

I felt my blood boil in my veins as I watched that beautiful carefree creature climb on the shelves to get the items on the prescription. I placed part of the drugs in my pockets, leaving the rest for the *Sanitäter* to carry. I wished I had taken the doctor's suggestion and come there dressed in civilian clothes. "Maybe next time," I thought.

"Come again," she suggested smiling, as I was ready to leave.

"*Aufwiedersehen!*" I said, waving my hand and stepping outside. The guard was still furious that he was forced to go against Rinke's orders. "When the *Kommando Führer* says you are to go straight back to the camp," he shouted, "you are to go straight back."

"Oh, shut up!" I said in disgust. "Nobody is asking your opinion."

He became wild over my reproach.

"*Pass mal auf, mein Lieber!*" he threatened. "Or I'll blow your brains out."

I paid no attention to his threats. Instead, I followed behind the rest of the prisoners, with the *Sanitäter* walking beside me. If Rinke was still at the company office, we had a good chance of getting the drugs into the camp. I gave the part I was carrying to some of the others to hide, since I was more likely to be searched. Besides, I was planning to see the prisoners on the construction job on our way and return to the camp later in the afternoon with George and the other men on the same shift.

The guard objected again to my request to stay behind and promised to send Rinke after me.

"I want to see what my men are doing," I said abruptly. "You can't stop me. Neither can the *Kommando Führer*."

This seemed to make him realize I had some responsibility that he had no authority to overlook. He gave up his objection and let me join George's group without any further argument.

This guard was one of the worst under Rinke's command. A mixture of Polish and German extraction, he was deadlier than any other, seeking in every instance to prove his fidelity to the Nazi party, in which he could not enjoy full membership and rights, because of his ancestry. He, thus, quite often caused unnecessary hardships to both prisoners and Poles, even in cases where a Nazi himself would have been less brutal and vengeful. Because of his treacherous personality, we referred to him as "The Stool Pigeon."

On Friday of the same week, I told Rinke that I wanted to take a hot shower. The Stool Pigeon stayed at the entrance of the building. I was trying to unlock the chain and lower my towel from the ceiling when I heard Polland's voice outside.

Polland was surprised that The Stool Pigeon was my guard and remained outside talking with him to avoid suspicion. I knew he must have wanted to talk with me.

I stepped into the shower room fully dressed, making sure that Polland saw me, while I tried to give the impression to the guard that I could not find something I was looking for. Five minutes had passed, and Polland had still not succeeded in finding an excuse to break away from the guard.

"I have forgotten to take along my key," I told the guard, who seemed to wonder why I had not taken the shower. "I'll see if they have a duplicate at the mine office."

I started to walk there while I cautiously pressed a note in Polland's hand, telling him where to wait for me. He kept walking along with the guard for a few yards and then stopped.

"I have to be back at my post," he insisted. "Thanks for telling me all about what happened between Rinke and the sergeant major," he told the guard and left.

The Stool Pigeon stopped outside the mine office to talk with one of the foremen who happened to have just come out of the pit. I entered the corridor leading to the office. I turned casually back to see if the guard was watching. Seeing that he was absorbed in his conversation with the foreman, I sidestepped into the narrow corridor past the office that led to a small exit into the back yard. Before the guard had time to become suspicious of my delay, I reached the building where I had told Polland to wait for me. I walked hurriedly up the old stairs leading to the top story of the shower building. Hans was already there.

"At last," I said with a sigh of relief, "I broke away from The Stool Pigeon."

"How have you been doing?" he asked anxiously.

"Same as usual."

"You remember the offer to come home with me and stay with my parents?"

"Yes," I said reluctantly.

"I'm going tomorrow on a two-day leave. We'll be there before Rinke knows you are missing."

"Why such a hurry? The war is going to be over in a few days, anyway."

"Because tomorrow night," Polland replied solemnly, "*Rinke is going to kill you.*"

"You expect me to swallow that?"

"I heard everything from *Unteroffizier* Hans!" Polland said.

"Oh, that rat! He's been telling stories again."

"Everything is planned," Polland continued. "It is going to look like you assaulted him."

I laughed at his frightened attitude.

"Look, Hans," I said. "I am thankful for your offer to help me save my life. Maybe tomorrow I will regret that I did not take seriously your warning. But I have been expecting something like this ever since Rinke became the *Kommando Führer*."

He listened quietly with fear shading his face. "Rinke has been waiting for this for a long time," he said, as if he were talking to himself.

I gazed at the empty walls for a few minutes while running through my mind the events of the last seven months. It seemed almost ages.

"Be sensible," Polland insisted. "You know there is no hope."

"I think there is," I said, and taking a notebook from my pocket, I wrote in German the following words:

Wenn alle andere Hoffnungen werden Sie verlassen, es bleibt immer eine: Gott!

When all other hopes have abandoned you, one always remains: God!

I had convinced Polland that I was going to stay.

"Watch your step," he cautioned. "It's going to be worse than you think."

"Don't forget I, too, have two hands!" I said, and began walking down the stairs. Polland remained on the same floor, to avoid suspicion. When I reached the ground floor, I heard steps outside the door.

"*Verflucht mal!*" the guard shouted. "*Wo ist der Kerl?* (Dammit! Where is he?)"

I hid behind the door, and as soon as I heard his steps disappear, I ran outside and started to walk indifferently toward the main entrance of the brick wall enclosing the mine.

I asked the sentry at the gate if the guard was already gone.

"*Ich weiss nicht!*" he answered, looking around as if he were making an effort to locate him. "I haven't seen him," he said finally, but just as he finished, The Stool Pigeon appeared, heading in my direction.

"*Mach doch keinen Spaß, mein Lieber!*" he shouted, turning his rifle against me when he came near, apparently thinking I had been with some girl.

"*Ach, wo!*" I exclaimed, "*Du bildest dich ein, Mensch!* (You are imagining things!)" I waved my hand in exactly the same way the Germans did whenever they intended to indicate that something they had heard sounded ridiculous.

"*Na, los!*" he shouted.

I started to walk back to the camp while he followed me with the rifle pointed at my back. Rinke was waiting in front of the guard room steps when I arrived back at the camp.

"*Kommen Sie mal 'rein!* (Get in here!)" he ordered.

I walked into his private quarters, which opened into the courtyard and into the office separately. Closing the courtyard door behind him, he grabbed the sick register and began to copy some numbers.

"*Diese acht Stücke gehen zur Arbeit morgen früh* (These eight men are going to work tomorrow morning)," he growled, after he finished copying the numbers of half the prisoners on the sick list. "I am holding you responsible if they don't," he warned.

I didn't say anything for a moment. Then, after some thought, I told him that they were not going anywhere but to the doctor.

"Whether they are fit to work," I cautioned, "is up to the doctor to decide. Not you!"

I had hardly finished when Rinke pulled his bayonet and pressed its point against my throat, twisting his grip a couple of times. Fortunately for me its round blunt point slipped, only scratching my skin. Trying to protect myself, I lost balance and fell back against the wall. I raised my arm to protect my face but he hit me on the elbow with the side of his bayonet. My arm was paralyzed for a moment, and I bent down in an effort to get away from the bayonet's swing, while in the meantime I tried to hit him on the crippled leg.

Suddenly, Rinke opened the courtyard door and rushed outside. I moved near the window to see the lieutenant stepping down from his motorcycle, while Rinke was straightening his coat trying to get ready for his usual Nazi salute.

They both entered the office while the lieutenant was removing his gloves, pressing his chin against his throat on account of the cold. He saw me in Rinke's quarters.

"What is the prisoner doing in the office?" he asked. "Send him out!" he ordered the Austrian *Unteroffizier* who had followed them to the door in order to carry out any orders Rinke might not have time to execute. Seeing that I hesitated in complying with the order, the Austrian *Unteroffizier* pulled his bayonet, trying to make me leave the room at once. I picked up my hat, which had been knocked off during the fight, and walked through the office back into the camp.

Joe was going over some Red Cross sheets when I walked inside the room.

"Where have you been hiding?" he asked, raising his head from the desk.

I didn't say a word. Instead, I went outside again and took a stroll around the billet, trying to regain composure and collect my thoughts. The lieutenant had saved me, for the moment, but Rinke would very likely get after me again as soon as the officer was gone. Where could I go that he couldn't find me? Any time he was ready to start again, all he had to do was send a guard inside to bring me to his office. And he knew that I still had an alternative — the same alternative other prisoners had. Just walk to his office, admit his might, send the sick to work instead of to the doctor, as he had ordered, sign a statement to the Red Cross that everything in the camp was in order, that my accusations against the Nazis were false, and then hope that Rinke would be kind enough to spare my life so that I could live to see the end of the war someday, after suffering every type of humiliation and injustice that would spring into his mind.

I stood by the fence behind the billet, looking at the tracks where a streetcar was rolling by. It did not matter to me if I were killed. I had nothing more to lose anyway. But I could not let myself give in to a Nazi. I knew that submitting to Rinke was submitting to defeat, and I did not believe I was yet defeated. There is a price each one has to pay, I kept thinking, in this struggle for freedom and dignity. Perhaps this was mine.

It must have been about an hour later when the lieutenant finally came out of the office. Rinke walked hurriedly into his room and came out a few minutes later, dressed in his Sunday uniform. He left with the officer for the company office.

I went back into the billet, trying to avoid the fate that awaited me upon Rinke's return. Polland's information was right, except that Rinke had planned it a day earlier than he had let the other *Unteroffizier* believe.

"Anything wrong?" Joe inquired.

"Is there anything right?" I asked, trying to keep him from suspecting anything. I did not want my sergeant major to know I was afraid. Still less did I want him to discover what was awaiting me upon Rinke's return.

The day shift crew were getting ready for sleep.

"I think I'll get some sleep, too," Joe said, yawning.

I walked outside again. I was too nervous to sleep. It was dark now except at the sentry boxes. The door of Rinke's office opened to let the Austrian *Unteroffizier* out. He headed in my direction, holding a small piece of paper, which he handed me.

"The *Kommando Führer* wants these men to get ready for work in the morning," he said. The sardonic smile on his face told me that Rinke had talked to his guards of his intention to strike at me. "Either Rinke finds them working," the German added, "or you are going on a long trip."

"They don't go anywhere before they see the doctor!" I said. "You damned pigs, what the hell do you want out of sick people anyway? You dirty, filthy bastards!" I kept shouting. "Get out of my sight, and stay out!"

I don't believe the Austrian *Unteroffizier* heard me, because he was hard of hearing, and by the time I was through shouting, he was already at the gate. Joe rushed outside half dressed.

"What's up?" he asked anxiously.

"The same old trouble," I said. "I have to shout at the Austrian *Unteroffizier* to make him hear anything."

"What did he want?"

"Nothing important," I said. "Let's get some sleep."

We both returned to the billet. Joe soon went back to sleep.

I was still awake when the guard walked in at five to get the morning shift for work. I put my clothes on and went to the *Sanitäter's* room to tell Harry that all the sick were to stay behind. Harry went along with me to each room and showed me the ones who had reported sick.

"You better go back to sleep!" I said to Harry.

Rinke was in the courtyard counting those for work. Not finding any of the eight prisoners he had mentioned the day before, he called me over to find out why they were not there with the rest of the working crew.

"*Wo sind die Kranken?* (Where are the sick?)" he growled.

I refused to answer.

"Keep him out here until I get back from the mine," he ordered the Austrian *Unteroffizier* guarding the gate.

As soon as he left, I tried to get back into my room, but the *Unteroffizier* turned his pistol against me. "You stay right where you are," he warned. I refrained from any further attempt to approach the gate. Instead, I kept walking in the courtyard, stamping on the ground, trying not to freeze. The *Unteroffizier* kept breathing into his hands to keep warm.

It was still dark when Rinke returned from the mine. He pointed at the door to his quarters, indicating that I should go in. He locked the door behind him, then stood with one hand at his belt, gripping the bayonet with the other.

"Why didn't you let those eight prisoners work?" he asked.

I didn't say anything. I waited for him to make the first move. Failing to receive any answer from me, Rinke angered himself with his own words. He pulled his bayonet and started to hit me on the head and shoulders. Surprised at the speed of his assault, I turned against the wall, trying to protect my face. I felt his bayonet hitting me on the back. I turned to face him. His expression changed when he saw me looking at him. He stopped, almost stupefied.

I felt like grabbing the bayonet from his hand and running it through him. It would have been easy. But then, his captain would make everyone pay for it. As I watched the sweat gather on his pale forehead, I realized that I could not go through with something like that. I needed someone else's help to get me out of the predicament I was in. I prayed. Rinke kept staring at me. He had gone as far as he could.

"Now," I said, "you have nothing left."

I opened the door and walked slowly toward the gate. The Austrian *Unteroffizier* gave me a peculiar look. Rinke stood at the door to his quarters.

"Let him in!" he ordered the Austrian *Unteroffizier*, who hastened to comply.

I started for the billet, thinking that I had made the best decision under the circumstances. I was willing to believe that Rinke would remain harmless, following this experience.

I felt very tired. I entered my room and sat by the desk. It was still dark outside. Everyone else in the room was still asleep. I folded my arms on the table, rested my head on them, and went to sleep. A little while later a noise in the room woke me up. I climbed on my bed with my clothes on, and went back to sleep.

When I woke up again it was already mid-afternoon. I took a cold shower. George Karaolanis appeared at the entrance.

"I received another letter," he said. "Will you read it for me?"

"In a few minutes," I said.

When I walked into the room where he was staying, George impatiently handed me the letter.

Mein Liebling,
Since the last time that I saw you I could do nothing else except think of you, worrying if something terrible has happened to you. How are you, my darling? Each time I go away from you, I always leave wondering if that meeting had not been our last. . . .

Deine Liebe,
Johanna

Joe interrupted the letter reading when he returned from the mine. He had gone there in the morning to check the Red Cross supplies, fearing that the Germans might break in and steal part of the food stored there.

"I would like to talk to you alone!" he said, standing at the doorway and twisting his moustache.

"What happened between you and Rinke yesterday afternoon?" he asked, when we were in the *Sanitäter's* room.

I wondered how much of the incident he had learned. I did not say anything, waiting for Joe to give me a hint of what he knew.

"Next time you are in trouble," Joe suggested, "I want you to tell me. I am not going to let Rinke lay a hand on you," he said.

I stood with my back against the stove, trying to get warm. He seemed determined to do as he had promised. I knew Joe was the best friend I'd ever had, and his interest in my safety was because of our friendship, rather than his sense of duty.

"I won't allow Rinke to touch you," he repeated.

"I don't think he will."

Harry returned to his room, bringing back with him some unused bandages.

"Somebody hurt his fingers," he said. "I went over to the billet to bind him up."

Twenty-Three

THE Rat walked in and handed me the allotted stationery for the week, late in the afternoon.

"Polland has been asking for you," he said. "You can talk to him over the telephone in the office," he suggested. "No one is there now."

I followed him to the office. He took up the receiver and dialed the number of the Russian labor detachment where Polland served as a clerk. I heard his voice on the other end.

"Go ahead," the German suggested. "He is on the line."

Polland was anxious to know how I managed to take care of Rinke.

"I can't tell you over the phone," I said. "But I am quite all right and very much alive."

"I checked with the kitchen here. You are right in your suspicions. You better come and check on it yourself," Polland said, confirming that the German cooks were taking our rations for their own men.

"Thanks," I said with a mild voice. I hung up the receiver and returned to my room.

Late at night I decided to write a letter home. Some of my friends had given me their stationery, as they didn't think there was any use to write any more letters. I wrote some five or six, each one with almost identical content. Joe busied himself with writing to his mother and sister, and I finally began to answer the letter I had received a few days before from my relatives in the United States.

> My Dear Uncle,
> I received your letter dated June 17th, as well as two letters from my Aunt written in September. How happy I felt receiving a letter from you after so long a time I cannot say. It came just in the moment when I most needed to hear from you. It is a great thing here for a man to know that he is not forgotten. I am always thinking of you and of my Aunt, your visit to us, the happy days that we all spent together in Corinth when, united in a short but real happiness, we forgot the distance that separates one from the other. I was then a little ignorant kid with a very infantile idea of life and the world. Will such a day come again? Certainly it will. And the joy then will be greater. I know how this letter will make you sad. Be sure, my dear Uncle, that everything here is all right. I found a good friend who has helped me more than anyone else to spend the hardest days. Later I will write you more about him. Kindest regards to all.
>
> Your nephew

"I wish I could write them the truth," Joe said when he finished writing his own letter.

"They know, just the same," I said, "even if you have to say that everything is all right."

I was getting ready for a cold bath, late the following afternoon, when the Austrian *Unteroffizier* dropped into my room.

"You are wanted at the office," he said. "Alone."

I wondered for a moment what the purpose of the sudden call could be, but I soon found out. When I entered the office, I saw Rinke, his captain, and some other officer of equal rank seated around the table while a woman stenographer was readying her notebook and pencils for some paperwork.

The new captain introduced himself as the *Gerichts-Offizier* (justice officer), and informed me that he was sent there to establish the facts in the indictment that the lieutenant had drawn up a few weeks before. He explained to Rinke that he was the accused and ordered him to refrain from doing or saying anything unless he was asked. He then took a Bible out of his bag, and raising its front cover, he asked me to lay my right hand on it and swear to tell the truth.

"Let us now proceed with the business of this matter," he dictated to the stenographer.

"You will have to remain outside," he suggested to the *Kommando Führer*. "You are to enter this room only when you are called."

Very much confused, Rinke reluctantly obeyed the officer's order. The off-duty guards gathered around him outside, curious to know what it was all about. Rinke, however, refrained from making any comments. He kept pacing in the courtyard. He could not understand why his own authorities were placing him in the defendant's role. He seemed confident, however, that as long as his captain was there, the trial was going to end with his triumph, and he worried little over what I had to say.

"Close the door," the officer ordered.

I did as he said.

"Please tell me," he proceeded when everyone seemed to be ready, "why you have accused the *Kommando Führer* of violations of the Geneva Convention as shown here under Count One?"

I remained silent for a few minutes, trying to guess how I could state my reasons without revealing to the Nazis the existence of evidence that they might seek to destroy after the hearing. I did not believe the officer was primarily interested in justice. Seeing Rinke's captain on the judge's side made me think that the purpose of this trial was merely to find and eliminate evidence that could be used against them later.

"I don't think your court is competent to handle this," I said finally. "No court can administer justice when the defendant, at the same time, is the judge."

The presiding officer swung nervously on his chair. "What are you driving at?" he asked, angered with my objections.

"That man," I said, pointing at Rinke's captain. "He is more responsible for Rinke's actions than Rinke himself."

The captain started to get up.

"Please, remain seated!" the judge implored, trying to avoid a fight. Then, turning to me, he continued.

"According to what I have here," he said, pointing at a bundle of papers that he began to lay on the table, "you have accused the *Kommando Führer* of certain serious offenses. You realize, of course, that as a prisoner you have no right to do that. You cannot accuse a German soldier and expect to get away with it. However," he said, looking this time at me, "I am here to see whether these offenses have actually been committed."

I did not put much faith in the officer's words. "The Geneva Convention," I said, "tells you distinctly that in a proceeding of this sort, a representative of the protecting power should be present. Not only is there no such person here, but the defendant's accomplice is allied with the judging party. From what you have said and from what I see, this is a mockery of justice and nothing else."

I started for the door. The justice officer called me back, indicating that he had to know the facts. His persistence made me think that he may perhaps have received instructions from some higher authority to hold the hearing.

"All right!" I consented and began to give an account of the events that formed the grounds for Count One: the incident at Udetfeld, when the Germans had tried to force the prisoners to load bombs, and had beaten the men when they refused.

"Wait outside," the justice officer suggested when I had concluded, "but don't go away. We haven't finished yet."

"Let the *Kommando Führer* come in, now," he told the captain.

Rinke hurried in as soon as the captain called him. He stood at attention for a sharp, impressive salute. The door closed behind him. I could not hear the questioning, so I started to walk nervously in the courtyard. Joe called me near the gate, anxious to learn what was taking place. A few guards gathered around.

"Don't let him get away with anything," one of them suggested. "Give it to him, now that you have the chance."

"Don't be afraid of him," another insisted.

I grinned at their encouragement. Rinke's conviction was certainly going to be their own redemption as well. Still, I was not certain that I shared their optimism. So I did not say anything; I only smiled nervously, and paced around the courtyard.

Late at night, the proceedings came to a close. Rinke was the last one called in to be questioned. I returned to the billet while Joe and the rest of the prisoners in the same room gathered around to learn exactly what had taken place.

"You can't trust any Nazi," Joe said. "They may be doing all this just to come out in the end and say that Rinke is right."

I shared his opinion, although I didn't make any comments. It did look like a lot of paperwork with only one verdict for the accused: Not Guilty — something they could easily decide without any trial at all.

"Well, if Rinke wins this trial," I said finally, "there is nothing more that can stop him. I hope the representatives of the protecting power arrive before this case is closed."

"And even if they do get here in time," Joe said, "there is very little they can do. The Nazis will jail them before they have a chance to get out of Germany."

I took my usual cold shower and lay on my bed, trying to get some sleep.

Why would the Nazis go through all this trouble, I kept wondering, to establish the facts in this case, unless they wanted to destroy them, or twist them in a way that would make them appear innocent? Maybe, I kept thinking, they are afraid to let the free world know of their crimes. Maybe they are trying to wash from the face of their government the shame of such acts by pinning the blame on one person. Or maybe it was just what Joe thought: a lot of paperwork. The answer to all these questions came the following morning when the captain returned to tell me that I had made a fool of myself for indicting him in the first place and that Rinke was to stay.

"You have a lot to gain," he suggested sarcastically, "by cooperating with my Rinke. You are our prisoners. You have to be content that we haven't killed you yet."

"Maybe that would be a favor!" I remarked. "Maybe that's why you haven't done it yet."

Rinke, who had been standing beside his captain, could hardly conceal his relief, hearing his commanding officer's advice to the prisoners. He seemed to forget that far to the west, along the German frontier, Allied troops were getting ready for the final blow against Hitler's last hideout. Inside the boundaries of Nazi Germany Rinke felt invulnerable and omnipotent. He thought the prisoners were abandoned and forgotten. He rubbed his hands in a gesture of contentment, and, then, standing at attention, he promised his captain that he would continue treating the prisoners in a manner satisfactory to the captain's wishes. He was very confident, in his promise, that he knew just what his commanding officer wanted him to do. Somehow, the presence of his captain seemed to give him the encouragement he needed for more criminal acts.

I left the captain and returned to the billet to warm up a little. I did not see Joe there, but suspected he would be in the *Sanitäter's* room chatting with Harry. I walked over to give him the news.

"I told you that's what they would do," Joe said. He had based no hopes on the trial.

"Well, I guess that's that!" I said.

After the evening roll call, I returned to my room accompanied by Joe and George, who preferred to be with the two of us, hoping to learn of new developments in Rinke's case or express his concern over the current trend of events.

An hour must have gone by when Rinke suddenly rushed into the camp, followed by two *Unteroffiziers* and a couple of guards. He posted one of the guards at the entrance of my room and the other between the partition separating it from the remaining hall to prevent any of the prisoners from interfering. Then, aided by the two *Unteroffiziers*, he began to confiscate every note or piece of paper he found in my room and on the desk. In his frustration, he took along letters I had received from home and Red Cross invoices, clearly marked with the censor's seal of Stalag VIII-B. My diary and all other records I had kept were confiscated. Rinke pretended that he was going to send them for censorship, but Polland later informed me that he had set them all on fire. Thus, he felt that any harmful evidence against him had been destroyed.

"Maybe it isn't over yet," I thought, seeing that Rinke was still afraid of possible evidence to prove his guilt.

While these events were taking place inside the camp, in the mine the situation had become equally serious. German civilians in the pits became abusive under the rights granted to them by the *Kommando*

Führer and began to attack prisoners whenever they found them isolated and off guard. The prisoners, however, managed to stay in groups and fought off these attacks without injury. One such incident was the case of Emmanuel, a young man around 25, who was attacked by five German civilians while working alone. Isolated from his group, he managed to defend himself with a coal shovel, the only "weapon" he possessed. His assailants were carried later from the mine in a pitiful condition, while he was escorted back to the camp with only a few minor cuts. Rinke did not intervene, fearing he might be revealed as the instigator of these assaults. The German civilians, however, came back a week later and succeeded in beating mercilessly one of the prisoners who was physically weak and feebleminded. The following day, to everyone's surprise, a mine gallery referred to by the Germans as "Veronica," collapsed, burying every one of these Germans. All the prisoners underneath Veronica came up safe and unscratched. The rest of the German civilians were unharmed, but Emmanuel's assailants died underneath the pile of coal. They went by God's hand, as a prisoner put it.

I was left undisturbed to sleep one morning a few weeks later, while the day shift was getting ready for work. I woke up to see one of the prisoners hit The Rat, while another managed to get the pistol away from the *Unteroffizier's* hand and was ready to fire at the German.

"What in the world are you doing?" I shouted. "Have you lost your minds?"

"He walked in here waving his pistol," protested the prisoner who hit him. "We told him to shut up, but he did not listen."

I laughed for a few seconds at their feat. "Fifteen men against one?" I asked. "Is that the way you settle your arguments?"

"Let him have it, Paul," a prisoner shouted to the one holding the pistol.

I grabbed Paul's arm and removed the gun from his hand. I threw it near the door.

"Take your artillery," I told The Rat, "and get out of this room before you get your head knocked off."

Still pale and shaking, the German walked to the door, picked up his pistol, and walked outside. I was confident he would feel ashamed to report or mention the incident to anyone else.

In the course of the same week I received a letter from Read informing me that two representatives of the protecting power had reached

Stalag VIII-B and that they were already on their way to our labor detachment. I passed the information on to Joe, and soon everyone in the camp knew of the situation. They crowded my room in an effort to learn the significance of this visit.

The two representatives arrived at noon the following day. A group of German officers and Rinke's captain accompanied them to the gate, protesting that they had no right to interfere with the affairs of the labor detachment, but they finally let them enter. The two representatives, along with Joe and I, walked into George's room, which was empty at that hour of the day, and sat at the long table in the middle, following a formal introduction by the captain of Rinke's company. The German officers left us alone to discuss our problems with the two representatives; they returned to the office of the *Kommando Führer*.

I can't very well describe my feelings when, for the first time in three and a half years, I could sit and talk with friends, sent there by the free world to take along our complaints and news of oppression and persecution at the hands of the enemy. I was glad they were there, but envied their luck, knowing that they were able to walk out of the camp free, and thinking they would soon be out of sight again of the Nazi spectacles of brutality. Yet we were to stay to witness and undergo these brutalities, with the hope at least of spending the days ahead in the way we had spent all the others, and not worse. I did not want to let these representatives know how I felt. I only wanted to see that they understood the situation through the evidence before their own eyes, and hoped that their intervention would bring useful results.

The first matter of importance was, of course, *Kommando Führer* Rinke, and the captain of the company to which he belonged. The two officials already had been informed of our situation by Read, the central Man of Confidence. It remained for me to acquaint them with the facts, as we had witnessed them and as we had lived through each one. I expressed my suspicions that the captain was behind every one of Rinke's moves.

"Rinke's actions are carefully planned," I pointed out. "He is too dumb to think that well."

The two representatives listened carefully, keeping a record of everything Joe and I said. We described the existing circumstances as impartially as was possible for soldiers, bearing always in mind that we would become as much a criminal as Rinke if we accused him of acts for which he was not responsible.

I provided all the help I could concerning the type and whereabouts of the evidence available. It was up to them to find and examine the evidence while the Nazis were still unaware of their purpose. Rinke's two victims — the two escapees — were not there to testify. Rinke had arranged to keep them at the construction job and went there later to make sure that they were not permitted to talk with the representatives of the protecting power. However, the two officials had already seen the report made by the German doctor at Udetfeld, and Read's own description of the beatings caused them to believe that there was no particular need to question the two at that time.

When finally Rinke's case was completely recorded, I introduced the matter of Red Cross supplies. There was nothing they could do about them, however, as the Germans refused to provide any means of transportation. It became apparent that we were to spend the remaining part of captivity living on German rations alone.

I introduced for discussion a number of minor questions, and, finally, the meeting was terminated three and a half hours after it had started. Harry prepared some tea at my request, the only gesture of hospitality we could afford under the circumstances. Joe stood up to make a toast. "To victory!" he proposed.

"To you!" the officials added.

As a last gesture of determination and hope, I told the two representatives of my own plans.

"If I don't get the *Kommando Führer* jailed for what he's done," I said firmly, "I am going to shoot him myself."

The two gentlemen sobered at my remark. "We'll do everything in our power to make justice prevail," they both affirmed. We shook hands and they stepped outside. Joe and I followed them as far as the gate. The sentry opened the door to let them out. We stayed and watched from inside the fence, and they waved as their new black car pulled away. We returned their farewell.

I stood by the fence, watching the black sedan disappear behind the walled mine complex, wishing I was in it going away to freedom. What an irony of fate! Only a few minutes before, they were inside the fence with us. Three and a half years had gone by inside this prison! Every single day was filled with tension, danger, and fear — the fear that the next day will take away what the previous day had spared. I wondered how they felt, asking me to tell them the things I wanted, when deep in their hearts they knew that they could not grant the most important thing. Rinke, the Red Cross supplies, and all the other things I was asking for were not important if I could be free. Yet, in spite of this, their presence inside the barbed wire, and their promise to solve all of our other problems, seemed to be the greatest service they had rendered. Their short visit meant relief, and their promise meant hope.

"Let's go inside!" Joe suggested. "We can get warm, at least."

The next morning, I decided to check on the kitchen racket that Polland had confirmed for me. Rinke was not in his office, so The Rat took me there. I stopped at the labor detachment by the mine kitchen to see Polland.

"I guess this was your day," he said, somewhat content that the representatives of the protecting power had come. We walked together into the kitchen next to the Russian camp while The Rat stayed behind, handing the guard duties over to Polland.

A middle-aged lady objected to my presence there: "Rinke has given me instructions not to let any prisoner in the kitchen," she protested.

"He did, eh?" I said, walking toward the corner where a couple of women were trying to chop carrots for our soup using a big, heavy axe.

"*Ja!*" the middle-aged lady replied. "What do you want here?"

"I am waiting for the mouse to come for the cheese," I said.

She burst into hysterical cries. "You are giving me a hard time," she protested. "I am going to call up Rinke and tell him!" she threatened.

That was exactly what I wanted her to do. If Rinke knew nothing of the food racket, he would not take her call seriously. If, however, everything in the kitchen was done with his approval, he would hasten to her rescue, fearing that she might give away everything she knew. I wondered if he was in the camp by this time, but I soon heard his voice when the lady called him on the phone protesting my interference. A few minutes later he was there, armed with his pistol and bayonet. He was furious and came swearing toward me. I tried to remain calm and waited to see what he'd do. I was convinced already that he was involved in this, but I expected him to find some excuse for his intervention other than demanding to know the reason of my presence.

"You know you are forbidden to talk with German women?" he growled.

"I came here to check on our food rations," I said, "and I am not leaving until I see our food go into the right container."

"Why do you want to do that?" he asked with some concern.

"Because I don't think we are getting the right amount!"

Rinke was offended by my answer. "Are you implying that. . . ." he started to say.

"I am not implying anything," I interrupted. "But I didn't come here because of some frustrated scullery maid."

"Where is your guard?" he demanded.

"Right behind you!" I said, pointing at Polland.

"Who brought you here?"

"I landed with a parachute," I said. "The guard was afraid to jump, so he stayed on the plane."

"*Du Verflucht!*" he spat, swinging his bayonet. Then suddenly as if he had thought of something past, he calmed himself to avoid a confrontation. Polland intervened to explain what had happened to my guard, who had gone into the Russian camp adjoining the kitchen.

Finding my escort's disappearance more important, Rinke went out to search for The Rat, telling Polland that the *Unteroffizier* should have known better than to leave me alone in the kitchen. I used this opportunity to find the directive of the German High Command specifying the amount of food to be issued for prisoners in the type of labor such as in a coal mine, and checked the actual supplies that the middle-aged woman had set aside for the day's use. She hastened to make up the deficiency by using the following day's supplies.

"Now I'll have to use the supply of the following day for tomorrow!" she complained. "Why did I have to be in this mess in the first place?"

"If you do what you are supposed to do," I said, "you wouldn't be in a mess."

"It was all Rinke's idea!"

Twenty-Four

THE lack of Red Cross food supplies already had begun to make its consequences felt among the prisoners in "Hell Dive" and starvation once more made its way into the camp, this time to stay until the war came to an end. We knew that only the end of hostilities could bring our rescue from this suffering, and as our physical strength kept sinking lower each day, the only question in everyone's mind was, "How long, yet?"

The Polish civilians working in the same locations with the prisoners managed to give us bread in spite of the German restrictions, but Rinke confiscated every ounce of food we brought into the camp by searching everyone on their return from work. He was not satisfied with confiscating the food alone, and beat the prisoners in an effort to make them confess the identity of the Polish civilians who had dared make such a gesture; but he also imposed upon the prisoners collective punishment by refusing to let the scant allotment of German rations be issued to them until they consented to give the names or description of those civilians. His madness was further aggravated by the prisoners' calmness. In spite of the beatings and hunger, they refused to give him the information he wanted.

For some strange reason, he avoided any contact with me or Joe, and whenever he was forced by orders from his captain to confer with us in his office, he always chose to talk to us in the open and only in the daytime, surrounded always by three or four of his guards. The Stool Pigeon, The Rat, Alex, and the Austrian *Unteroffizier* usually comprised his bodyguards. He never came into the camp for a roll call. Instead, he sent one of his loyal watchdogs to count the prisoners.

This made it difficult for me or Joe to put an end to his conduct. Some of his guards persisted in warning him that he had already pushed things too far, and that the more he made us feel desperate, the closer came the possibility for one of the prisoners to "bump him off," but Rinke had gone mad and was unable to reason any more. The news of German defeats from all directions had changed him into an insane, bloodthirsty beast. New, more abusive rights bestowed upon him by the Nazi party enabled him to increase his reign of terror over the other Germans in the area. And the anticipation of an order from Heinrich Himmler — the number-one agent of Germany's internal security at that time — for the annihilation of war prisoners increased his impatience to the extent that he kept promising to us openly that such an order was going to come.

In spite of this situation, however, I sought repeatedly to meet him alone, intending to make him realize that while he could do as he pleased with Germans, the prisoners in E.757 were a group he still had to deal with. When occasionally I succeeded in speaking to him face-to-face while his bodyguards offered him their protection, I made it clear that his might had not impressed me in the least and that if anything like what he was threatening came about, he would be the one to answer for it in the end. Rinke responded by ordering that the prisoners be searched on their return from work before they could be let into the camp. He suspected that guns might be smuggled in, furnished by Polish civilians outside. It was such a fear, perhaps, that kept him from attacking me personally, even when killing me seemed the only reasonable thing for him to do. At times, I thought of carrying a gun for protection; I felt that Rinke must have been aware of this. I was prepared to sell my life at a price he would have to pay; but he was not willing to buy it.

Following the failure of the first trial, Read succeeded in inducing the German commandant of Stalag VIII-B to order a new hearing in Rinke's case through some ingenious way which I was never able to discover. A week before Christmas 1944, another "justice officer" was sent in from Teschen to draw a new indictment against Rinke, in spite of my insistence that his captain was also to blame. The Germans did not want to let this case reveal that someone of definite authority and responsibility was behind these brutalities, and they were anxious to shape the entire case in such a manner as to appear that some irresponsible person had caused these hardships and that as soon as a responsible authority learned of the problems, they took steps to punish the transgressor.

The indication that a new trial was about to start was taken seriously by Rinke, as he spent most of the time visiting his captain, seeking his assurance that he was going to protect him, as he had at the first trial. Rinke's failure to receive such an assurance was manifested through a change in his behavior. He seemed to pay very little attention to the affairs of the labor detachment anymore, spending most of his time at the company headquarters. He avoided his own friends in the mine and the camp, telling them flatly that he could do very little to solve their quarrels with war prisoners. The mine director threatened to report Rinke's indifference and "neglect of duty," but Rinke paid little attention to his threats, and even cautioned the mine director about the way he talked to "a soldier in uniform." Rinke felt betrayed by his captain, and this became his main concern.

The liberties that he had given, however, to the German civilians and the hatred he had indoctrinated in them against us were something he could not revoke. Fights in the mine pits between prisoners and civilians continued, and disorder replaced the regular production hours. The civilians claimed that the prisoners attacked them first, while the prisoners claimed that the civilians were the ones who had started the whole thing. The mine director endowed himself with special rights for bringing the situation under control by disposing of those prisoners who proved themselves to be "aggressive" and reluctant to work. Joe made a special trip to the mine and warned the director that if any harm came to the prisoners because of his instruction, he would be the first one to be dumped into the mine shaft.

The judge who was to preside at Rinke's second trial arrived at the labor detachment a few days after Christmas, accompanied by the captain of Rinke's company and the usual secretarial staff. They both came to "Hell Dive" from the mine where, disguised as mine workers for several days, they had tried to learn from their own observations the cause of the disorder there. Most of our men failed to recognize them, but some who had seen the captain before passed the word to the others that they were being watched. It was probably only the Germans who were unaware that the two officers were spying on their actions.

Rinke's office was converted into the courtroom in which he would be indicted on my charges. Both Joe and I were called to testify this time. I was permitted to use Rinke's two victims, the escapees from Udetfeld, as witnesses for one of the counts. No one, outside of myself, Joe, Rinke, his captain, the judge, and the court staff were allowed in the room. My witnesses were allowed in only during the brief period of their testimony, which was to my detriment, because they both refused to admit that it was Rinke who had beaten them, fearing a reprisal as soon as they were left at Rinke's mercy.

Rinke smiled with contentment at their refusal to admit the truth; he hoped that he would still be found innocent on every one of the remaining counts.

After a brief but precise account of the grounds behind my charges and a thorough cross-examination of all the testimony, I was called to make a final statement.

"I know," I started to say with a clear voice, "that whatever I have said or will say in support of my charges, whatever was brought up by the sergeant major as serious offenses against common decency and justice, committed by the ruling authority of this camp, whatever ours and your own evidence has proved in the course of this hearing, I know," I repeated, "that we will be the ones to be found wrong, because we are prisoners and have no right to be otherwise. The acts of cruelty and savagery committed under the jurisdiction of the present camp authority, were the result of this concept of justice, not merely 'acts of anger' or the temporary need for discipline, as the defendant has claimed them to be.

"Had Rinke believed," I continued, "that a form of justice other than this still exists in Nazi Germany, he would not have felt encouraged to commit any of these offenses of which he is now accused. Had the prisoners believed in the sincerity and competence of this court, my two witnesses, a few hours ago, would have testified to the truth as it is — as Rinke himself knows it to be — instead of concealing it along with every other suffering. They would have told this court that on a September afternoon, they absorbed the fury of the defendant's punches for a whole hour, tied to a chair, until he felt satisfied with the results he had produced. They would have told this court of the "enjoyment" Rinke had had by asking them the cause of their injuries and then beating them again for saying either yes or no; they would have explained how, instead of being admitted to the hospital for treatment of their wounds, they were forced into hard labor while Rinke amused himself at their suffering."

The judge listened carefully to my statements, rubbing his chin occasionally, with an expression of smothering embarrassment. "Let us forget for a while," he said, "that we are enemies, and talk to each other as man to man. For this short while we are not at war but in court, trying to bring to justice the same trespasser. That is the purpose of this trial, to bring to light the facts and punish the offender if the evidence produced points in that direction."

"If you really want to find the offender," I said, "there is the man you want!" I pointed at the captain, who seemed as if lightning had struck him.

"I!" he exclaimed, jumping from his seat. "I never told Rinke to do things like that!" he protested.

I was hoping that Rinke would be able to produce the orders he had received from his commanding officer in the past and free himself from a part of his guilt. But when he was asked to do so by the judge, all he could do was to say that the orders he had received from his captain were given to him orally.

The trial eventually came to an end. The verdict in the case was to be delivered a few days later, but it was certain that Rinke at least would be found guilty. The judge left no doubt as to the nature of the verdict when, at the end of the hearing, he hinted at what Rinke should expect. "You are to stay here at this post," he said, "for only a few more days. But while you are still here, don't make the mistake of bothering the prisoners again. If you are mad," he continued, "put your hands in your pockets and keep them there. Because if you don't, I'll have both those hands cut off. Remember that as long as you live."

"*Jawohl, Herr Hauptmann!*" Rinke said, standing promptly at attention.

His captain was getting ready to leave with the judge. Rinke hastened to secure a promise similar to the one the captain gave him at the end of the first trial.

"I am afraid, Rinke," the captain replied to Rinke's astonishment, "that I will have to lock you up."

Rinke bowed his head, and gazing at the ground, he began to walk toward his quarters at the other end of the guard room. The captain did not bother to reprimand him for retiring without the customary salute.

During the four days Rinke remained as *Kommando Führer* of our labor detachment, he spent most of his time in his room, not making any effort to talk to any of his guards, not even those still loyal to him. He was completely demoralized and confused. Finally, on New Year's Eve, his successor arrived to take over the duties of *Kommando Führer*.

Rinke accompanied him inside the camp and acquainted him with Joe and me. On the morning of the new year — 1945 — he was no longer in command. The new *Kommando Führer* had taken over.

It was a big day for everyone. It remained in my life as the one day out of my three and a half years in captivity that I did not feel I had spent as a prisoner, in spite of the fact that I was still confined inside the barbed-wire fence, for, right there in the heart of Germany, after eight long months of struggle against crime and injustice, I had won my battle. And for the first time, a Nazi, instead of a prisoner, was the loser.

The impact of Rinke's defeat was felt strongly among his friends, who remained helpless and stupefied. It was felt even stronger among those Germans who feared him, who suddenly and unexpectedly found themselves freed from the horrifying nightmare that his terror had created. These Germans celebrated Rinke's defeat while his friends mourned his misfortune.

The enthusiasm, however, was greater within the camp where our men, for the first time, were free to do as they pleased while the guards hastened to place themselves at their service, "because," as they put it, "of the admiration and respect they felt for good soldiers," regardless of the fact that we were their enemies.

While thus far we had not been allowed to use any coal at all, now tons of coal were piled inside the camp. The work at the mine became only the mine director's business, as the guards refrained from telling the prisoners what to do. It was the prisoners who made the decisions now; the Germans simply obeyed.

I received permission to use one of the empty buildings in the next compound as an infirmary, something I had been trying to do for months without success. The prisoners were no longer searched when returning from work, and they were able to bring into the camp the food that the Polish civilians had given them at their working places. But the greatest privilege of all accorded them was the freedom they obtained to associate with females, as long as they made no effort to escape.

Rinke watched all this, but he was not allowed to say or do anything. In his presence, the new *Kommando Führer* had told me that he had been sent there to "calm the spirits" and ease the tension that Rinke had created and to help everyone return to a normal state of body and mind.

When I saw Dr. Tsapla again he was smiling and happy.

"What did you do to Rinke?" he asked grinning.

The same week, I went to see the dentist, as usual. The Stool Pigeon escorted me there.

"Dr. Tsapla told me the news!" the dentist said smiling as soon as I walked in, while the guard remained in the waiting room. I kept pacing around the room while the dentist busied himself with the patient, telling me at the same time of the latest war developments.

"The Russians have reached Charkov!" he said, but before he had the chance to say anything more, the guard broke in and turned his rifle against me, overrun with emotion and excitement.

"Come on!" he ordered. "Let's go!"

I knew this guard was one of Rinke's closest supporters, and I wondered what had caused all the excitement.

"Come on!" he ordered again, seeing that I made no effort to move. "I heard everything through the keyhole. You are lost now!" he said. "You can't prove that you were not spying this time."

"You heard what?" I interrupted abruptly. I looked at the dentist. He had become pale and frightened. His hands were trembling.

"I heard the doctor give you war information," he hastened to reply.

I did not know whether he had really heard our conversation or merely thought he did. I laughed at his explanation. "We were talking about ancient Greek history," I said casually.

"What did he mention Charkov for?" he asked, pointing at the doctor.

"Oh, that!" I said. "That is the name of a town in ancient Greece. Poland is not the only place where there is a town with that name."

He seemed to doubt himself for a minute, and I was sure I had him confused when upon leaving the dentist's office, the doctor called him back and admitted everything, begging the guard to avoid mention of the incident and spare his family. That was something, however, The Stool Pigeon just would not do. He had been trying to pin me against the wall, and this was the first time that he had the opportunity to do it.

"*Mein Lieber*," he threatened, "don't make any mistake and lie about it," he warned.

I did not want to admit the truth even if the doctor did give us both away in his effort to spare his family's lives, so I kept insisting on my story that I knew nothing of what he was talking about.

Upon our arrival at the labor detachment, he let the other prisoners back into the camp but ordered me to wait in the courtyard while he went into the office alone to report the incident, still nervous and excited. He came out a few seconds later to lead me into the office.

The new *Kommando Führer* was seated behind the desk. Rinke was standing behind him. A guard was in the same room at the time.

"Well," Rinke growled at the new *Kommando Führer*, "you have your evidence, what are you waiting for? Put him against the wall! You'll never get a chance like this again."

I wondered for a minute what Rinke would have done if he were still in command, but his threats made me feel glad he wasn't.

The new *Kommando Führer* did not ask me any questions. "Come into my room," he suggested, indicating for me to lead the way.

"You don't have to pretend," he said. "I have enough evidence to shoot you right now. What the guard told me is true and you can't disprove it. Don't you think," he asked "it is rather foolish for a man at your age to die now, when he is so close to freedom?"

I looked with surprise at the old man in the gray-green uniform. "I'm a soldier," I said, "and as a soldier the only thing I expect is that someday I will get killed. My army did not guarantee me a long life."

The old man gazed at me with a peculiar expression. "I'll do anything I can," he said after a moment, "to save your life, but as a soldier I have to report the incident to my superiors. You can go back in the camp now."

I did not say anything. There was something different in his promise that made me suspect that he was not going to report the incident at all, and that his talk was just a bluff to appease Rinke's eagerness to finally eliminate me. I opened the door to the courtyard and walked outside. Joe was waiting at the gate, anxious to know why I was kept in the *Kommando Führer's* office.

"I went in to see if there is any mail for us," I said, "and ended up arguing with Rinke." I didn't want to worry Joe.

Two guards arrived the following morning to take Rinke to the company headquarters, where the sentence against him was pronounced. Joe and I were standing near the fence when Rinke walked out of his room for the last time. He was different from what he used to be. Beaten, confused, and demoralized, with his head down, he stepped into the courtyard.

"Ready?" one of his guards asked.

Rinke nodded.

"Let's go!" the same guard ordered, and the party of three, with Rinke in the middle, left for Beuthen.

Twenty-Five

I left Joe and started to walk toward the **Sanitäter's** room, which Joe and I were occupying now that we had a separate building for an infirmary. Joe made a gesture to follow me.

"I want to be alone for a few minutes," I said. "There is someone I want to talk to."

Joe was embarrassed by my refusal to let him join me, but refrained from interrupting the privacy I had requested. I walked into the room alone and closed the door behind me. The stove inside was red hot from the heat of the burning coal, which I had shoveled in an hour before. It was quiet and peaceful outside. I removed my hat, knelt, and, folding my hands, I prayed. "My God," I said solemnly, "please forgive me if I was wrong."

Joe came in a few minutes later, accompanied by George and a number of other prisoners who followed him there casually while talking about the "liberation day" and the possible length of time we might still have to spend as prisoners. Every indication at last had begun to point in the direction of freedom. The fighting front was now but 30 miles from our labor detachment. Artillery fire could be heard occasionally, and the guards began to visualize themselves inside the barbed wire already, each one trying to gain sympathy for himself, begging for our mercy on the day when the situation was to be reversed. There seemed to be no doubt in anyone's mind that "this was it," that we were definitely going to be free, and that our freedom was only a matter of days, if not hours. Even the captain himself changed his attitude and let the spirit of defeat manifest itself in his actions and words, looking upon Joe and me as the ones on whom his fate depended.

The old military spirit was soon revived in Joe, and once again he was the same old company sergeant major, ready to shout orders and enforce discipline as he knew it.

We were no longer forced to work. The Germans decided to spend the remaining time showing us the better side of their nature — the one we had never known, the one that would induce every one of us to forget the hardships and suffering we had received at their hands during the years of captivity. The side that never really existed.

On the 16th of January 1945, with the front as near as 15 miles to the coal mine, the order for a mass evacuation of all prisoners from eastern Germany arrived from the German High Command.

Behind this move every Nazi or German saw the chance to escape even temporarily from a fate like the one they had engineered for us. They believed that somehow, at the last minute, they were going to surrender on terms to the Western Allies and that they would never have to experience life behind the barbed wire.

The forced march to the west began the following morning, January 17th. We were not told how far we would have to go. We were not given any food or water. All we were told was that we had to keep moving, lined up in fives, at the pace that the officer set riding his motorcycle in front of the column. Anyone stepping out of line was to be shot; the sentries at the end of the column had orders to make sure those who could no longer walk did not remain behind alive.

We were joined in this march by all the labor detachments for which the same company of Germans were responsible. Most of us were in good physical shape to walk. Some, however, who had been kept in hospitals, were not. They were to be shot, according to the instructions of the German High Command, but we succeeded in persuading the captain to let them return to the camp. We were allowed to take them along in the large wooden boxes used as sleighs. We took them as far as the snow-covered road lasted and as far as our own reserve of strength permitted. Pulling those boxes was not very hard, except when passing through cities where the ice had been removed from the brick pavement. We used snow for water whenever we could stop for a few seconds without being fired at.

The first day of the march ended at midnight, when the entire column was allowed to rest in three little barrooms 30 kilometers west of Beuthen. There was no room for us to stand one alongside the other, but the Germans squeezed everyone in by firing on those in the rear, thus forcing everyone to move inside. In these small rooms, packed one on top of the other, we spent the night, four hours in all. The Germans were in a hurry to get the column started as the Allied front line kept approaching at the same rate, a few miles behind us. The city of Beuthen and the labor detachment we had left were captured that same day.

In the morning, under the falling white flakes of snow, wet, hungry, and exhausted, we were put back in fives, ready to leave for the day's marching assignment. In their hurry the Germans did not waste any time to count the prisoners; with the help of well-trained police dogs, they detected any who might have tried to remain behind hiding.

The sergeant major, George, and I were in the same row. Occasionally we relieved those carrying the prisoners who were unable to walk. The number of these prisoners increased, as new ones became fatigued during the march. In the afternoon of the same day, we saw the first prisoners from another group lying on the side of the road with a bullet through each of their foreheads. The sight of these victims, lying on their backs at the slanting edge of the road with their feet on the pavement, their heads down the slope, and their hands spread wide, formed a terrifying spectacle for everyone. As we passed by, all our hopes for a better fate were chilled by these cold-blooded murders. Many, frightened by the sight of these silent witnesses of our own end, began to believe they were already exhausted. One prisoner from our group, a middle-aged man, believed he had become paralyzed and began to cry and scream.

"I can't walk!" he screamed desperately. "My knees! I can't walk any more! My feet!" he kept yelling amidst cries of fear, as he found himself gradually nearing the end of the column, where the last sentry was to make sure that he was left behind dead.

I managed to get to him before he reached the end. I placed his arm around my shoulder and tried to help him walk, doing my best at the same time to encourage him that he had the strength.

"You are all right!" I kept telling him. "You can walk if you want to. You just think you can't because you were frightened at the sight of the dead prisoners."

"My knees," he protested, crying. "My knees, they don't hold anymore."

I tried to lift him, but I could not, so I let him ride on my shoulder the same way I had seen the *Sanitäters* carry wounded at the front lines four years ago when there were not enough men to carry a stretcher. I was thus able to walk faster and reach the part of the column made up of prisoners from our camp. Joe saw me approach, but he thought I could carry the prisoner for some distance before he came to my relief. I was already tired from the prisoner's weight and the fast pace at which the column was marching. Soon, I started to lose pace and remained behind my group, getting closer to the last German guard. "Now we are both lost," I whispered to myself.

Joe, meanwhile, seeing that I had disappeared with my cargo behind our group, eventually came through the column looking for me. When he saw me nearing the last guard, he hurried his step to get to me. I put the prisoner on the ground and each of us placed one of his arms around our shoulders. "Thank heaven," I whispered. Gradually we rejoined our group far ahead. We carried the prisoner all the way until finally we were allowed to stop. This time we were thrown in a castle, and there was just enough room to stretch our legs and lie on the ground. I sat with my back against the wall trying to rest.

The result of the first two days of the march and the fear of the fate awaiting each one when his feet and knees no longer could hold the strain and fatigue were apparent in every face. It was not hard to feel the tension.

"I am not staying here!" a prisoner began screaming all of a sudden. "I am not going to wait for them to shoot me!" he started yelling. "I am going home! You understand? I am going home!" he yelled, getting up, as if he was trying to leave. He laughed at himself, as if he had managed somehow to solve his problem. "I am going home! Ha, ha," he kept laughing. Before anyone could realize what he was doing, he ran to the door. His friend got up and went after him to bring him back, but he was already outside, yelling and shouting. "I am going home! Ha, ha, haaa. . . ."

His shouts and laughter ended with a sudden gunshot. Inside the room, we looked nervously at each other. There wasn't a thing we could do.

I could not sleep that night. From what I had seen during the first two days of the march, the only thing I could expect was more days of the same, without any food or water, until one day, somewhere along the road, some German soldier would use one more bullet for me. This seemed to be the only conclusion I could draw as to the motives of this Nazi move. It did not seem possible that any of us were going to live to be free.

"What a funny place to die!" Joe remarked with a certain bitterness in his voice. George was lying with his back against the wall, silent.

"What did you do with the girl?" Joe inquired.

George gave no answer.

I did not make any comment, although I shared his feelings. "You can't have anything," I said finally. "Not as a prisoner, no matter how much it may mean to you."

"If there is ever another war," Joe said, "and I have no choice but to be taken prisoner, I will have a bullet, one single bullet saved up. That bullet is going to be for me. I will save myself all this."

I made up mind to escape without telling any of my intentions to Joe or George. Harry had not been around for some time, but he returned in the late hours of the night. "I was trying to take care of frostbites," he said. "Quite a few of our men are suffering from it already." His hands were frozen; they had cracked open from the frost and were bleeding, but he didn't seem to mind.

"If we ever get out of this hell alive," Joe commented, "I will recommend you for a citation by the Greek army."

"I am only trying to do my duty," Harry contended.

Early in the morning, we were marching again, still without any food. The abundance of snow had partly quenched our thirst. Two prisoners who had tried to escape during the night had been shot by one of the guards from our group. All day long I kept fixing in my mind the location of those forests and villages along the way that were crowded by German front-line troops, intending to stay clear of such nests after my escape.

This day, more prisoners were lying dead along the roadside than the previous day. Fortunately, we didn't recognize them; they belonged to other groups before us. We crossed the Oder River at the town of Ratibor that same day. It was frozen already, which would make it possible for me to cross the river after my escape without having to look for a narrow section to swim across in the freezing water.

The Germans were getting ready to blow the bridges linking the city of Ratibor west of the Oder with the scattered small outskirts east. While climbing up the last hill before the city, a number of horse sleighs, which thus far had been kept in front of the column, were stuck on the icy slope. A large number of prisoners used for traction were striving painfully, but without success, to push them uphill under the beating of German rifles and whips. On these sleighs the Germans had stored all their belongings. A number of guards, overcome by fatigue and frostbite, were carried on the same sleighs. With leather whips, they kept beating the prisoners, infuriated over their inability to move the heavy wagons up the hill.

It was a terrifying and pitiful spectacle for everyone. We kept passing by the dead bodies on the roadside, wondering where the road was going to end.

"They are lucky!" prisoners remarked at the sight of the dead. "They can't do anything more to them now."

"Yes, they are lucky!" I kept thinking. For them the march was over. Their suffering had ended. They couldn't hear the Germans anymore. They did not have to worry whether tomorrow they would live or die. They had nothing more that the Nazis could take away from them. For them, it was over for good. For us, there was more yet to come.

We marched past Ratibor, and we were finally told to stop at the little village of Annahuette, eight kilometers west of the river. The *Kommando Führer* of our labor detachment told us that we were to have a day of rest. No mention was made about giving us anything to eat. That was not important as far as the Germans were concerned. The important thing was that we were on the "other side of the Oder," as our *Kommando Führer* had announced.

I used the whole night to get all the rest I could before my escape. In the morning I decided to shave, thinking that if I were seen, I would not give the impression of a deserter or a runaway convict. There was no water or soap, so I contented myself with just plain snow as shaving cream.

"What in the world are you doing?" Joe inquired.

"Just trying to look handsome!" I said. I did not tell him of my plans. I knew he would object — especially if he knew of my reasons for escape. I had made up my mind to be free. That was all I wanted, all that mattered. For how long was of no consequence.

Late in the afternoon, I told Harry of my decision.

"When do you plan to leave?" he asked.

"Tonight, at midnight! It'll be dark enough then," I said. "Do you have an extra pair of underpants?"

"I have two pairs on," Harry replied. "I'll give you one if you need it."

"That'll be fine!" I thought. If he didn't know any more of my plans, he wouldn't have to lie for me.

"What are you going to do about the hounds?" he asked.

"I just hope they won't notice me," I remarked hastily. "I'll take that pair of pants when it gets dark. I don't want anyone to see you."

I spent the remainder of the afternoon planning different ways to get away unobserved from the barn where we stayed. I convinced the *Kommando Führer* to let Joe, Harry, and me sleep in the adjoining barn, separated from the rest of the prisoners. Without attracting the attention of the guards, I carefully spread the contents of a small pepper box, which I managed to retain from the last issue of Red Cross parcels, around the perimeter of the barn, hoping that the police dogs would not be able to detect me. Harry gave me the extra pair of underwear as soon as it was dark enough. A few hours before midnight, everything was ready. All three of us retired in the barn to get some sleep before the next day's march.

I soon went to sleep. Joe did the same, but Harry did not succeed, though he tried for hours. When I woke up at midnight, he was still awake. He shook my hand. "Good luck!" he said.

"I'll write to you in Australia," I said, and slid down the heap of straw where we slept. The movement annoyed Joe.

"Why the hell don't you go to sleep?" he murmured.

I slid through the bales of hay, deep enough so that nothing could pierce through. I did not let Harry suspect I was still in the barn. I preferred that he thought I was gone.

The morning found me asleep. Growls, thrashing of rifles, orders flying in all directions woke me up. Soon, the Germans would know I was missing. One came into the barn to make sure it was empty. I heard the sound of sleighs mixed in the grunts of men trying to get them moving, the stepping of boots. I waited for the sound of hounds in the barn. Moments seemed like hours. Finally, the sounds grew weaker, the shouts less frequent. They were leaving without me. I could breathe at last.

About noon, I decided to open slightly the door panel and look into the yard. I heard voices nearby, and I closed the panel quickly. They belonged to the militiamen with rifles on their shoulders, searching for me. It must have been reported that I was missing. Once more I slipped through the bales of hay and waited.

When night came, I walked quietly to the back entrance of the barn. I started to open the door, removing first the log that held the two panels together. The door creaked as the heavy wooden panels fell back. I pushed them in again and held them closed with my knee, while I pulled a heavy rock near, to keep one of the two panels firm. I held the other open a little to see where the militiamen had gone. They were not in sight. I closed the second panel, avoiding any noise that could give me away. It held there without any support. I put a long-sleeved wool T-shirt over my khaki coat and pulled Harry's underpants over my trousers, stuffing inside the remaining part of my coat. I took some snow through the opening underneath the door panels and spread it over my hat.

When I finished with this camouflage, I opened the same door panel to see whether the militiamen were around. I did not see them, so I stepped out and pulled the door panel until it closed. I started to walk away from the barn. I did not stop to look behind me, anxious to get far enough from the building before the militiamen came. I was certain they would not be able to see me if I moved as far as a hundred feet away. I had tried a similar experiment the first night by hanging a white piece of cloth at a closer distance and then trying to locate it in the darkness. The result was quite satisfactory. It was too cold for anyone to see without protective glasses, something which neither the guards nor the militiamen had.

I had moved as far as 30 feet from the barn when I thought I heard voices. I fell on the ground, into the deep snow. I could hide completely without being seen, even at a distance of a few feet unless someone was standing directly above me. Being near to the earth, the sounds were amplified. Every noise seemed to come from very close at hand.

Finally, I decided to stand up and look. I did not see anything moving or hear any more voices nearby. I started to walk again, while my heart was beating like a drum. All I would hear if I were caught, I kept thinking, would be just a shot, and maybe not even that. Somebody else would hear that. I heard no hounds bark or move in my direction. I was far from the barn now, but still not far enough to feel safe. I kept walking until finally the barn and the village of Annahuette disappeared completely in the white glittering snow.

It was still cold. I was hungry and exhausted. But the pressure and tension of prison life were no longer there. The fears I had maintained yesterday, the fate that awaited me where the road of marching, death, suffering, and human endurance ended, were not there anymore. Walking over the snow-covered hills, in the freezing dark winter night, far off where the horizon ends, I could see, through my mind, hope — and, beyond the horizon, freedom.

in which others saw a reef in the vast ocean called the future.

In Athens, in 1946, Joe Kavroudakis had remarked in awe, "Do you realize what we did? We took on Hitler's Germany! I have recommended you for the Distinguished Service Medal."

Joe became a lieutenant general in the Greek army. Basil Peirasmakis reached Egypt, then went on to Rhodesia and became a navigator in the RAF. He flew missions over Heracleion, each time diving over his home several times. His mother said that she knew it was him. Two years later, he was transferred to the Free Greek Force that had been formed in the Middle East. He retired from the Greek air force with the rank of colonel.

My journey, which began when the *Hereward* sank, has not ended; it has yet to reach port. All becomes clear when I look to the greater power, who is steering my raft, keeping the stormy waters from swallowing me. He knows the harbor it is destined to reach.

Appendix

A Greek POW in World War II 235

Principal bombing area and German landing sites near Heracleion, Crete, by Anastasios Aslanis.

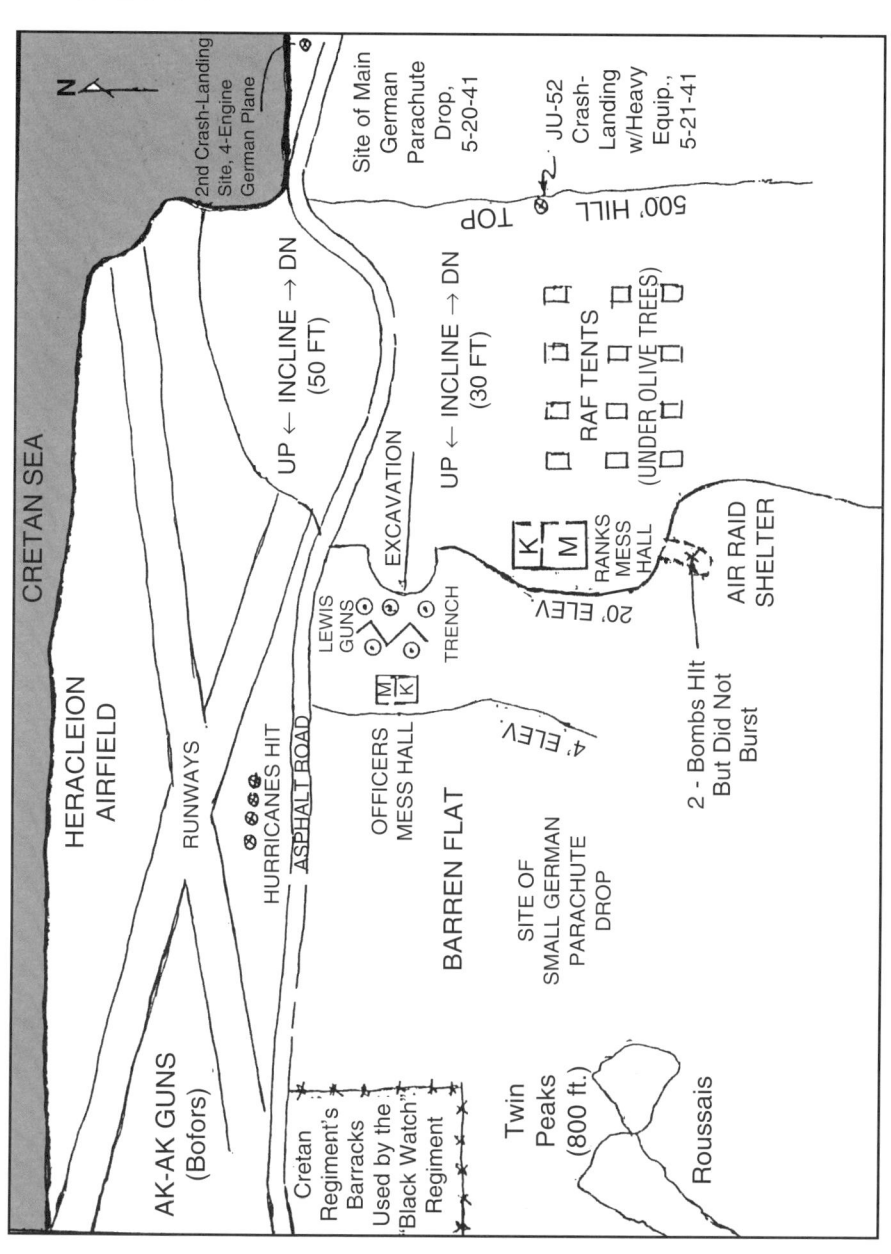

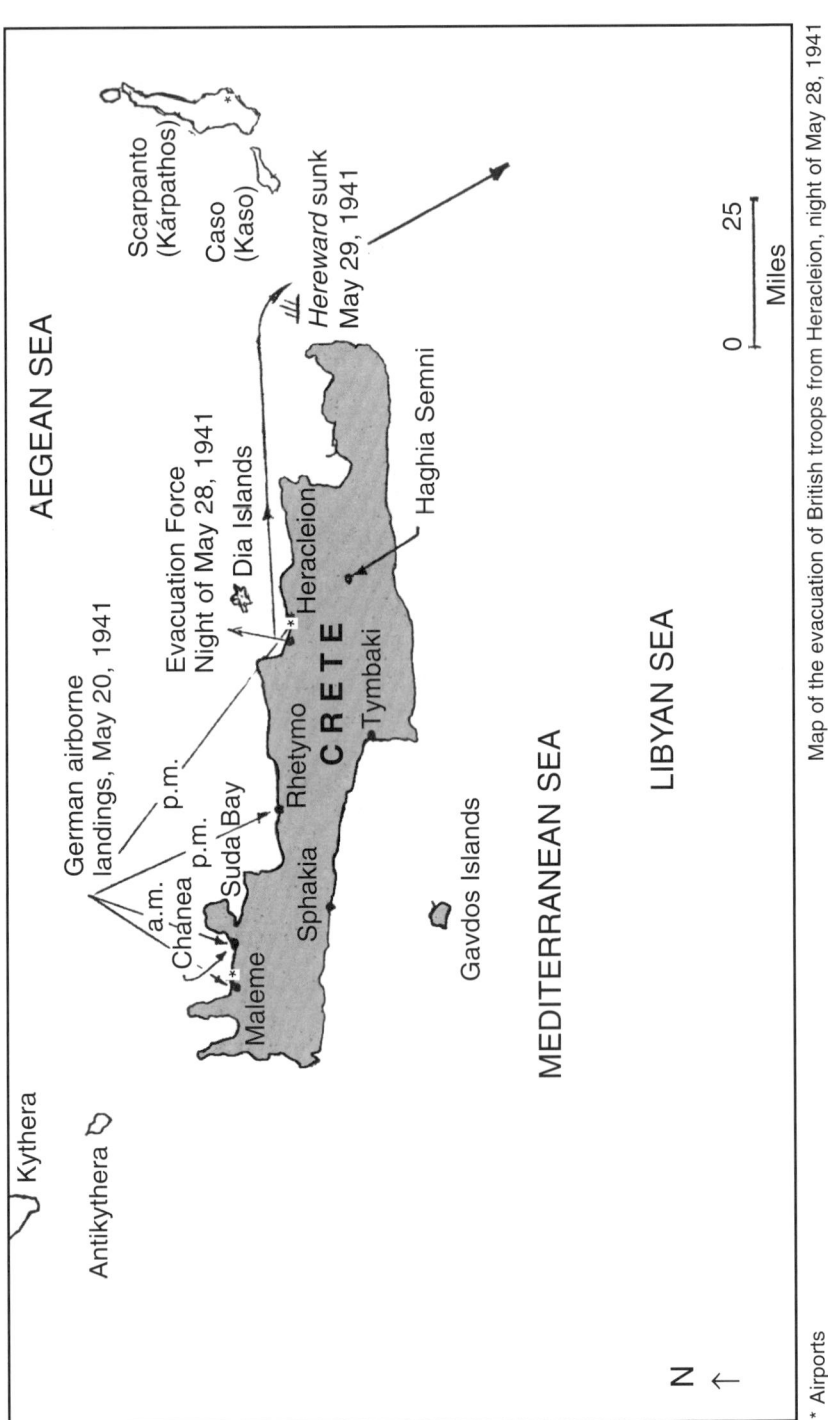

Map of the evacuation of British troops from Heracleion, night of May 28, 1941 (by Anastasios Aslanis).

A Greek POW in World War II 237

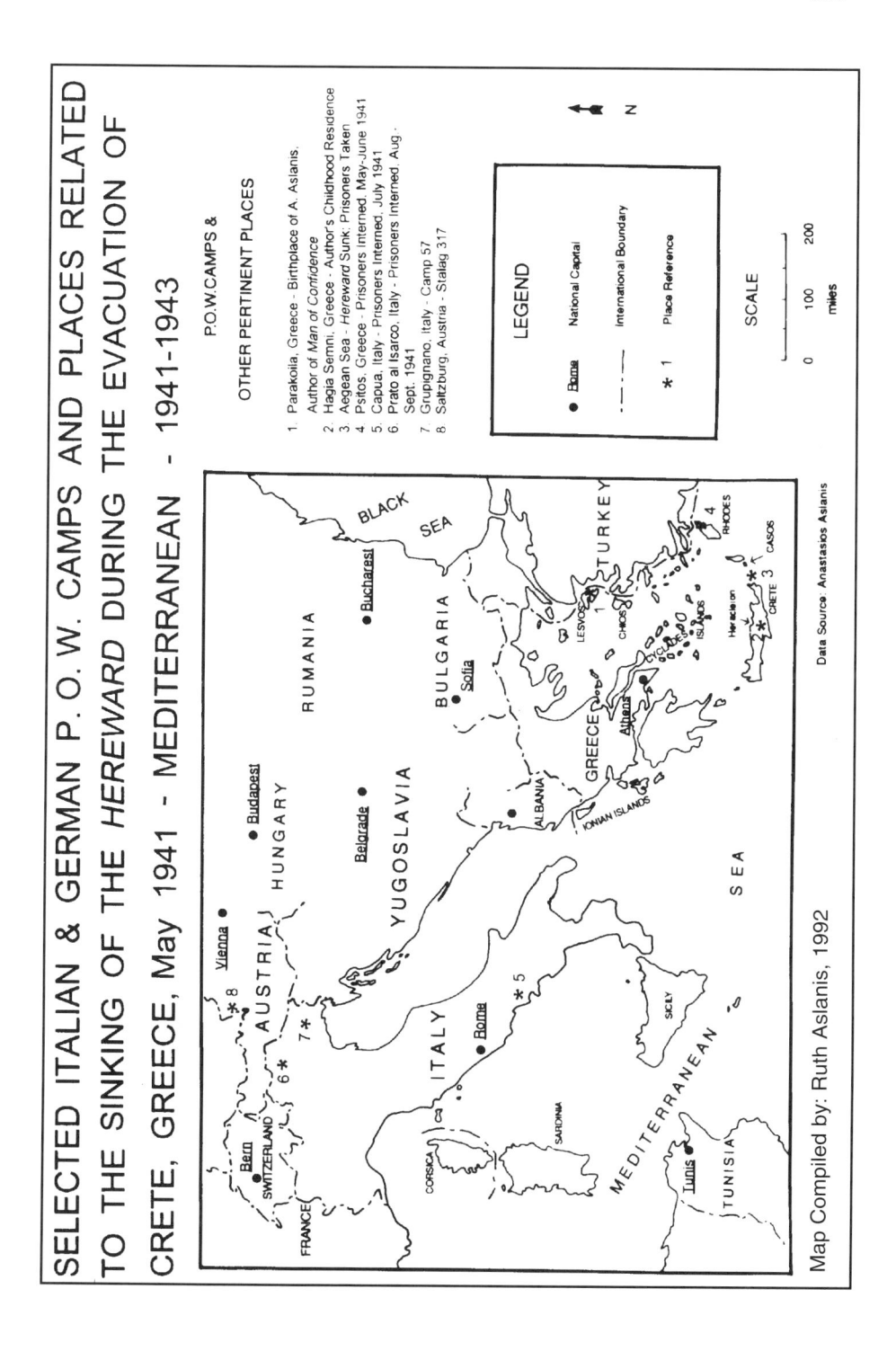

SELECTED ITALIAN & GERMAN P.O.W. CAMPS AND PLACES RELATED TO THE SINKING OF THE *HEREWARD* DURING THE EVACUATION OF CRETE, GREECE, May 1941 - MEDITERRANEAN - 1941-1943

P.O.W. CAMPS & OTHER PERTINENT PLACES

1. Parakoila, Greece - Birthplace of A. Aslanis. Author of *Man of Confidence*
2. Hagia Semni, Greece - Author's Childhood Residence
3. Aegean Sea - *Hereward* Sunk: Prisoners Taken
4. Psitos, Greece - Prisoners Interned, May-June 1941
5. Capua, Italy - Prisoners Interned, July 1941
6. Prato al Isarco, Italy - Prisoners Interned, Aug.-Sept. 1941
7. Grupignano, Italy - Camp 57
8. Saltzburg, Austria - Stalag 317

LEGEND

● Rome — National Capital
--- — International Boundary
*1 — Place Reference

SCALE
0   100   200
       miles

Data Source: Anastasios Aslanis

Map Compiled by: Ruth Aslanis, 1992

Dear uncle

I hope that you have received my message sent to you through the American Embassy in Switzerland. I am writing this letter a week after that message has been dispatched from the camp, wishing to find you in happiness and health. I have been interned into the P.o.W. camp with many other British P.oW. twenty one months ago, during which I addressed to you several letters. I spent all that time in completing my knowledge of French, German and Italian, so to day I am master of these three foreign languages. Fortunately, amongst the books of our camp library there are many ones referring to my school training of the last three years. I have not been able, owing to war consequences, to finish the gymnasium's course, leaving so my uncompleted education in its fifth school year. My family unfortunately is not in case to support the expenses of the continuance of the last two years training in the intermediate school as well as those of the University, in the future. Myself, I am doing everything that I can to keep always in mind all that matter which I have been taught, making thus profit of the time, which otherwise might be lost. This is all my news. I expect to have yours very soon. I would also like to hear from my dear aunt.

yours affectionately
Anastasios Aslanis

Letter from the author to his uncle in the U.S., from Camp 57 in Italy.

A Greek POW in World War II 239

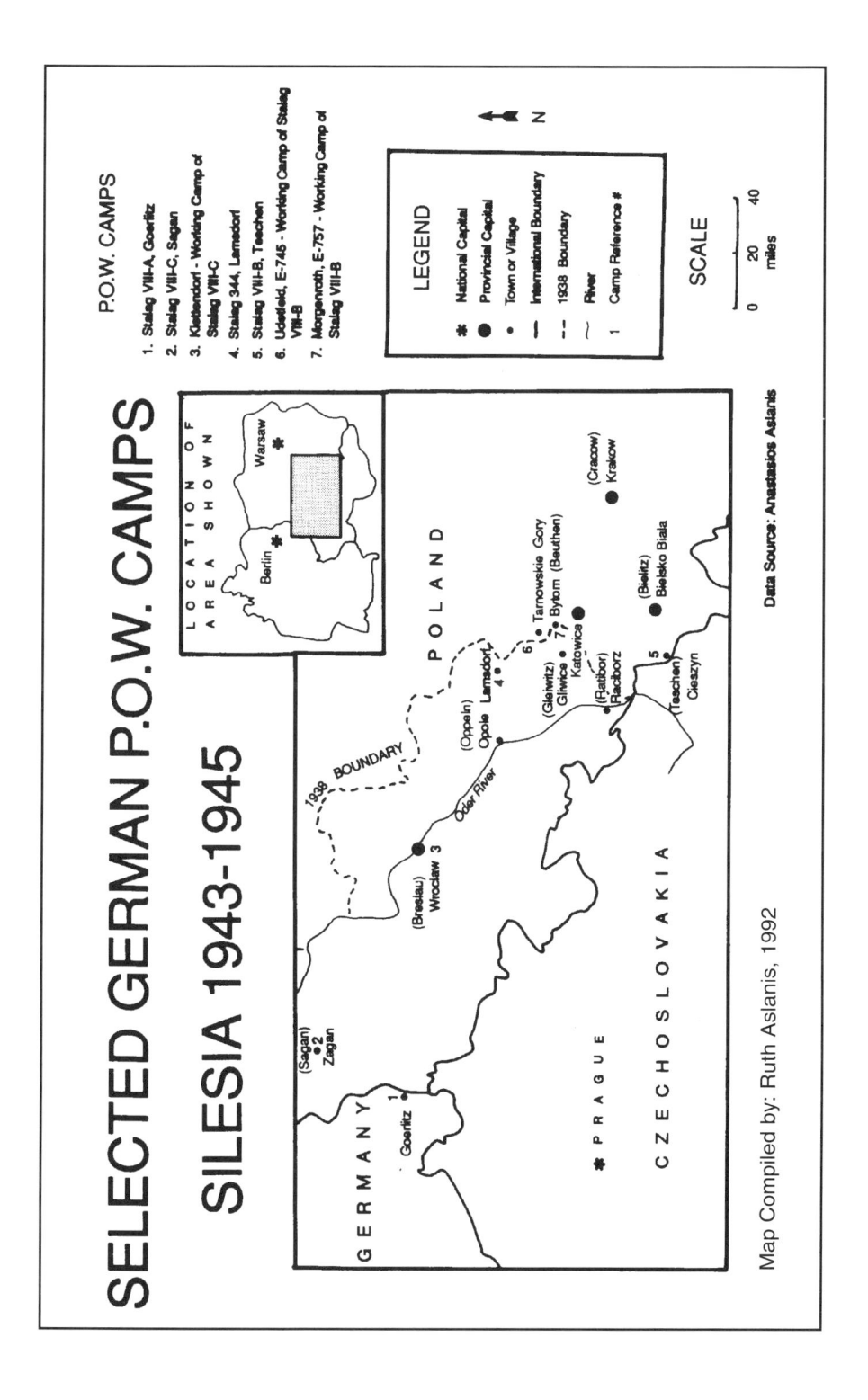

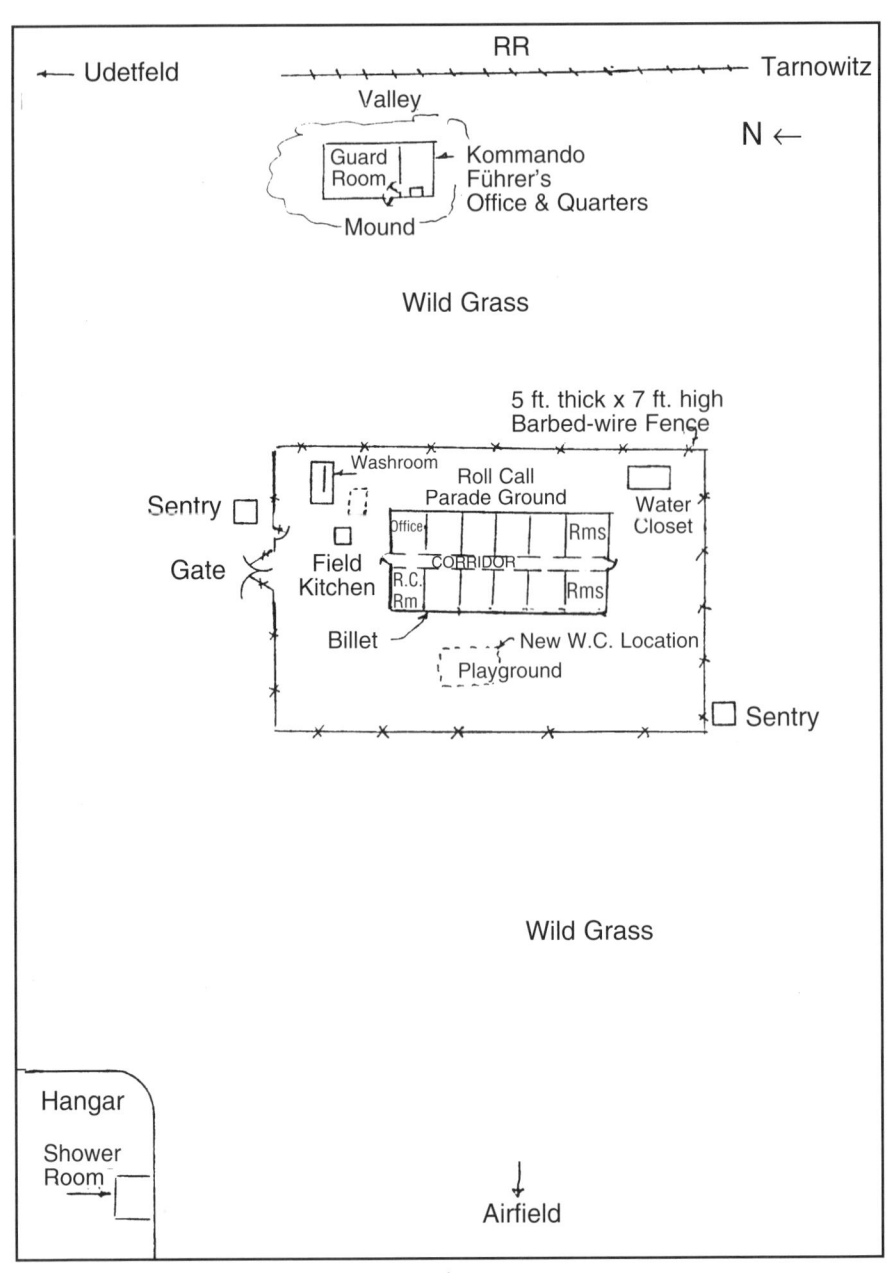

Plan of E.745, Udetfeld (by Anastasios Aslanis).

A Greek POW in World War II

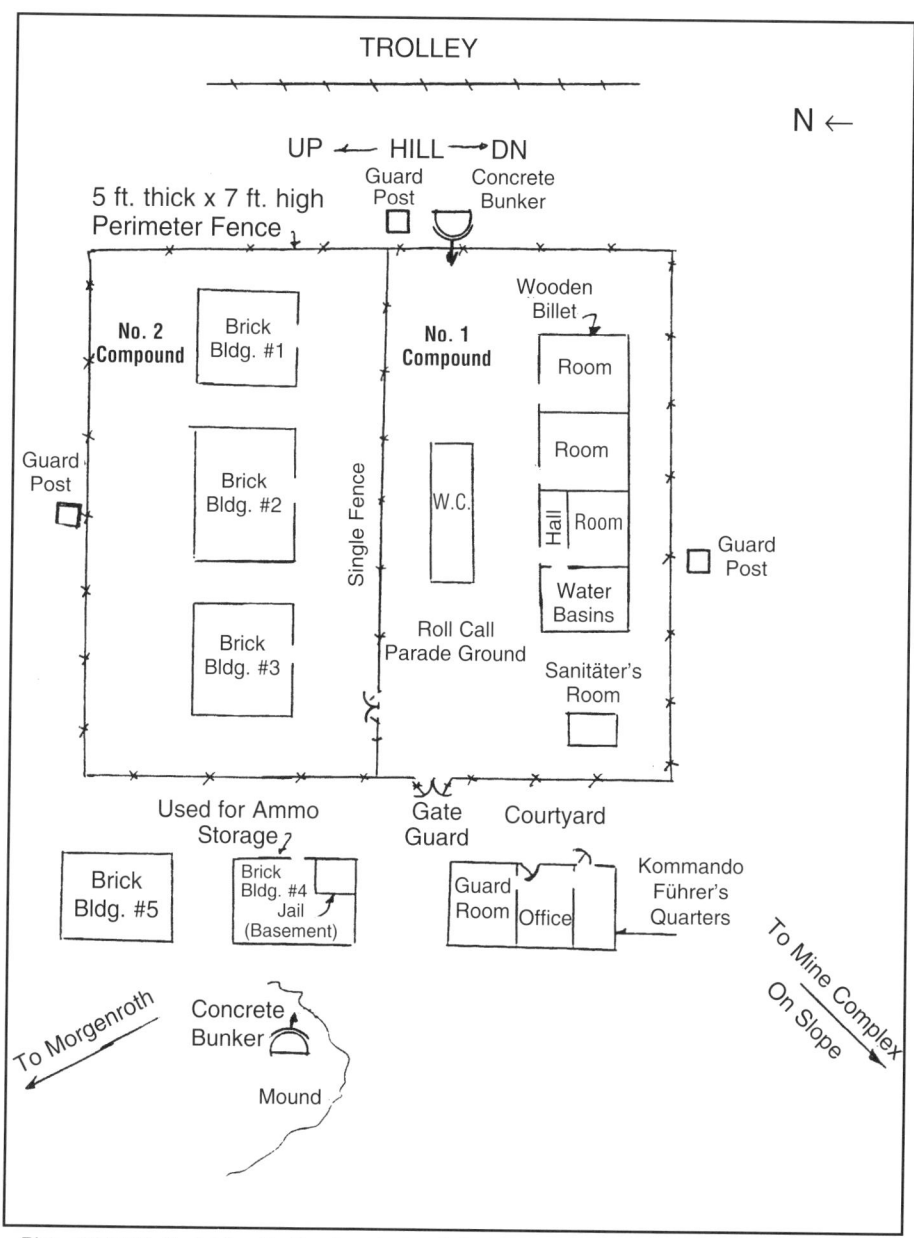

Plan of E.757, Godulahuette (by Anastasios Aslanis). (Two additional concrete bunkers were located northwest of the brick buildings.)

Above and opposite: Letter from the author to his aunt in Wilmington, Delaware, November 26, 1944. Mailed from Camp E.757.

A Greek POW in World War II

Auf diese Seite schreibt nur der Kriegsgefangene!
Questa pagina è riservata al prigioniero di guerra!
Deutlich auf die Zeilen schreiben!
Scrivere soltanto sulle linee e leggibilmente!

26/11/4?

My dear aunt,

I am writing again few words to you with the hope that they will give you the same pleasure as yours and that of my uncle received few weeks ago. Everything here is much the same. I am always looking forward to the day when freedom will replace imprisonment.

I am thinking of you all the time, of home, of all my beloved persons from whom the supreme duty keeps me away. How long still? Certainly not very.

I am reading your letters over and over, trying to immagine, once I cannot be there, how things are really knowing. I am compelled to satisfy my curiousity with your pleasant information, that everything goes well.

I do not know wether I shall receive your answer to this letter. However I wish that everything continues to be alright. Someday we will all meet in different circumstances of course. Then we shall relate everything old, or new. God propose! Kindest regards to my uncle. Yours affectionately

244 THE MAN OF CONFIDENCE

Above and opposite: Certificate and translation from the Greek Ministry of the Army, sent to the author two months after his return home.

Translation

(Γ.Δ.Υ.Σ.)

General Directorship
Ministry of the Army
Div. of Casualties, Section IIIa

Ser. Number
3355

CERTIFICATE

It is certified that the Soldier Aslanis Anastasios of Joannis class of 1946 is registered in the Rolls (Metroa) maintained by us, he was prisoner in Italy from 29-5-41, he returned the 16th of May 1945.

The present is issued for all legal use, at the request of the interested person.

Athens the 15th of August 1945

SEAL &
Signature of Director

Pratikakis Emm.
Lieut. Colonel of the Infantry

Fee

Left to right: Raymond, Dédé (?), and Jacques, October 1943, in Stalag VIII-A, Goerlitz.

A boxing match in Lamsdorf, Stalag 344, 1943.

Prisoners in Lamsdorf, Stalag 344, 1943.

A Greek POW in World War II 249

Funeral cortege of a Greek POW, Lamsdorf, Stalag 344, winter 1943.

British POWs, officers and ranks, at the funeral of a Greek POW in Lamsdorf, Stalag 344, 1943 (the officers were doctors interned in Lamsdorf).

A Greek POW in World War II

British POWs in Lamsdorf, Stalag 344, 1943.

Greek POWs in the *Arbeitskommando* attached to Stalag 344, which the author visited in 1944 to check the living conditions provided by the Germans. These prisoners were later moved to Udetfeld, Camp E.745.

The author (on horse) in July 1945 with his brother Constantine.

Index

— A —

Addison, Fred, xviii, xxiii-xxiii
Africa
  Libya, 10, 12
    Tobruk, 10, 12
  North, 15
  South, 70
Albania, xix
Alex _____ (guard), 123, 143, 157-158, 161, 167-168, 176-177, 180-181, 185, 212
Alexakis, General, xviii, 230-232
Algiers
  Oran, 28
Allies, 12, 15-16, 25, 58, 68, 86, 97, 103, 111, 115, 123, 128, 130, 139, 149, 205, 221-222
Alps, 11
America, 230
American, 15, 115, 164

Anzac (Australian-New Zealand), xx, xxiv
Asia Minor, xvii, 7
Aslanis
  Anastasios, vi, xv
  Constantine, xvii
Australia, 10, 12, 18, 24, 156, 226
Australian, 3
  army, xxiv
Austria, 17, 25
  Salzburg, 17, 23, 30, 37
Austrian, 183, 186, 195, 197-198, 201, 212
Axis, 12

— B —

Bassett, Jack, xviii, xxii, 80-81
Battle of the Atlantic, xix
Behandlung der Kriegsgefangenen (Treatment of War Prisoners), 140-141

Belgian, 27
Belgium, 64
Berliner (guard), The, 123, 139-140
Beste, Sergeant, 70-71, 75-76, 78, 85
Bohr, General, 115-116
Borneo, 13
British, xviii-xx, xxii-xxiv, 1, 2, 6, 12, 33, 50, 51, 59, 61, 70, 72-73, 75, 79, 81, 86-87, 100, 111, 115, 118
   air force, xx-xxi, 80
   Air Ministry, xx
   army, xxi, 34, 72, 156
   Black Watch Regiment, xxi
   camp, xxii
   government, 111
   Intelligence Service, 15, 86, 119
   Navy, 9
   RAF, xiii, xviii-xix, xxiv, 80, 233
      camp, xx
Bulgaria, xix

— C —

Calcaterra, Commandant, 12-14
Concentration camp, 11, 17-18, 29, 85, 87, 101, 132, 136-137
Crete, xvi, xviii-xxii, 1-2, 6-7, 9-10, 67, 80-81
   Haghia Semni, xvi-xvii
   Heracleion, xiv, xvi-xix, xxi-xxiii, 1-2, 80, 230, 233
      Gymnasium, xvi-xviii, 230
      Military Academy, xxi
      Pateles, xxiii
      Square Venizelos, xxiii
      Tris Camares park, xxiii
         Venetian walls, xxiii
   Rethymo, xxii, 80
   Spylia, xxiii
Czech, 91, 127

— D —

Das Reich, 116, 163
Day, Sergeant Cyril "Bill," 34-37, 39-40, 43-51, 54, 56-57, 59-63, 86
Dédé _____, 28-30
Delaware
   Wilmington, xiii, xiv
Dia, xxi
   Ida mountain, xxii

Distinguished Service Medal, 233
Dodecanese Islands, 7
   Rhodes, 2, 7-9
      Psitos, 8

— E —

Egypt, 9, 72, 80, 85, 233
   Alexandria, xxiv, 2
Emmanuel _____, 206
England, 80, 139, 183
   Beaconsfield, 230
   Liverpool, 230
   London, 10, 68, 139, 230
   Newcastle-under-Lyme, 230
English, xviii, 19, 33, 39, 66-67, 104, 139, 149-151, 155-156, 164
Europe, xxii, 72
European, 1
Extermination camp, 17, 109

— F —

Finns, 48
France, 58, 64, 114, 139
   Bordeaux, 139
   Cherbourg, 123
   Dieppe, 81
   Dunkirk, 2
   Le Havre, 28
   Lyon, 27, 139
   Paris, 28, 139
   Saint Lô, 123
Frank _____ "The Deacon" (guard), 101, 103, 106, 111, 113, 115, 135, 137, 139-140, 143-146, 150-151
Free Greek Force, 233
French, 24-28, 30, 32-33, 35, 44, 51, 57-58, 85, 89
Freyberg, Major General Bernard, xix

— G —

Geneva Convention, vii, 11-12, 17, 20, 24, 28, 33, 35, 40, 44, 46-47, 57, 61, 71, 86-87, 96, 106, 110, 118-119, 121-122, 149, 202-203
German, xviii-xxiv, 1-2, 5-6, 9, 12, 16-18, 20, 22-30, 33, 35-42, 44-48, 50-51, 55, 58-61, 64-68, 70-73, 75-91, 93-100, 104-106, 109-111, 113-114, 116-120, 138-141, 144, 148-153, 155-157, 160,

German *(continued)*, 162-165, 168, 170, 173, 175-176, 178, 182, 185-187, 190-192, 194, 197, 199-201, 203, 205-206, 208-209, 211-214, 216-217, 221-225, 227, 229
  air patrol, 9
  army, 9-10, 160, 166
    Panzer battalion, 16
  Block *Führer*, 68, 70-71, 76
  government, 20
  High Command, 22, 104, 106, 115, 136, 141, 150, 210, 221-222
  Intelligence Service, 98, 100, 103
  Luftwaffe (air force), 108, 117
  planes, xx-xxi, xxiii, 2-3, 5-6, 114
  POW camp, xiv, 97
  SS (*Schutzstaffel*), 110, 136
  War industry, 101, 109
  Wehrmacht, 101, 116, 132, 136, 141
Germany, xvii, 17, 19, 21-22, 46, 49, 55, 58-59, 62, 87, 89, 91, 96-97, 100-101, 103, 110, 114-116, 132, 148-149, 159-160, 164, 168, 170, 175, 180, 204-205, 212, 214, 216, 221, 230, 233
  Berlin, 24, 123
  Dresden, 24, 229
  Eisenach, 229
  Erfurt, 229
  Frankfurt, 230
  Gleiwitz, 120, 132
  Goerlitz, 24-25, 32, 34-37, 40, 42, 44, 51, 61, 66, 229
    Stalag VII-A, 31-32, 42, 51
  Gotha, 229
  Jena, 229
  Klettendorf, 34, 36, 53, 61-63, 65, 67, 73, 87, 171
  Lamsdorf, 62-63, 66, 70-72, 74-75, 81, 92, 105-107, 110, 122, 152, 159, 176, 179, 181
    Stalag VIII-B (Stalag 344), 62, 66-67, 71, 74, 81, 159, 177
  Leipzig, 229
  Munich, 24
  Oppeln, 64, 66
  Sagan, 40, 42-43, 46, 50-52
    Stalag VIII-C, 42
  Silesia, 55
  Teschen, 87-88, 91-92, 100, 111, 119,

Germany *(continued)*
  Teschen *(continued)*, 127, 149-150, 159
    Stalag VIII-B, 87, 91, 96, 100, 110, 118, 125, 127, 130, 150-152, 155-156, 159, 172, 184, 205, 207, 213
  Weimar, 229
  Ziegenhain, 229
    Stalag IX-A, 229
Gestapo, 57-58, 131
Gigli, Benjamino, 133
Great Britain, xix, 11, 231
Greece, xvii-xix, xxi, 2, 10, 49, 85, 100, 110, 175, 218
  Athens, 230, 233
  Corinth, 9, 201
    Canal, 9
  Pireus, 9, 230
  Thessaloniki, xix
Greek, xvii-xix, xxiv, 24, 66, 72, 82, 100, 171, 217
  air force, 233
  army, xiii, xvii-xix, xxiii, 100, 168, 224, 232-233
  civil war, xiv
  Embassy, 232
  government, xiv, 72, 230-231
Goebbels, Paul Joseph, 97, 116, 160, 163-165
Goodie _____, 71-72, 77-79, 83, 85, 91

— H —

Hawaii
  Pearl Harbor, 12
Himmler, Heinrich, 212
Hitler, Adolf, xvii, 21, 25, 28, 49, 95, 97, 116, 121, 129, 132, 136, 173, 178, 180-181, 184, 205, 233
Hitler-Jugend, 132
HMS *Hereward*, 1, 3, 6, 10, 178, 233
Hungarian, 91

— I —

Italian, xix, 6-16, 22, 133, 230
  army, 9
  Front, xvii
Italy, 9, 11, 13, 15-16, 18, 36, 46-47, 64, 68
  Bari, 9-10
  Bolzano, 11

Italy *(continued)*
  Capua, 10-11
  Genoa, 16
  Grupignano, 11
    Camp No. 57, 11, 15, 17-18, 32, 36, 68
  Naples, 16, 230
  Rome, 16
  Taranto, 230
  Udine, 11, 16-17

— J —

Jacques ____, 27-30
Japan, 12
Japanese, 12, 15
Jew, 31, 164
Johanna "Joan" ____, 89-90, 99, 102, 105, 123, 157-158, 161-162, 168, 178, 182, 199
Joyce, William "Lord Haw Haw," 12, 15

— K —

Karaolanis, George, 88-90, 99, 102, 104-105, 115, 117, 123, 133-135, 138-139, 145, 147, 155, 157-159, 161-165, 168-170, 178, 182, 192, 198-199, 205, 207, 221-222, 224
Kaso, 6
Kavroudakis, Joseph "Joe," 67-72, 74-76, 78-83, 85-91, 94-96, 98-101, 105, 109-111, 115, 117-121, 124-132, 134-135, 137-139, 143-145, 147-150, 152, 156, 158, 163-172, 175, 178-180, 182, 184-188, 196-197, 199, 201, 203-205, 207-209, 212-214, 216, 219-220
Kommando Führer (camp commandant), 37-45, 48-51, 53-57, 59, 61-64, 86-88, 91, 93-95, 97-98, 104, 129, 150, 152, 161-162, 165, 177, 179, 186, 190, 192, 194, 197, 202-203, 205-208, 216-219, 225-226

— L —

Lager Feldwebel, 82-84
Lager Offizier, 19, 22, 31, 73, 77
Libya, 13

— M —

Maltese, 10

Man of Confidence (*Vertrauensmann*), vii, 16, 18-20, 23, 27, 32, 35-36, 38, 71-73, 77-78, 88, 98, 118, 130
  Central, 40, 43, 46, 50, 61-62, 88, 91-92, 100, 109-111, 149, 207
Mason, Squadron Leader, xviii, xx-xxi
Mediterranean Sea, 4, 11, 178
Metaxas, General, xix
Metaxas Line, xix
Michigan, 231
  Detroit, xiv, 231
    General Electric, xiv
  East Lansing, xiv, 231
    Michigan State, 231
      University Press, xiv
  University of Michigan, xiii
Middle East, 72, 85, 231, 233
Morgenthau, Jr., Henry, 164
Morgenthau Plan, 164
Mussolini, Benito, xvii, 16

— N —

National Greek Independence Day, 84
Nazi, xiv, 4, 9, 13, 15, 17-22, 24, 26, 31, 33, 35, 38, 40, 43-45, 51-53, 57-58, 62, 64-66, 70-76, 78, 83-86, 90, 94, 96, 98, 100-101, 110, 115-117, 119, 129, 132, 136, 140, 148-150, 152, 159-160, 164, 166-167, 170, 175, 178, 183-184, 192, 195-196, 202, 204-205, 207-208, 212, 214, 216, 221, 224-225, 231
  death camp, 124
  government, 64, 116
  POW camp, 17, 20
New Jersey
  Upper Montclair, xv
New York
  Hastings, 232
New York Consul, 232
New Zealand, xix, 24, 34, 39, 60, 86
No Price for Freedom, xiv
Norman ____, 2

— P —

Pacific Ocean, 15
Peirasmakis, Basil, xviii-xxiii, 80, 81, 233
Peter ____, 179-181, 184
Philippakis, George, xvii

Philippine Islands
  Corregidor, 12
Planes
  Hurricane (British), xxi, 5
  Junkers 52 (Ju-52), xxi-xxii
  Messerschmitt (German), xxi, xxiii
  Stuka (German), xxi-xxiv, 2, 4
Poland, 64, 86, 115, 156, 218
  Annahuette, 225, 228-229, 231
  Beuthen, 133, 137, 152, 156, 159, 219, 222, 230
    Camp E.757 "Hell Dive," 152, 154-155, 159, 170, 172, 182, 211-212, 214
  Bielitz, 91, 127, 130, 132
  Breslau, 34, 48, 54-56, 132, 175
  Godulahuette, 191
  Kattowitz, 91, 130
  Morgenroth, 152, 190-191
  Ratibor, 225
  Sosnowitz, 91-92, 130
  Tarnowitz, 91-92, 105, 127, 132
  Udetfeld, 86-88, 91, 101, 104, 108, 113, 116, 123, 126-127, 132-133, 135, 152, 155, 168, 182, 203, 208, 214, 230
    Camp E.745, 87, 92, 98, 104, 108, 133, 135, 144, 146, 149, 152
  Warsaw, 116
Polish, 62, 85, 87, 91, 101, 105, 108-109, 113-114, 123-124, 134-135, 143, 156, 160, 164, 170, 192, 211-212, 217
  army, 135
Polland, Hans, 96-98, 106, 111, 119-120, 123, 125-129, 131-135, 137, 139-141, 143-145, 149, 152, 185, 192-194, 196, 200-201, 205, 209-210
Potter, Senator Charles E., 231
POW, 65
Propaganda, 97-98
Protecting power, 148-152, 156, 159, 167, 175, 179, 203-204, 206, 208-209

— R —
Raymond _____, 27-29
Read, _____ (central man of confidence), 91-92, 101, 109-112, 119, 125, 129, 149, 151-152, 156-157, 159, 171-172, 206-208, 213
Red Cross, 11, 16, 18, 20, 28-29, 31, 36,

Red Cross (continued), 38, 42-44, 48, 50, 60, 62, 70, 72, 79-80, 85, 87-88, 91-92, 100-102, 108, 110-111, 119, 130, 138, 152, 184-185, 196, 199, 205, 208, 211
  International, 11, 28, 60,72, 85, 106, 183
  parcel, 11-13, 51, 56, 90, 92, 100, 108, 124, 134, 153, 226
Rhodesia, xiv, 233
Rinke, Fritz, xiv, 94-101, 104, 106-107, 109-112, 115, 117-126, 129, 132-158, 160-162, 164-189, 191-200, 202-219, 230, 232
River
  Fulda, 229
  Hudson, 232
  Nile, 12
  Oder, 225
  Seine, 114-115
Robert _____, 27, 29-30
Russia
  Charkov, 217
  Moscow, 68
Russian, 18-21, 30-33, 48, 51, 95, 115, 152, 155, 200, 210, 217
  front, 115, 132, 137
  POW, 17

— S —
Sanitäter (nurse), 43, 46-50, 52, 54-56, 88, 104-105, 117, 122, 147, 151, 156, 158, 167, 171, 176, 178-181, 186-187, 190-192, 197, 199, 205, 220, 223
  Harry _____, 156-157, 159, 163-165, 167, 171-172, 177-180, 188, 197, 199, 205, 208, 224, 226-227
Scarpanto (Kárpathos), 6
Schmeling, Max, xxii
Scottish, xxi
Sicily, 15
Simmons, "Shots," 13, 14
Singapore, 12
Spanish, 139
Stool Pigeon (guard), The, 192-194, 212, 217-218

— T —
Terrorangriffe (terror raids), 115
Thomas, Sergeant, 68, 70, 79
Toby _____, 10-11

Tsapla, Dr., 156, 159, 189-191, 217
Turkey, 9
   Constantinople, xxi

— U —

United States, xiv, xix, 12, 139, 164, 184, 201, 231
   Congress, 231
   First Army, 229
   Immigration and Naturalization Service, xiii
   Justice Department, 231
Unteroffizier, 20-21, 212
   Hans "The Rat," 123, 125, 134, 152, 176, 181, 184, 193, 200, 206, 209-210, 212

— V —

Vardakos, George, 13, 26, 30, 33-35, 47-48, 54-56, 61-63, 66, 175-177

Verpflegung (ration) office, 88, 103, 105

— W —

Washington, D.C., 232
Weapons
   Bofors 40mm gun, xix
   Enfield rifle, xxi
   Lewis machine-gun, xx
   V-2 rockets, 139
Wintermute, Edwin, xiv
World War I, 15-16
World War II, xiv, 231

— Y —

Yugoslavia, xix